ADDICTIVE STATES
OF MIND

ADDICTIVE STATES OF MIND

Edited by

Marion Bower, Rob Hale,
& Heather Wood

Routledge
Taylor & Francis Group

LONDON AND NEW YORK

First published 2013 by Karnac Books Ltd.

Published 2019 by Routledge
2 Park Square, Milton Park, Abingdon, Oxon OX14 4RN
52 Vanderbilt Avenue, New York, NY 10017, USA

Routledge is an imprint of the Taylor & Francis Group, an informa business

British Library Cataloguing in Publication Data

A C.I.P. for this book is available from the British Library

ISBN: 9781780490052 (pbk)

Edited, designed, and produced by Communication Crafts

CONTENTS

Margot Waddell

Since it was founded in 1920, the Tavistock Clinic has developed a wide range of developmental approaches to mental health which have been strongly influenced by the ideas of psychoanalysis. It has also adopted systemic family therapy as a theoretical model and a clinical approach to family problems. The Clinic is now the largest training institution in Britain for mental health, providing postgraduate and qualifying courses in social work, psychology, psychiatry, and child, adolescent, and adult psychotherapy, as well as in nursing and primary care. It trains about 1,700 students each year in over 60 courses.

The Clinic's philosophy aims at promoting therapeutic methods in mental health. Its work is based on the clinical expertise that is also the basis of its consultancy and research activities. The aim of this Series is to make available to the reading public the clinical, theoretical, and research work that is most influential at the Tavistock Clinic. The Series sets out new approaches in the understanding and treatment of psychological disturbance in children, adolescents, and adults, both as individuals and in families.

"Ground-breaking" is a much over-used and abused cliché perhaps, yet it does seem the right term to describe *Addictive States of Mind*. The three editors are also significant contributors to this excellent collection of papers on some of the most recalcitrant and disturbing pathologies so often manifest in addictive states of mind. Much has been, and is being, written about the aetiology and treatment of addiction, but there is little from the coherent and enlightening perspective offered by this book. Here we have set out for the reader a comprehensive, scholarly, and moving exploration of a wide spectrum of different addictive behaviours and of some of the settings in which they are clinically—that is, psychotherapeutically—addressed. The book also, unusually, includes work across the life-span, with chapters on infancy, young childhood, and adolescence as well as on adult addictive states.

As editor, I am especially proud to have it in the Series because much of the work on which the chapters are based has been taking place in the Tavistock Clinic and its sister Clinic, the Portman. As one author puts it, various conceptual frameworks are drawn upon: "psychiatric, developmental, neuroscientific, genetic, legal, moral, social, and psychoanalytic". The necessity of being able to draw on all these complementary perspectives is particularly characteristic of the Portman Clinic's approach to offering psychotherapy in the areas of severe pathology and co-morbidity that typify its patient population, who present with problems of violence, criminality, and compulsive sexual behaviours. But in this volume the net is thrown wider than that: it includes material on the work of other teams, institutions, and services and their varying responses to addictive presentations. The emphasis is not so much on discrete symptomatology than on a developmental picture of the whole person and of the defensive structures that have been in place from early on and have intensified over the years. The chapters collected here, from diverse contexts and describing a range of interventions, are unified by a psychoanalytically informed approach to the subject of addictive behaviours and states of mind.

The authors' drive to understand such cases is underpinned by a strong commitment to tolerate, and to work with, often very extreme degrees of trauma, disturbance, perversity, and horrifying cycles of self- and other-destructive behaviours of a kind that makes such patients very hard to reach. Throughout, the maintaining of a psychoanalytic attitude of mind can be seen to support the capacity to contain anxiety and also to "think under fire". This capacity typifies the work described here, alongside the ability to maintain hope and to instil that in colleagues and patients, despite everything.

ACKNOWLEDGEMENTS

T his book has been a long time in gestation. We are grateful to our authors for their patience and for their thought-provoking and scholarly contributions.

Our series editor Margot Waddell has been a constant source of encouragement and gentle prods into action.

Rob Hale and Rajeev Dhar's chapter, "Flying a Kite" (chapter six), is based on an earlier version originally printed in *Criminal Behaviour and Mental Health* and is reprinted with kind permission of John Wiley and Sons.

Rob Hale's chapter "In Search of a Reliable Container" (chapter ten), was first published in *The Psychodynamics of Addiction*, edited by Martin Weegman and Robert Cohen (published by Whurr publishers/Wiley-Blackwell) and is reproduced by kind permission of John Wiley & Sons Ltd.

Angela Foster gives sincere thanks to David Hogsholt for his permission to use his photograph, which she came across in a world press award publication. It is one of a series in a study entitled "Mia—Living life trying".

Thanks to Bruno Bower for his typing and instruction in the use of the comma.

We are grateful to our families for their support and patience during the preparation of this book.

Finally, thanks to our patients, from whom we learn all the time, and without whom this volume would not exist.

ABOUT THE EDITORS AND CONTRIBUTORS

Marion Bower is a Consultant Social Worker in the Learning and Complex Disability service at the Tavistock Clinic. She is also a psychotherapist in private practice. She edited *Thinking Under Fire: Psychoanalytic Theory for Social Work Practice*. She is currently working on a biography of Joan Riviere.

Vanessa Crawford is currently Lead Practitioner with Special Interest, Shropshire Community Substance Misuse Team. Prior to this post she was Consultant Addiction Psychiatrist and Clinical Director, East London and the City Specialist Addiction Services based in Hackney, East London. Much of her working life as a doctor has been spent in the East End of London, with two years at St George's Hospital as Clinical Lecturer in Addictive Behaviour.

Raj Dhar is a Consultant Forensic Psychiatrist and non-practicing barrister. He has worked as a senior clinician in a variety of clinical settings and was previously a Clinical Director of General Mental Health Services in London. He is currently in private practice in central London and is an honorary academic at the Institute of Psychiatry.

Angela Foster is a social worker, psychoanalytic psychotherapist, and an organizational consultant working in the public sector and voluntary sectors with clinical teams and managers in mental health, substance misuse, child care, and student counselling. She gained considerable experience in therapeutic communities and social work education before moving to the Tavistock Clinic to develop consultancy and training in community care. She is co-editor of *Managing Mental Health in the Community: Chaos & Containment* and continues her involvement with the Tavistock Clinic through teaching on post-graduate courses.

Rob Hale trained as a psychiatrist and psychoanalyst and since 1980 has worked at the Portman Clinic and the Tavistock Clinic. His initial clinical interest was in self-destructive acts moving to perverse acts, particularly of those individuals who seek help for paedophilia. This clinical experience has provided the basis for the consultative work, both clinical and organizational, in other institutions, starting with the work in drug dependency described in this volume. For the past two decades he has spent increasing amounts of time working with Medium and High Secure Hospitals as an external consultant for the clinical staff and managers of those institutions.

Alessandra Lemma is the Director of the Psychological Therapies Development Unit at the Tavistock and Portman NHS Foundation Trust and a Consultant Adult Psychotherapist, Portman Clinic. She is the Clinical Director of the Psychological Interventions Research Centre at University College London (UCL). She is a Fellow of the British Psychoanalytical Society, Honorary Professor of Psychological Therapies in the School of Health and Human Sciences at Essex University, and Visiting Professor, Psychoanalysis Unit, UCL. She is the General Editor of the New Library of Psychoanalysis book series (Routledge) and is Regional Editor of the *International Journal of Psychoanalysis*.

Luis Rodríguez de la Sierra is a training and supervising adult and child psychoanalyst of the British Psychoanalytical Society. He works at the Anna Freud Centre, at the London Clinic of Psychoanalysis, and in private practice. He has published papers on child analysis and drug addiction.

Susannah Rose is a psychoanalytic psychotherapist and Lead Psychotherapist for the Eating Disorder Services at the Priory Hospital Roehampton. Before joining the Priory in 2004, she worked in psychological services within the NHS. Prior to training as a psychotherapist, she worked in the field of substance abuse, running therapeutic music groups for current and former heroin users. She has a particular interest in the presence of autistic traits within anorexia nervosa and is currently undertaking research in this area at the University of Essex.

Richard Taylor is a Consultant Forensic Psychiatrist at the North London Forensic Service, Camlet Lodge Regional Secure Unit. He is a member of the London Strategic Management Board for Multi-Agency Public Protection Arrangements (MAPPA). He has an interest in prison psychiatry, forensic outreach, inpatient services for women who are mentally disordered offenders, and homicide assessments. He has also been involved in the assessment of a number of alleged and convicted terrorist detainees and is a member of the Royal College of Psychiatrists' Special Committee on Human Rights. He has published articles and book chapters in the areas of MAPPA, ethics, confidentiality, prison psychiatry, and the interface between general adult and forensic psychiatry. He is currently involved in research on risk management decision making.

Heather Wood is a Consultant Adult Psychotherapist and Clinical Psychologist at the Portman Clinic, Tavistock and Portman NHS Foundation Trust and is a psychoanalytic psychotherapist with the British Association of Psychotherapists. She has a special interest in the problematic use of internet pornography and virtual sex and the related subject of paedophilia, and she has published chapters and papers on these and other topics.

Jessica Yakeley is a Consultant Psychiatrist in Forensic Psychotherapy at the Portman Clinic and Director of Medical Education and Associate Medical Director, Tavistock and Portman NHS

Foundation Trust. She is also a Fellow of the British Psychoanalytical Society. She has a long-standing interest in medical education and has published papers on risk assessment, MAPPA, prison health, and antisocial personality disorder; she is the author of *Working with Violence: A Contemporary Psychoanalytic Approach*. Current research includes a trial of mentalization-based treatment for men with antisocial personality disorders.

Biddy Youell is a consultant child and adolescent psychotherapist and Head of the Child Psychotherapy Discipline at the Tavistock Clinic. Before taking up this role, she was Head of Training at the Northern School of Child and Adolescent Psychotherapy in Leeds. As part of her clinical experience, she worked for several years as an expert witness in the family courts, and it was in this work that she first came across the full impact of parental addiction on children of all ages.

FOREWORD

Alessandra Lemma

In the film *Shame* (2011)—a British drama directed by Steve McQueen—the central character, Brandon, a casually slick, reticent man, is addicted to sex. Sex is pornography, prostitutes, one-night stands, and, if all else fails, masturbating alone in a toilet cubicle at work. He obsesses about doing it, getting it, and wanting it. Normal life, like a porn-clogged hard drive, has simply ground to a halt. He inhabits a sensory world where bodily sensation is everything. When he takes the risk to date a woman who does not immediately leap into bed with him, and they eventually have a sexual encounter, he is impotent. Since she presents herself to him as someone who wants to relate, and indeed desires him, his desire is literally crushed by the threat of her real otherness.

In Brandon we recognize a man whose compulsive sexuality is an outlet for unspoken, perhaps even unknown, anxieties. That which remains unmentalized traps him into repeatedly fashioning a sexual orgy out of developmental tragedy. Undigested residues of unsatisfactory or traumatic experiences with others, only hinted at in this film, are typically live in the transference in our clinical encounters with addicted individuals.

Control and impotence are a central axis in many addictive presentations. The sealed loop of Brandon's addictive behaviour is what the inspiring chapters in this volume explore from different perspectives, giving us a rich insight into the plight of individuals trapped in this kind of self-destructive cycle. They remind us of the struggle facing the clinician in helping such individuals to step out of the narcissistic and often perverse enclaves they have retreated into in the sway of internal objects that may be felt to be terrifying, seductive, bullying, or corrupt. The clinical constellation where the patient uses particular thoughts or object relationships in a tenacious and repetitive fashion is the hallmark of addictions and is a central aspect of the type of pathological organization described by Steiner (1993).

To begin with, within psychoanalysis addictions were seen largely as a direct expression of drive derivatives; hence their suitability for psychoanalytic treatment was considered poor. In the theoretical and clinical vacuum that this created, the treatment of substance addictions became disproportionately dominated by cognitive behavioural interventions and 12-Step programmes. The Editors of this book are thus to be congratulated for putting together a collection that restores psychoanalytic thinking as relevant to our understanding of substance addictions and of addictive states of mind that can manifest in addictive behaviours. Reminiscent of Fenichel's (1945) focus on the compulsive nature of eating disorders, defining them as "addictions without drugs", this book addresses a range of addictions beyond substance misuse.

Early psychoanalytic theory on substance misuse specifically stressed pleasurable/aggressive drives and the symbolic meaning of drugs to explain their appeal. By contrast, the modern psychoanalytic perspective elaborated in this book places greater emphasis on how intolerably painful or confusing affects and states of mind are managed through the addictive behaviour, which could be seen as a way of self-medicating states of subjective distress and suffering.

The central thread uniting the chapters, and what distinguishes these contributions from other approaches to addictions, is a compassionate focus on understanding the perverse mindset that fuels addictive behaviour—that is, the focus is on the dynamic function of the addiction (Kernberg, 2007).

Perversion is taken to mean different things within psychoanalytic discourse. In this book the authors view perversions, not in terms of specific behaviours, but as a type of blueprint for object relations. While perversions may involve a quest for excitement through sex, drugs, or gambling, for example, the focus here is on the underlying incapacity—or indeed at times refusal—to relate to the other as separate from the self and not as a narcissistic appendage. It is the anxieties aroused by intimacy and relatedness that drive the pursuit of ecstasy and excitement.

The extent of self- and other-destructiveness manifest in some of these individuals bears witness to a determined commitment to destructiveness that can stymie therapeutic efforts and requires constant vigilance of our countertransference. Reflecting on the therapeutic challenge facing the clinician, which the authors of this book call to our attention through generously sharing their clinical experiences, I was reminded of the poem, *Cheers*, by the American poet, Raymond Carver. Carver, as is well known, suffered from a serious addiction to alcohol. In this poem, he vividly conveys how the addicted individual envelops himself in the addiction—in the anticipation of the ecstasy or oblivion this will bring about *for sure*—without needing to relate to another person. The other is the threat and has to be kept out, as Carver evocatively captures:

Vodka chased with coffee. . . .
I hang the sign on the door: OUT TO LUNCH.

The Editors of this collection have offered us a rare insight into why these patients invariably greet the therapist with their own version of "the sign on the door". It is indeed hard to reach them because the therapist, like other people in their lives, is felt to be the one who "steals the vodka", as it were. For this reason, and as the clinicians in this book exemplify, this work requires getting *alongside the mind* of addicted individuals before attempting to get *into their mind*. It also requires attention to be devoted to the way the setting in which this work unfolds may itself become corrupted. Psychoanalytic thinking can help multidisciplinary teams to stand back and respond to the addictive state of mind in humane and containing ways that are not collusive. This book thus provides rich food for thought not only for the individual practitioner but also for those responsible for shaping services for addicted individuals.

Introduction

Marion Bower, Rob Hale, & Heather Wood

It is virtually impossible to open a newspaper these days without finding an article about addiction. Almost invariably, we are told that the addiction is increasing, that it is affecting younger people, and that there are conflicting views about how to treat it. New forms of addiction are frequently diagnosed. Addictions are not only a private matter; partners and children are affected. Addictions may affect public spaces and government policies. Crowds of young drinkers, for example, have had a major impact on our city centres; drug-taking equipment litters the stairwells of inner-city flats. Currently there are initiatives to raise the price of alcohol in the UK in order to deter consumption.

Given the high incidence of addictions, it is perhaps surprising that the psychoanalytic literature on addictions is sparse, with a few notable exceptions (Glover, 1932; Hopper, 1995; Rado, 1933; Rosenfeld, 1960; Yalisove, 1997; Yorke, 1970). The traditional psychoanalytic view is that addicts need to be "clean" or "dry" before they are treated. However, many patients do not consider their addiction a problem and arrive in therapy for other reasons; a significant number of addicts who did not arrive with the label of addiction are therefore probably receiving psychotherapy or analysis. We hope to show that psychotherapy is an effective form of treatment for many addicts, but also that psychoanalytic ideas are useful not only in the practice of psychoanalytic psychotherapy: an understanding of the internal world of addicts has implications for the way services are structured and for social policy. We have 24-hour drinking, but on-the-spot fines for possessing drink. Such contradictory policies mirror the internal world of the drinker, which contains both harsh and indulgent figures, and may only serve to compound the confusion that exists around alcohol consumption.

This book is aimed not only at psychotherapists and psychoanalysts, though they may find much of interest, but also at all those who work with addicts, whatever their professional perspective. Our aim is to present contemporary psychoanalytic thinking about addictions and addictive behaviours, expressed both through work in the consulting room with individuals and groups, but also in thinking about services and policies with respect to addictive behaviours.

The phenomenology of addiction

Although this book is about addiction, this term is often used interchangeably with dependency. This is particularly true when it is a specific substance, rather than an activity, that is the source of the addiction. We would suggest that by studying the features of addiction to drugs or alcohol, one can see many of the features of other activities that we would term addictive. In their seminal paper of 1976, Edwards and Gross describe the eight separate features of alcohol addiction, which are seen as equally applicable to drug addiction, and they note that each part of this syndrome relates in some way to each other part. In summary, the eight features they document are:

1. *Primacy of drug-seeking behaviour.* This is also called the "salience" of drug use; the drug and the need to obtain it become the most important things in a person's life, taking priority

over all other activities and interests. The consequence is that the addict ignores other needs, whether for social relationships, health, solvency, or morally based behaviour. Despite the warnings, he or she continues the drug use.

2. *Narrowing of the drug-taking repertoire.* The addict moves from using a variety of drugs to a single one used to the exclusion of all others. The social setting in which the drug use takes place and the way in which the drug is administered become stereotyped in an almost ritualistic way.

3. *Increased tolerance to the effects of the drug.* To achieve the same change in mood state, an increasing amount of the drug is required or a more immediate route of administration is employed. Another feature of increasing tolerance is that the individual shows few signs of intoxication at blood levels that in normal people would render them highly intoxicated.

4. *Loss of control of consumption.* The person finds it impossible to regulate further consumption of a drug once he or she starts using it. If the addiction is to gambling, more money needs to be thrown away.

5. *Signs of withdrawal on attempted abstinence.* These are both physical and psychological and are characterized by a craving for the drug. They are often most marked in the morning when blood levels are likely to be low.

6. *Drug-taking to avoid withdrawal symptoms.* Typically this would involve having the drug available on waking. Fruit machines in betting shops are probably an example of this.

7. *Continued drug use despite the negative consequences.* These may include bankruptcy, marital breakdown, job loss, or imprisonment. This is an extension of the first criterion.

8. *The rapid reinstatement of previous level of drug use after abstinence.* If, after successful withdrawal, addicts return to drug use, they become dependent much more rapidly than those who were not previously addicted.

These features refer to processes that are both psychological and physical; they also bring together the propensity to become addicted and the consequence of that addiction. It is a feature of addictive processes that it is often hard to differentiate between cause and effect. Although this book considers addictions to drugs and to alcohol, we extend the concept of addiction to activities that we would contend share many of these features, although the primacy of physical addiction may not be so obvious.

There are many conceptual frameworks used to understand addiction—sociological, behavioural, biological, psychoanalytic. Each has its merits, and all must ultimately be reconcilable. The American psychoanalyst Brian Johnson (1999) proposes a useful framework for approaching the subject of addiction. He outlines three perspectives on addiction, documented below: the neuro-biological perspective, the view of addiction as a way of tolerating negative affect, and an object-relations conceptual framework. Johnson sees these as different ways of understanding the same clinical phenomena.

The neurobiological concept

Central to this hypothesis is the concept that addiction is accompanied by (and possibly caused by) changes in brain biochemistry and brain circuitry. The precise nature of these phenomena is set out by Kalivas and Volkow (2005), who describe three stages in the process of addiction:

1. acute effects of the drug
2. transition to addiction
3. end-stage addiction.

Each involves a separate set of brain centres and brain connections, and each has a different set of neurotransmitters (the chemicals that facilitate the connections). Furthermore, the longer that the brain is under the influence of the drug, the greater is the likelihood that there will be changes in the structure of the individual cells of the brain as well as their connections to one another.

The point is made that there is a difference between liking a drug and craving a drug (one may crave something that one does not like). Liking and craving are subsumed by different neural systems: liking predominates in the acute phase, shifting to craving in the addicted phase. Some of the changes in connectivity of brain centres and cellular structure may be permanent, accounting for the fact that craving may persist long after abstinence.

Addiction as affect regulation

The second perspective identified by Johnson, is a "self-medication" hypothesis; it proposes that drugs ameliorate a negative affective state and that different forms of dysphoria will respond to different drugs. Khantzian (1985) believes that opiates attenuate feelings of rage and violence, central nervous system depressants such as alcohol relieve anxiety and emptiness, and stimulants augment hypomania and relieve depression. Whether the drugs achieve a real treatment for the "disorder" or whether, as seems more likely, it is apparent and temporary, and at what cost, is open to question. The theory also leaves unaddressed the reasons for the underlying negative affective state, which may have a genetic component but are also generated by the distortions in object relations occurring in the processes of childhood development, as described in the next section.

Object-relations theory and addiction

Object-relations theory is the third perspective outlined by Johnson. This psychoanalytic model was developed by Fairbairn, Klein, and Winnicott. It assumes that all humans are object seeking from birth. The word "object" is used to refer to the object of an instinct, and it denotes the possibility that the object of an instinct may not be a whole person, but may be only a part-object, a particular representation of a figure, or a part of the body. Internal object relationships are built up from birth, based on actual experiences of parents or carers as well as unconscious phantasies[1] about them. These internal object relationships act as a template for the way in which we will perceive relationships later in life. Thus, closeness may be perceived as reliable or as suffocating, depending on the internal object relations.

Klein's model of development has two stages (see Segal, 1973). In the first few months of life, the early ego is fragmented, and initially the infant is driven to internalize what is good and to get rid of what is bad. The mother is accordingly experienced as either very good or very bad. When feeling bad, the infant may attempt to communicate this state, or to rid him/herself of this experience, through the psychic mechanism of projective identification. This is the paranoid-schizoid position. The characteristic defence of this stage is splitting, and the leading anxiety is survival of the self. If all goes well, the infant becomes aware of the mother as a whole person with good and bad qualities. This is the depressive position, and the leading anxiety is the survival of loved objects. The leading defence of this position is the manic defence, which involves the denial of the importance of loved people.

Addictions can be used to defend against both paranoid and depressive anxieties, and, because of their qualities and effects, specific substances lend themselves to becoming incorporated into particular defensive phantasies. The phantasies fulfilled by the ingestion of the substance or the addictive behaviour may be many, varied, and contradictory.

Examples of such phantasies might include

» achieving a state of oceanic, conflict-free, union with the primary object (heroin is often reported by addicts to engender such feelings)
» control of one's own state of body and mind
» being able to feed the self and not depend on anyone else for psychic "nourishment" or "supplies"
» revenge: damaging one's own body as though it were the body and mind of the other (excited vengeance-seeking is often reported in those misusing alcohol, as expressed, for example, in the phrase "getting hammered" to describe a gratifying assault on the brain and the liver through alcohol intoxication)

» the control of external events by rituals, which may become imbued with a "magical" quality, as if believed to be capable of transforming reality

» risk-taking in order to hand over the responsibility of the outcome to fate

Part of the unconscious function of the addiction will be the enactment of these and other unconscious phantasies.

Addictive behaviours represent an enactment of something that cannot be contained and metabolized through thought. In infancy, an attentive mother helps the baby process unmanageable feelings. The baby projects these feelings into the mother, who metabolizes them and returns them to the infant in a more digestible form. If all goes well, the infant after many such experiences internalizes the mother's capacity for thought (Bion, 1959, 1970). If this process fails to take place, an addiction may represent an attempt to substitute for containment. Thus, someone may "drink to forget" or drink to "drown their sorrows", or take drugs hoping to engender a state of being "out of it", deliberately pursuing a state of dissociation or mindlessness where whatever it is that cannot be held in mind and digested is somehow negated or erased. Other addictive behaviours may represent a symbolic enactment of experiences that cannot be contained. Thus, the addict may behave in such a way that he or she courts shame or loss, or censure by society, as an enactment of punitive and vengeful feelings towards self and others that cannot be explicitly thought about and managed.

As well as those behaviours that specifically involve the ingestion of substances, there are a number of other compulsive behaviours—notably gambling, eating disorders, and compulsive sexual behaviours—that are also often said to have "addictive" elements, or addiction-like qualities, and these are also considered in this volume. A theme addressed in the chapter by Yakeley and Taylor on gambling (chapter seven), and in the chapter by Wood on compulsive sexual behaviours (chapter eight), is the way in which addiction-type behaviours may become ritualized, in ways that are highly significant. The gambler may have a lucky charm that must be touched or kissed, the sex addict may have a procedure to guard against interruptions, or a ritual cigarette before or after masturbating. Like obsessional rituals, these may function intra-psychically to foster magical thinking and an illusion of control, warding off misfortune and courting chance, or, in the case of sex addictions, precluding the intrusion into the solitary ritual by a real or symbolic other.

However, over and above this, the compulsive act itself may involve the creation of a drama, in which pathological internal object relationships are externalized and replayed. In sex addiction, there is often a tightly scripted sexual fantasy in which one person with particular characteristics will act on another in a particular way. The person may find others with whom to enact this drama, or may seek its realization in pornographic materials, but either serves as an externalization of the internal object relationships. The specific object relationships that are replayed compulsively in this way are never those of love or affirmation, but are those that cannot at that point be fully known and assimilated within the mind. Thus, it may be that the person cannot bear the inadequate, "victim" part of him/herself or a potentially sadistic, abusive part of him/herself, and so seeks scenarios in which this sadomasochism is enacted between others. In drug addiction, as Rosenfeld (1960) describes, the internal scenarios enacted may be of the internalization of an idealized breast, the ever-present source of continuous nourishment and contentment, and of the submission to a deadly, persecuting external force. As these parts of the self are projected and enacted or are rehearsed in fantasy, they are effectively evacuated from the mind and so cannot be understood and assimilated.

The relationship between addiction and perversion

Addictions and perversions have much in common. Leaving aside the physiological dimension of addiction to substances, at a purely psychological level both involve the pursuit of a manic "high", achieved through the ingestion of substances, or through intense sexual excitement. This may be used to counter internal feelings of deadness, depression, and inadequacy. There is an omnipotent fantasy that the source of pleasure is under the person's own control, and they are not dependent on another.

Both addictions and perversions may be characterized by narcissistic object relating in which the separateness and difference embodied by the other are denied. In substance misuse, partners or friends often become accomplices in the procurement of the substance, or in endorsing a substance-misusing sub-culture, but there is an avoidance of genuine dependency on an other; it is only the substance, which is under the person's own control, that can truly be relied upon. Similarly in perversions, there may be an other who is a participant in the enactment of the sexual script, but often he or she is only tolerated while complying and playing the role assigned to him or her; there is no celebration of the other's capacity to be different, to challenge expectations, and to surprise.

In both addictions and perversions, there is often the creation of a ritualized scenario, which allows the repetition, either through action or in fantasy, of an internal drama. Serving as a dramatic realization of the pathological internal object relationships, this drama is often one of abuse, mistreatment, cruelty, and contempt. Alongside this, there may be aspects of the drama which provide a realization of an idealized fantasy, of incorporation of an idealized object in substance misuse, or of getting right inside an idealized object in a perversion—for example, through cross-dressing (see Glasser, 1979). Because these dramatic realizations function to evacuate rather than metabolize intolerable internal scenarios, both addictions and perversions are often characterized by endless, compulsive repetition.

Both addictions and perversions are underpinned by sadomasochistic currents. Perversions, as Glasser (1979) and Stoller (1975) have described, represent a sexualization of aggression, or "the erotic form of hatred" (Stoller, 1975). Similarly, Rosenfeld (1960) draws attention to the incorporation and enactment of a toxic, destructive force in drug addiction. In both, there is the generation of excitement regarding an act that potentially destroys.

In substance misuse, there is a strong suicidal current, and the fantasy of destroying the self. In addition, there is the destruction, in phantasy, of a dependent feeding relationship in which one must rely on another to be nurtured and fed. The addict feeds him/herself with his or her supply of drink or drugs. Thus he or she feels insulated, ultimately, from the terrors of dependence on another. In perversions, it could be argued that what is destroyed, in phantasy, is the creative couple, the coupling of masculine and feminine elements which can potentially give rise to life. Such creative coupling can occur in heterosexual or homosexual couples, where there is a coming-together of valued differences, and it is not confined to a meeting of male and female anatomy. It is obliterated in sexual acts when there is no other but an inanimate object, or when the other is treated only as an object for the enactment of the individual's internal drama. Limentani (1989) and others have pointed out how in perversions the crucial facts of life are overridden: the fact of gender difference in transvestism, and the fact of generational difference in paedophilia. Freud, in his classic paper on fetishism (1927e), argues that the fetishist cannot be allowed to know the "truth" of the mother's castration, because of the intolerable castration anxieties that are aroused in him, and so takes as his sex object an inanimate object under his control, which effectively substitutes for the mother's penis. In all of these, there is a regression from the knowledge that it is a couple who have conceived and given birth to the individual.

Another difference between addictions and perversion is that while addictive behaviours may be infused with an excitement that at times appears almost sexual, in perversions there is not just a quality of sexualized excitement, but a specific behaviour or fantasy enacted in order to achieve physical sexual arousal and, usually, orgasm. A patient may describe, for example, an "orgy" of drug taking, drinking, or compulsive eating, in which there is frenzied consumption, building to an almost ecstatic state or climax, followed by a sense of release and relaxation; although this mimics and may symbolize sexual behaviour, it does not involve physical sexual arousal and orgasm and so is not a perversion. Conversely, someone appearing to enact a perversion—for example, compulsively downloading pornography, but doing so in order to categorize, sort, and collect images, but who feels no sexual arousal—may be seen to be perverse, or to be behaving in an obsessional way, but cannot be said to have a true perversion.

This introduction has moved from a phenomenological description of the addictive process, through a biological understanding
of the changes in brain structure and function which are both the
drivers and the result of the addiction, to a psychoanalytic conceptualization of the complex and often contradictory fantasies
that lead to addiction becoming an effective, albeit self-destructive,
defence mechanism. Psychoanalysis is not a single, unified theory,
and within this volume a range of psychoanalytic perspectives
is represented, including Kleinian, post-Kleinian, Freudian, and
object relations. It will be for the reader to decide which theory
best fits the phenomena described, and to what extent the particular behaviour depicted within each chapter fits within the overall
characteristics of the addictive process.

Rather than a detailed introduction to each chapter being provided here, a short preface is included at the start of each chapter,
to introduce and frame each contribution.

Note

1. The term "phantasy" will be used throughout to denote fantasies that are
unconscious and inferred, and the term "fantasy" retained for those fantasies
that are conscious. The latter accords with the popular use of the term "fantasy"
as something imagined and elaborated in the conscious mind.

CHAPTER ONE

Challenges
in a substance misuse service

Vanessa Crawford

This chapter, written by a psychiatrist working with people with severe and complex addictions, sets the scene. We are provided with a graphic account of the multiple problems—physical, psychological, social, financial—of someone with severe drug addiction, where sex working and the risks of pregnancy, infection, and assault compound an already challenging presentation. The personal history of trauma and abuse means that the patient requires highly skilled and sensitive management, and adaptations in service provision—such as no morning appointments—that respect the individual's lifestyle.

The conflict for professionals is encapsulated in a brief description of the responses of Vanessa Crawford's patient group when asked what messages they would like to be conveyed to future doctors: don't prejudge us, treat us as individuals, give us proper pain control—and "don't trust us". Implicit in this is the recognition that they are in the grip of something that leads them to deceive, probably themselves, but also others—a wish to pervert a relationship to someone who is trying to help.

Crawford conveys the importance of being knowledgeable, but not omniscient; of helping the individual to overcome the barrier

of shame, which may lead to information being withheld; and the
crucial contribution of a collaborative and coherent staff team in
containing such challenging patients and in helping them to turn a
corner towards recovery.

D
rug and alcohol (substance misuse) treatment services are delivered by both statutory and non-statutory services in the UK. Medical cover is largely provided by psychiatrists or general practitioners. Substance misuse treatment services in England have started to undergo radical changes, and this is set to continue. Under the current Coalition Government, services are being re-tendered, and partnership bids between the voluntary and statutory sector agencies are encouraged. Jobs are being lost, and, due to economics, specialism will be diluted in order to achieve the cost to win a tender. Addiction psychiatry as a specialism for doctors in training has become very insecure.

The 2010 Government Drug Strategy has at its core the theme of abstinence as the definition of "recovery". The Coalition Government set out the following goals for the drug strategy:

Reducing demand—creating an environment where the vast majority of people who have never taken drugs continue to resist any pressures to do so, and making it easier for those that do to stop. This is key to reducing the huge societal costs, particularly the lost ambition and potential of young drug users. The UK demand for illicit drugs is contributing directly to bloodshed, corruption and instability in source and transit countries, which we have a shared international responsibility to tackle;

Restricting supply—drugs cost the UK £15.4 billion each year (Gordon, Tinsley, Godfrey, & Parrott, 2006). We must make the UK an unattractive destination for drug traffickers by attacking their profits and driving up their risks; and

Building recovery in communities—this Government will work with people who want to take the necessary steps to tackle their dependency on drugs and alcohol, and will offer a route out of dependence by putting the goal of recovery at the heart of all that we do. We will build on the huge investment that has been made in treatment to ensure more people are tackling their dependency and recovering fully. Approximately 400,000 benefit claimants (around 8% of all working age benefit claimants) in England are dependent on drugs or alcohol and generate benefit expenditure costs of approximately £1.6 billion per year (Hay & Bauld, 2008, 2010). If these individuals are supported to recover and contribute to society, the change could be huge. [HM Government, 2010, pp. 3–4]

East London Substance Misuse Services

In the area I work, in East London, there is a statutory service providing care to complex cases and the non-statutory service for those service users who may have lesser complexity. Complexity is defined by the level of problems caused by the drug(s) or alcohol used. This may be psychological, psychiatric, or physical and is usually a combination of all the above factors. An example of a complex patient would be a 30-year-old female, opioid-, alcohol-, benzodiazepine-, and crack-cocaine-dependent with tuberculosis and HIV, involved in the sex-working (prostitution) industry with a history of sexual abuse, depression, and suicide attempts. There will be some variation over time in the way patients are split between the two services depending on the skill mix of the teams and, to a lesser degree, on patient choice. In a low-patient-number, high-intensity service such as ours, clear throughput with care pathways into and out of treatment are essential to prevent the system clogging up. Patients may become very attached to one key worker or a system, and well-planned and transparent disengagement can alleviate a lot of distress in the patient. Initial engagement takes place over 12 weeks and may continue for years if the presentation is extremely challenging. The majority should transition into a service for more stable cases within months. Our service takes referrals from any professional, but predominantly referrals come from the local non-statutory sector community drug service and GPs.

At the Specialist Addiction Unit, we are commissioned to see case loads of approximately 30 per worker, and the staff group consists of psychiatric nurses, psychiatrists in training, sessions from a clinical psychologist, and the invaluable resource of a general nurse. We provide addiction treatment for any substance, prescribed or illicit, alcohol, and drugs. Our speciality is complex interactions of drug use, challenging behaviour, mental illness, physical health complexity, and hard-to-engage populations.

Substance misuse services are generally catchment area, based on borough of residence; attachment to registered GPs can cause problems as the area of residence may no longer match with the GP. This is important in that ease of access may significantly improve engagement in treatment; with a substance-focused lifestyle, short geographical distances can become huge barriers psychologically. Also, the funding for any residential or paid day programme will be paid by the budget holder only if the individual resides in the borough funding his or her treatment.

In many individuals, an addiction is linked with a desire for instant gratification, so delaying treatment may negatively affect engagement. However, instant treatment may only promote initial, but not continued, engagement. An excellent compromise is to make early telephone contact with a patient, explaining what the service can offer him or her.

Specific substances

I have focused on three of the most common substances. Easily accessible information for all other substances can be found on the Internet at DrugScope (www.drugscope.org.uk/resources/ drugsearch/drugsearch-index.htm) and, for the ever-expanding catalogue of mind-altering chemicals, at Erowid (www.erowid. org). Erowid also provides a fascinating insight into personal experiences with named chemicals under their "What's New" section (www.erowid.org/new.php).

Alcohol

For a detailed description of the Alcohol Dependence Syndrome, see Edwards and Gross (1976). The definition of alcohol dependence can be transferred to all other drug addictions; it is useful in understanding what dependence can involve:

1. narrowing of drinking repertoire (i.e., drinking in response to a large number of cues); also described as a stereotyped pattern of drinking
2. salience (prominence) of drink-seeking behaviour
3. increased tolerance to alcohol
4. repeated symptoms of withdrawal from alcohol
5. relief or avoidance of withdrawal symptoms by further drinking
6. subjective awareness of compulsion to drink
7. reinstatement of dependent drinking after a period of abstinence.

Follow-up by Edwards of alcoholics over 10 years found that 25% had continued troubled drinking, 12% were abstinent. The remainder had a patchwork of abstinence and troubled drinking.

For approximately 90% with symptoms of alcoholism and of depression, the primary diagnosis is alcohol dependence. Up to 70% complain of mood dysphoria during heavy drinking, and there is a 10–15% risk of completed suicide with alcohol dependence. Symptoms of depression should abate after three weeks of abstinence; diagnosis of major depression reduced from 67% to 13% in one group of alcohol-dependent patients following detoxification (Davidson, 1995). Increase in alcohol consumption is more likely during relapse of bipolar affective disorder, potentially creating havoc in conjunction with already disinhibited behaviour.

Cocaine

Acute effects last about 20 minutes and include exhilaration and decreased hunger. Excessive use leads to an acute toxic psychosis marked by agitation, paranoia, and hallucinations that may be visual, auditory, or tactile. These include a sensation of insects crawling under the skin, known as formication. Cocaine can cause respiratory and cardiac failure. Chronic use can lead to tolerance or withdrawal symptoms (mainly dysphoria and fatigue) and to a chronically anxious state. Seizures, heart attacks, and strokes are not uncommon; the commonest cause of chest pain to be considered in males in their forties presenting to casualty is cocaine use.

Crack cocaine

> The first hit is always the best. . . . I've never had anything like it. With crack once you've got that hit of the day, no matter how much you take you don't get it back. If the rock is there, I can't leave it, even though I don't get anything off it. But you can't just have one [rock] and leave it; you've got to have more. [quoted in *Crack and Cocaine in England and Wales*; Home Office, 1992]

Crack cocaine is the base of cocaine powder, the latter being the hydrochloride of the substance; crack cocaine has a faster onset of action than the hydrochloride and wears off more quickly, promoting its image as a "greedy drug".

Heroin

> Oh! just, subtle, and mighty opium! that to the hearts of poor and rich alike, for the wounds that will never heal, and for "the pangs that tempt the spirit to rebel," bringest an assuaging balm; eloquent opium! that with thy potent rhetoric stealest away the purposes of wrath; and to the guilty man, for one night givest back the hopes of his youth, and hands washed pure of blood. . . . [de Quincey, 1821]

> It is probably one of the most pleasurable experiences I've had. All the pain goes. All the anger is gone. I was lying on the sofa floating happily. It makes you feel safe and warm like being wrapped up in a blanket. [Anon; quoted in DrugScope, 2012]

Heroin is an excellent pain killer and is best viewed in those terms when looking at its role as a drug of addiction. It cushions the user: some become upbeat and more active, others slow down and worry less about day-to-day issues as if dissociated from the emotion of an event. It can be smoked, inhaled, and injected, and the purity varies considerably when buying from the street. It is often used in conjunction with cocaine; a combined injection is known as "snowballing" or "speedballing". The addition of cocaine is problematic due to its action as an anaesthetic; this kills the pain and therefore may lead to damage to the veins, as any pain that would have been felt is numbed by the anaesthetic effect. Withdrawal from heroin, contrary to that from alcohol, is not physiologically life-threatening, but the treatment (e.g. methadone), when given to an opioid-naïve patient, is potentially life-threatening. Of note, the majority of those taking up heroin use will stop without accessing any treatment service.

Engaging with substance misusers

The NHS Specialist Addiction Unit in Hackney, East London, forms part of the Mental Health Trust and is based on a general hospital site. This has the benefit of reducing stigma in that individuals seen visiting the site could be there for any health issue. The biggest problem we deal with in terms of achieving good-quality treatment is attitudinal. This is largely outside the addiction services, but not exclusively. We were recently told we were "dumping" a seriously ill, alcohol-dependent patient in casualty. We had sent a junior doctor (the key worker) and a general nurse with the patient to explain the presentation. The same presentation of confusion and vomiting would not have elicited the same response if the patient had cancer. It is very clear that, as health care professionals, we have no right to withhold treatment on the basis of the cause of the condition. Unfortunately those with substance misuse problems are often denied compassionate, empathic treatment on this very basis. Equally there are many examples of good practice and excellent staff, but we must challenge colleagues who use their professional standing punitively on the basis of their personal beliefs. Our patients are highly unlikely to formalize complaints, some believing that it is their own fault, others that the system will close ranks, and therefore they are wasting their time.

I teach future doctors and spend time on issues such as stigma which cannot be learned so easily from textbooks. We talk about not allowing age, gender, social class, and religious affiliation from stopping them asking the patient questions: "I ask everyone these questions—they may not apply to you, but I don't know without asking." We have patients of pensionable age using opioids and crack cocaine, and you would not know by looking at them. We see people with religious affiliations that would condemn drug use who are addicted; it may then be even more stigmatizing for them to disclose, so we need to enable them to do so. I encourage the students to reflect on their own religious and personal beliefs. How does wearing Muslim dress affect the patient's transference, is it useful to pre-empt this with a personal statement, and should health care professionals self-disclose when asked? Many of these issues will come up for young doctors starting work in a hospital setting. We discuss how they would respond if they have concerns about a colleague's substance misuse; they have a range of resources available to them, rather than ignoring the situation, hoping it will disappear. The aim is also to instil an adequate knowledge level so that they can take a good drug and alcohol history and know how to treat alcohol and opioid withdrawal and signpost into further treatment. Brief interventions/comments can be very powerful and remembered; junior doctors may not realize how much positive impact they can have even just by asking about an issue such as nicotine addiction. These same themes equal apply to anyone working professionally/ therapeutically with a service user/client.

I asked some of our patient group what key messages they would like me to convey to future doctors. They came up with four themes of "Don't prejudge us", "Treat people as individuals", "Don't trust us", and "Give us proper pain control", which have been reiterated by those in recovery. I have been working closely with members of Narcotics Anonymous (NA) who come and talk to the students about their organization and their own life stories. This receives very good feedback, challenges stereotypes, and enables students to ask any questions before testing these questions out with "live patients". They can ask questions in their group of about 50 students or come down at the end and ask questions individually. It enables students to also disclose family and personal issues and receive appropriate signposting advice from the consultant lecturer. It also forms part of the "work" of those in 12-Step (NA) recovery, and so it has a linked positive effect. In smaller group teaching on site, I favour the involvement of expert patients—patients already in treatment who feel able to speak to future doctors either alone or with a doctor as facilitator. Of note, students have said that one of the reasons psychiatry is unappealing to them as a career is that they do not see recovery. This may represent more than just seeing recovery, as oncology and many other areas of medicine will provide this same perception of little recovery. More community care has led to those being admitted to hospital being much sicker, thus feeding into this perception. Patients are discharged home earlier, and their recovery is not witnessed by medical students on the whole. Involving NA has been very positive in this respect as they are addicts in recovery, and I hope to be able to introduce this teaching earlier in the curriculum. There is a national medical student curriculum for addictions, and the plan is to ensure that this is embedded throughout the curriculum, as addiction touches on every system of the body and can be seen in all patient groups.

Building trust through a therapeutic relationship takes time, especially where there is a history of difficult and abusive relationships in a person's life as a child or as an adult. Given the risk of staff changes over time, it is important to engender a therapeutic relationship with the service, rather than the individual, although both are very important. Ensuring that staff avoid repetition of questioning and have a good knowledge of the patient's notes is to be developed within teams. Recently one of my new colleagues was faced with a patient's concern that it would be necessary to start again after a change of key worker. The staff member's duty is to reassure that holidays, sickness, and other changes should not affect patient care; we all have access to the patient's notes and a duty to read them prior to seeing the patient. Listening, empathy, and unconditional positive regard are the attributes we would like all staff to develop. Sharing of case management in team clinical meetings enables all staff to look at different ways to manage complex and challenging cases while maintaining a positive therapeutic relationship. All staff are encouraged to keep patients apprised if they are running late and to apologize if this is the case. We have a general nurse on site every day, so delays allow a great opportunity to link the patient to the general nurse while waiting for the appointment with the key worker. We telephone patients during their appointment time if they do not attend and impress that attendance and alerting us to delayed arrival is important. When people—whether staff or patients—feel valued, they are more willing and able to give to the system.

Central to engagement is flexibility, non-judgemental attitudes, and an ability to extract and hear the narrative. Childhood and adult abuse is common in our patient group. We seek to form boundaried and therapeutic relationships. This should start with the first letter inviting the individual in to an appointment, to first contact with reception, through assessment and key-working. Communication and appropriate information sharing is incredibly important, and the reasons for doing this are outlined from the start of treatment. We are in regular liaison with social services and frequently attend child protection conferences and core group meetings. We work closely with social services to identify protective factors within the parents, while being very open about perceived areas of risk. The most commonly used substances we see are nicotine, alcohol, crack cocaine, and heroin. Corroboration of the patient's report is essential—for example, drug testing, obtaining hospital records for reported medical conditions, confirming medication prescribed with the GP. There is often a desire within addiction services to want the individual to do well, a temptation not to report on concerns and to develop a relationship with conditions that make it difficult for the patient to disclose the reality. It is rare for a parent to tell me that his or her drug or alcohol use has a current negative effect on the children. Working as a clinical team provides an environment for advice, questions, and the challenging of ideas and views within a safe, supportive team. This can naturally be difficult for junior staff, but also for some senior staff.

Team leaders of all disciplines must try to enable all staff to be actively involved in team decisions and remember that knowledge levels and ability increase over time and at different rates in different individuals. In a busy, manpower-lean environment, this is a challenge for any practitioner. Currently changes are occurring in the addictions field, services are being re-tendered, and staff may find themselves working across statutory and voluntary sector organizations.

The clinical governance issues are a challenge: as doctors and other health care professionals, we are under the guidance of our own accrediting bodies and the linked levels of clinical governance. Different organizations will have different incident-reporting and incident-monitoring systems and a differing focus on research and audit, to name just three of the clinical governance key headings. This can be a very challenging transition for any practitioner and also leads to a sense of instability for the patients. Organization names and personnel may show greater turnover than in previous years, and this patient group appears to be sensitive to such changes and able to vocalize their concern.

Our work begins with the initial information gathering, medical check, and consideration of prescribing needs. Controlled drugs carry their own risks of overdose and of potential death in the opiate-naïve, so they are not prescribed without careful assessment and team discussion. We work as "the team", and this has become a known and powerful advisory body. Patients come to know that if they have a specific request during their treatment, perhaps less frequent attendance, this will be taken to "the team". This is then discussed at the clinical meeting and "the team" decision passed back to the patient. This helps towards greater consistency in decision making, ensuring that all the information required has been gathered, and reduces the risk of individual workers being criticized for blocking the treatment plan or indeed facilitating it when another patient with the same request has it declined. I encourage transparency of decision making to be given to patients and intelligent explanations of why the decision was made. If the answer is expected to be received with a volatile response, then we can plan that meeting, the location, how many staff need to be present, and whether we need the backup of our security staff. We have a full team handover at 9 a.m. every day to ensure all staff, and in particular our receptionist, is prepared for the day. In addictions, the family interactions have often been and remain very dysfunctional; the aim with "the team" is to model a functional family that sets appropriate boundaries.

The role of the whole multidisciplinary team in providing a welcoming, positive clinic is incredibly important. The telephone manner of the receptionist, the timely communication and response to messages received, and a well-designed waiting room all promote a space for positive recovery. We had a wonderful year or so when we had a cleaner in the unit who was committed to and passionate about her work. We chatted together in the evenings when the other staff had left. The unit was kept spotless; she became animated when she could not get the supplies she needed to keep the service at the standard she felt was required. She would tidy up the leaflets, news-papers, and magazines in the reception area. She got to know the staff from their rooms and a brief crossover as they left for the day; when I experienced a bereavement, she was an unexpected source of support. When she left, some time after her potential retirement date, we held a party for her and gave her a gold clock. It was notable that our team's appreciation of her contrasted with the fact that her employer did nothing to mark her leaving. My intention is to run an inclusive team where no member of staff would feel his or her role was too important to prevent him or her from covering for all other staff. Occasional reception cover is a humbling and enlighten-ing experience for all staff; the multitasking, the interface with all the patients who tell a lot to the receptionist in informal chats, the fact that to go to the toilet or get a drink requires the post-holder to call a colleague to cover them. A good receptionist can maintain a happy waiting room, pick up any unusual or concerning behaviour and tell the key worker, and prevent incidents of aggression escalat-ing by early action.

An addictions team can achieve a huge amount even without expertise in the many substances that may be used problematically. When we recruit new nursing staff, the emphasis is on recruiting those with strong psychiatric nursing experience and a good atti-tude, more than on addictions experience. However, there may be inappropriate psychiatric diagnoses made, missed physical illnesses, and poor formulation leading to weak treatment plans if there is not a deeper understanding of substances of addiction and their complications.

Team discussion is incredibly important to enable a well-informed decision that can be explained clearly to the patient. There are few absolute answers, and flexibility and the ability to challenge the deci-sion-making process are very important. Being able to give patients a positive goal to aim for while not saying "yes" to all requests is an important balance to achieve. The patient group has a shared theme of low self-esteem mixed with an externalization of blame in some; this can be very hard for even the most competent of staff at times. Working as a team provides the support to carry what at times seems to be a personal attack, and to see if there is indeed some reality in the "blame" or whether it is entirely projection.

Case example

Jane is 29 years old, with a heroin and crack cocaine addiction. She was referred to our service by a local organization, working with sex-working women, who had been meeting her out on the streets for some months, getting to know her and inviting her to their weekly drop-in where food, housing support, and access to psychiatric and physical health care is available. The organization also has a male worker to engage the men involved in the sex-working woman's life and has also managed to bring Jane's partner into contact with us. We undertook a brief initial assessment to enable immediate methadone prescribing; a long assessment with no apparent reward may inhibit engagement from a very chaotic, entrenched lifestyle. Morning appointments are not practical when someone has been out working all night, and long appointments with lists of questions may lead to irritation and premature termination of the interview. A Care Plan was initiated with Jane early on, looking at the journey required from the start of treatment to stabilizing enough to move out of specialist treatment into primary-care prescribing. One of the key issues to address was the sexual abuse history from childhood and traumatic abuse in her adult years while sex-working. Jane has been tested for HIV and hepatitis B and C and has been found to be hepatitis-C-positive. She has been offered treatment for her hepatitis C, but she does not yet feel able to commit to the weekly Hep C treatment appointments and the risk of feeling unwell and possibly depressed. The offer will remain open until she feels ready to access treatment. After six sessions with her allocated key worker, she attended with a black eye; with exploration, it emerged that her partner regularly assaulted her when she returned after a night's work, and they were both using crack cocaine and alcohol. She was given information around the options for domestic violence services, including the emergency helpline number. Four weeks later, Jane presented complaining of feeling sick, particularly in the mornings; a pregnancy test was positive. The work then became even more intensive, with more frequent discussion in supervision, at the team clinical meeting, and with regular interagency communication. All pregnant women with our service are automatically referred to our addictions liaison midwife and children and families social services. With good introductions, patients can realize how helpful engaging with social services can be. Jane decided that if she stayed with her partner, she would not be allowed to keep the baby; she therefore decided to move into a women's refuge and to re-contact her family, with social services' support, so that she could have a chance of keeping the baby with the support of her mother. Jane went on to residential detoxification, while her mother cared for the baby for two weeks, and then on to three months' rehabilitation within a mother-and-baby placement. She remains drug- and alcohol-free and has the support of her mother and social services, helping her to maintain the care of her baby.

Undertaking a basic assessment

A basic assessment would look at the following:

Taking a drug history

» Which drugs? Name them (e.g. gas, cannabis, alcohol, ecstasy, ketamine, GHB, GBL). Patients will not volunteer drug names so have to be asked; there is a stigma and a fear of the consequences of disclosure.

» Prescribed or bought?

» How much? Weights and price. Where does the money come from?

» How often, to what effect, still enjoyable?

» By what route? Name venous access sites. People are embarrassed to admit that they may inject into their neck or groin but will often answer if asked in an open manner. Patients need to know that the questioner is knowledgeable and is not going to judge them negatively for disclosure.

» Criminal history: drug/non-drug related, imprisonment—longest sentence, violent/non-violent.

Complications of drug use

» Physical: for example, sharing of injecting equipment, sexual risk factors can lead to HIV, hepatitis B, and hepatitis C; liver cirrhosis with alcohol.

» Psychological: often difficult to separate cause and effect—needs a very thorough history, if possible with a friend or relative of the person.

» Social: without addressing these issues or at least heading the person in the right direction to do so, we limit the efficacy of a prescription (e.g. sharing a flat with other drug users, no electricity or gas, not receiving appropriate benefits).

Guidelines for assessing drug-using parents

» Is there a non-drug-using parent, is drug use stable or chaotic, can you compare with levels of care when the parent was a non-drug-user?

» Is accommodation adequate, bills being paid, food, clothing, warmth?

» School attendance, age-appropriate activities, emotional needs being met?

» Are the children assuming parental responsibility?

» What happens to the children when drugs are being procured?

» Where are the drugs kept, used?

» Is there a wider support network?

» Do the parent(s) see any problems?

To be able to gather the information regarding drug use does require knowledge of drugs used; it is not normal for patients to volunteer a list of illicit drugs used beyond that which will secure them treatment. Stigma is a huge issue; there may be a fear of a change of perception by the health care professional, coupled with the risk of informing social services, the police, their family, or their employer. Many will have experienced attitudinal changes when they have self-disclosed previously and therefore will be reluctant to be let down again. If they see a professional who appears to be comfortable and confident in his or her specialty, then there is a much greater likelihood of information sharing. Even a lack of knowledge can be overcome by an interest to know more: "I'm afraid I don't know a lot about the drug you've just mentioned—can you tell me some more about how you use it and what it does for you in a positive and nega-tive sense?" As mentioned earlier, there are many useful websites to access more information; be mindful that there is very powerful weighting on pro-drug websites that may not give the most balanced view, though nor will anti-drug sites. The website www.drugscope. org.uk is an excellent resource for a drug search and describes the history, effects, side-effects, and legal issues related to each drug. Throughout, never lose sight of the fact that alcohol remains the most destructive substance of all; cocaine carries a much greater risk to physical health than heroin, but society's view would rank those substances with heroin as the most problematic drug, based on the media and political presentation.

The creation of a Care Plan is incredibly important and may be difficult to achieve when our patients come in with an agenda and perhaps a personal crisis on that agenda. We repeat our Care Plans every six months, unless there are any major changes in the interim; there can be a tendency for staff to get caught up in drug monitoring and the prescription and to fail to move on to issues for recovery. Without a plan for alternative activities, it is difficult to imagine recovery: finding the goals and desires for each individual can be challenging, but it is essential. There is a risk that individuals may embark on a reduction of their opiate prescription, while also quietly increasing their alcohol intake, without it being noticed. Our patient population tends to be much less worried about the implications of their alcohol intake than about their opiate intake. The internal push to get off methadone at all costs is sometimes difficult to stall; this is contrary to the view of an addicted individual as drug-seeking. We often have great difficulty encouraging patients to increase their dose of methadone. There is a view that a level of saturation of the opiate receptors in the brain needs to be achieved before craving can reduce. Many are more fearful of the addiction to methadone than to heroin; this is due to the fact that the half-life of—and so the withdrawal from—methadone is protracted compared to withdrawal from heroin.

Conclusion

I was drawn to the title of a *British Medical Journal* article recently: "Do Not Sit on the Bed". It outlined the health-and-safety restrictions placed on hospital wards, the widespread banning of flowers and of sitting on beds. The author of the article expresses concern at this extraordinary sanitization of health care, which is unevidenced and demonstrates an ignorance of the compassion essential for recovery. Somewhere in the world of targets, we must not allow our teams to lose sight of why we came into the health care field. Patients (I have reverted to this term as a majority have a preference) are our customers and, I believe, as in any good shop, should be offered a good service and be treated with respect by caring, knowledgeable, and skilled staff. All team members should carry equal importance in creating a secure and effective team. Without listening, empathy, and positive regard, we will never fully know our patients. With the stigma experienced by those with addictive disorders, this becomes even more important to embed in treating teams.

To ascertain information on a sensitive, emotionally charged, illegal, and stigmatized activity is difficult. Meeting with a patient for the first time and asking a series of very personal questions can be a difficult task; for inexperienced practitioners, it can be particularly challenging. Where there is prejudice in a staff member, the role of the clinical meeting enables team members to challenge and question the presenter. Equally, frustrations and difficulty in engaging patients can be shared, along with support and ideas given by colleagues. Most teams will have limited psychodynamic psychiatry skills to enable them to produce a high-quality psychodynamic formulation; when this is available, it is incredibly helpful in enabling teams to manage and treat very challenging patients and to tolerate the emotional intensity of the work. The power differential in teams working with vulnerable adults, especially in the context of prescribing controlled drugs, needs to be carefully managed to prevent it becoming punitive towards the patients. There is also a risk that staff can feel that challenging behaviours are tolerated; when keeping patients with challenging behaviour in treatment, a clear, well-communicated Care Plan—for example, contracts, warning letters, copying correspondence to key individuals—is essential. Changes of key worker should be carefully considered, while acknowledging that in an outpatient service the old key worker will still see the individual in question in the waiting area. Ideally, the difficulties would be best worked through with the same key worker, but this may not be appropriate. Taking the discussion to a team clinical meeting enables other colleagues with previous knowledge of the patient to discuss the aspects of the history that they are aware of; in this way, a better informed and more balanced decision can be made.

Access to drug- and alcohol-specific information is now well supported by the Internet. However, readers need to be mindful that Internet sites that come to the top of an Internet search are the pro-drug websites. The website www.drugscope.org.uk is an excellent source for basic information about drugs, effects, side-effects, and legal issues.

Assessment in addictions requires a basic knowledge and the ability to search for additional information when required. Substances alter our mental state, and it is very important to be able to hold the conversation with patients as to how their drug use affects them, what they like about it, and what they no longer like about it. What does the drug do for them, in what context, and is it consistent each time or variable depending on the mental set and setting? Can we corroborate their story, with information from a friend, relative, GP, and other health care professionals? Retrospective memory can be rose-tinted or, indeed, make a situation appear much more negative than it was at the time. What does the patient want to achieve from being in treatment, and is it something our service can offer?

The skill in addictions is to be able to assess the whole person, determine what in his or her presentation is physical, psychological, or psychiatric symptomatology, and then decide on a plan of action that encompasses the whole person.

In summary, stigma and attitude are the key enemies to successful treatment of those with addiction-related problems. As individuals and health care professionals, we have a duty to provide high-quality care to people regardless of the cause of their presenting problem. In spite of resource implications, it is possible to provide a compassionate and boundaried service by working closely as a team and daring to challenge colleagues who violate their professional obligations. The patient group in addictions may present us with a challenge, but also present as one of the most grateful and satisfying to work with.

CHAPTER TWO

Parental addiction and the impact on children

Biddy Youell

Biddy Youell's chapter comes from the perspective of an NHS child psychotherapist, experienced not just in treating children and assessing for treatment, but also in conducting assessments to advise family courts about the safety of the child.

Youell focuses on the emotional and psychological impact on the child of having a parent with an addiction. She provides a graphic account of an infant with an addicted mother, a baby in whom the urge to make an attachment seems to have been almost extinguished and replaced by a passive hopelessness. Youell also describes teenagers who have little chance to attend to their own development as they struggle to support and rescue their addicted parents. In her words, what children of addicts have in common is that "The parent is preoccupied, most if not all of the time, with something other than the child". As she vividly conveys, this represents not just an absence of a functioning parent, but the replacement of a potentially containing, attentive parent by someone who behaves more like a child, needing to be cared for, and even berating the adolescent for being a puritan when attempting to be responsible and set limits. The adolescent is then not just a "parental child" with respect to providing care for the parent, but becomes a quasi-parent having to bear the hostility of his or her (actual) parent, which presumably derives from and belongs with the parent's own introjected parental figures or internal objects.

Youell describes the plight of these young people, burdened by a sense of guilt and responsibility towards their parent(s) and wary of dependency themselves. In some cases, the need to protect an idealized image of the parental figure makes it impossible for them to separate, and they remain in thrall to the family culture and extremely difficult to reach through psychotherapy or other interventions. In unfortunate cases, the parent sees the young person's psychic pain and offers the only solution they know—ingestion of substances—and so the cycle of addiction can become transmitted through the generations.

Youell's chapter is not just of interest to those working with children, but is an invaluable reminder, for those working with adults who are the children of addicts, of the psychological deprivation, conflicts, and assaults that these people may have experienced in childhood and adolescence as their own development is eclipsed by the need to preserve the life or sanity of their parent.

This chapter looks at the impact of parental addiction on the health and well-being of children. It is inevitable that some of what is said is broad generalization, since each case is different, depending as it does on a range of factors, most significantly on the nature and severity of the addiction and the age and developmental stage of the child or children. The chapter aims to focus on the emotional and psychological impact but without understating the importance of the physical neglect and material deprivation that almost always accompanies substance misuse and other forms of addiction, particularly where the addiction is expensive and/or illegal.

There is an argument that holds that being an addict does not necessarily make you a bad parent, or, at least, no worse a parent than many. I will return to this later in the chapter. It is well documented, nonetheless, that serious addiction often goes hand in hand with financial insecurity, unemployment, poor diet, poor health care, and other manifestations of neglect (Kroll & Taylor, 2003). Even where money is not an issue, children are inevitably caught up in the chaotic lifestyles of their parents and may be exposed to all kinds of danger and risk. Domestic violence and child sexual abuse are commonly associated with excessive drinking, gambling, or drug use. School attendance is often adversely affected and academic achievement is compromised (NHS Choices: www.nhs.uk). Children of parents with hidden, socially "shameful", or illegal addictions are required to keep secrets and often become adept at lying to people in authority. Addictions cause rifts between generations, and young children may be deprived of contact with their extended family as a result of estrangements between partners, among siblings, or between parents and the grandparental generation.

The most common forms of parental addiction impacting on children's lives are, of course, addiction to alcohol and to mind-altering drugs. Less common, but increasingly significant, are addictions to Internet social networks, Internet gambling, and Internet pornography. Some women are addicted to eating; others to dieting or exercise. Both men and women can become obsessed with sex, with plastic surgery, or with body piercing. These may seem much less dangerous or less fixed than drug or alcohol dependency, but they all have a potentially devastating effect on the individual personality and therefore on family relationships.

Other chapters in this volume concern themselves with the particular aspects of different addictive behaviours. However, in terms of the impact on children, all addictions have one thing in common. The parent is preoccupied, most if not all of the time, with something other than the child. The child does not have the invaluable experience of feeling that his or her welfare is the mother and/or father's absolute priority. Children have described feeling themselves to be insignificant or even invisible. They talk about having to accept that they cannot stop their parent drinking, gambling, taking drugs, or whatever it is. They live with knowing that they were not "enough" to make their parent's life satisfying. For older children or adolescents, this is distressing and damaging in ways I explore later in the chapter. For babies and very young children, it can be catastrophic.

Infants and very young children

Much of the literature on babies of addicted parents focuses on the physiological impact of alcohol or drugs on the unborn infant. Research has, understandably, been preoccupied with the long-term effects of excessive alcohol consumption during pregnancy and the particular characteristics of foetal alcohol syndrome (FAS). It is reported that alcohol consumption is now one of the three most common causes of birth defects. In its most serious form, foetal alcohol syndrome can result in physical abnormalities, deformities of the brain or skull, and damage to the central nervous system. Children with mild forms of FAS have problems of impulsivity, poor coordination, impaired speech, and idiosyncratic social skills (www. nofas-uk.org).

An increasing number of babies are being born dependent on drugs, and there is a growing body of knowledge as to what are likely to be the long-term effects on development of having to go through a controlled withdrawal programme in the first days of life. Descriptions of babies going through withdrawal are harrowing in the extreme, and these children often share the developmental challenges that are listed above in relation to FAS.

Equally well researched and documented in the social care literature and in the popular press are the risks to babies' safety which result from living in chaotic and often violent families. One such case in Scotland involved the death of a 2-year-old at the hands of the new partner of his heroin-addicted mother. Brandon Muir's death in March 2008 brought forth the now all too familiar outpouring of public outrage and disgust, particularly as it became clear that he had sustained a number of undetected injuries over a period of time. Neighbours reported on a noisy and disorganized household, and they had their suspicions about drug use and prostitution, but there was little concern about Brandon. Children in such circumstances tend not to draw the attention of the authorities until there is a disaster such as that which befell Brandon, or until the child enters school with social, emotional, and behavioural problems. There is still a tendency, even among child care professionals, to think of new babies as requiring little more than food, clothing, protection from physical harm, and some kind of routine.

In ordinary circumstances, however, babies respond not only to the physical care offered by the mother or primary carer, but also to the lively, pleasurable interaction that develops within the relationship. Most babies are welcomed into the world by parents who are interested in getting to know their baby, committed to offering care and protection, and enthusiastic about every small development. Babies soon learn that they can rely on their mother (father or carer) to respond to their cries and that they bring with them food and comfort. When things go well, they also quickly learn that they can delight their mother with a smile or with some small appreciative sound. They "learn" that it is this same person who can help them when life seems to be full of discomfort and fear, transforming moments of terror into periods of peace and security. This is the process that Bion (1962) describes in his theory of "container–contained".

So what happens when the parent is not able to fulfil this function because of an addiction? Observations of babies in assessments conducted for the family courts have produced compelling evidence of the anti-developmental effects of parental neglect and self-preoccupation. In some instances, babies seem simply to give up, to shut down. In the absence of a lively relationship, they become passive, undemanding, and sometimes almost entirely silent. It is as if they demand nothing and expect nothing. Of course, this may occur as a result of organic damage from drug or alcohol ingestion in utero, but in some cases it is a withdrawal from a bleak and unrewarding world. I have written elsewhere (Youell, 2005) about one such baby, who presented as brain-damaged at 7 months. I quote very briefly here from a session in which an attempt was being made to draw Kylie into contact.

> I made encouraging sounds but she soon flopped her head onto the floor and remained very still, showing no response to my voice. I turned her over onto her back and she seemed more comfortable. However, she did not meet my gaze as I spoke to

her and her head remained in the mid-line regardless of what was going on to either side of her. She showed no response to sound or movement. When I put a toy in her hand she held it for a moment but it quickly slipped from her grasp. . . . Eventually we made eye contact and I felt hugely rewarded and redoubled my efforts to maintain contact with her. I tickled her tummy gently and her mouth moved in what I thought was the beginnings of a smile or a giggle. At this moment I was interrupted by somebody at the door and when I turned back to Kylie it was as if she had switched off. She was staring blankly ahead and made no response when I spoke to her and took her hands again. [p. 51]

Kylie later thrived with a lively, attentive, and determined foster carer. She was fortunate in that she was given the chance of a different life, and her early withdrawal could be seen as having been protective against the full impact of her experience. If she had remained with her mother for longer, she might have become beyond the reach of her new carer and unable to respond to new opportunities.

While some babies withdraw, others become hyper-anxious, restless, and extremely demanding. These babies "put themselves at risk" by crying loudly, eating hungrily, and sleeping little. They are difficult to comfort and difficult to ignore, and a relationship takes shape that is characterized by frustration and resentment. The following is an extract of an observation of an 11-month-old baby, Clint, during a contact session with his crack-cocaine-addicted mother. She was on a rehabilitation programme at the time of the observation.

Clint lay in his mother's lap, clawing at her jumper with insistent fingers. She was pulling his hands away and, at one point, gripped all ten fingers in one fist and glared down at him, her teeth clenched with suppressed anger. He stared up at her with wide, challenging eyes and began to kick wildly. He let out a piercing scream and she looked desperately towards her partner, who shrugged and said, "What do you expect me to do?" Reaching into the bag by her side, she pulled out a dummy and shoved it first into her own mouth and then into Clint's. He arched away from her and twisted his head from side to side. The dummy dropped to the floor, and he screamed again. His mother grabbed him up roughly and stared into his face begging him to be quiet and then turned him to sit on her lap facing away from her. He wriggled and almost fell between her legs. She yanked him back up and, complaining that he was impossible, reached down for the bottle that he had discarded some minutes earlier. As she approached his mouth with the bottle, he pushed it away. For a few moments this developed into a game, and at one point both mother and son giggled. He took the teat in his mouth. However, when Clint inadvertently pinched his mother's arm, she swore at him and took the bottle away. She began to range around the room with her eyes and looked at her watch. Clint slipped down onto the floor, where he settled for a moment or two. He lay down and stared blankly at the ceiling. His mother looked at her watch again and looked towards her partner, who said "What?" in exasperated tones. Clint jerked up and, twisting over, regurgitated some milk onto her shoes.

The relationship between Clint and his mother was not without liveliness, and there were moments of shared pleasure. Clint was not an unwanted baby, and his mother was fierce in her belief that she was a good mother. However, it became apparent to those observing the pair that the relationship was reliant on one or other of them providing challenge or excitement. There was a great deal of giggling and tickling as well as physical "fighting". If both fell quiet, there was a feeling of absolute emptiness and despair. It is possible to imagine that, in his early months, Clint's experience would have been of an unpredictable mother—sometimes warm and loving, sometimes agitated and hostile. She would also have been simply unavailable for periods of time. Williams (1997a) has drawn attention to the way in which some mothers not only fail to contain their baby's distress (Bion, 1962) but actively add to it (unconsciously) by projecting their own state of mind into the baby. She contrasts what Bion called "alpha function" in a mother's relationship with her baby with what she has called "omega function". Bion defined alpha function as the means by which unmetabolized, affective experience is transformed into conscious thought. In Williams's formulation, "'Omega function' derives from the introjection of an object which is not only impervious, but is both impervious and overflowing with projections. Just as the introjection of alpha function is helpful in establishing links in organizing a structure, the introjection of 'omega function' has the opposite effect, disrupting and fragmenting the development of personality" (1997a, p. 126). She suggests that some babies are porous to these projections, while others manage to shut them out but, in the process, withdraw from contact.

Mind-altering substances literally change states of mind in ways that infants and young children cannot process, although they do come to recognize the signs and signals at an early age. Toddlers of parents with addiction become very watchful and extremely sensitive to changes in emotional temperature. They learn when it is safe to make demands on their parents and when to steer clear. The danger is that they also learn how to manage their own feelings of anxiety or neediness in ways that are anti-developmental. It is common to see autistic-like behaviours in toddlers whose parents have been neglectful or emotionally unavailable. Such children often fail to develop the ordinary playfulness that is a vital part of early relationships, and they have very real difficulties when they go to school and are expected to mix with other children and to focus on organized activities. Of course, going to nursery or to school can also be a protective factor, and many children begin to emerge from withdrawn states when offered new opportunities for making relationships.

Older children and adolescents

As children get older, they may be able to articulate something of their experience. This will only happen, however, if they are able to trust the people who are showing interest or concern. Very often, children of addicts are adept at concealing the reality of their home lives. They may also have developed hardened, cynical attitudes to the adult world in general, unable to believe that anybody is capable of altruistic concern.

The examples that come to mind are usually drug or alcohol related. One thinks of latency children who are repeatedly humiliated by their parent turning up at school drunk and argumentative. Children who never bring a note from home, who repeatedly "lose" permission slips, and who cannot muster the cash for the next outing are sometimes covering for parents whose focus is on the next drink or how to achieve the next "high". Social workers describe the ways in which children are observed trying to hide the alcohol or, conversely, are discovered trying to buy alcohol or drugs so as to relieve the pain of the parent suffering from withdrawal. Many children, often supported by organizations such as Al-Anon and Alateen, tell stories of the ways in which they tried to persuade their parent not to drink, often managing to extract promises that they knew the parent would not be able to keep. A sibling pair who had recently been removed from their home, along with five younger siblings, told me that their mother would make tearful promises after every binge. They believed her, until the whole family was made homeless and they were all received into care. They still wanted to believe that she could do it, and they were proud of her when she managed a few days. They insisted that if she did manage to stay off the bottle, the youngest two children should go home to her because "she would give them a good start"—just as she had given them. They were astonishingly forgiving of her, convinced that it had been their violent father who had driven her to drink and that she had done what she could to prevent him from hurting them. These remarkable children had a great deal of insight into their family life but, sadly, were unable to make lasting relationships with foster carers, social workers, or teachers. Their loyalty to their mother and overwhelming sense of responsibility to her and to their younger siblings was such that they could not break away. They could not manage the expectations of their foster parents, nor bear the hopefulness expressed by professionals who thought them charming and resilient. The boy found his way into a street gang and from there into youth custody and the girl into a relationship with a violent man and an early pregnancy. Both drifted back to their mother's care as soon as they could and cocooned themselves in a tight-knit family unit, which projected all the disappointment into the professional network. It was clear that these two children did not have an internal parental object that could support them in developing along separate and different pathways. In the internal world, as in the external reality of their family life, the "healthy, sane but weak" part of the personality (Steiner, 1982) was held in a Mafia-like grip (Rosenfeld, 1971), which demanded total loyalty to the idealized mother.

It is not only alcohol and drug dependency that impacts on children in this way. A 12-year-old boy told me on one occasion that his mother's new-found commitment to religion was no different from her earlier addiction to alcohol. His view was that the church would take her away from the family in just the same way. An adolescent boy told me that his mother could not be coaxed away from Internet chat rooms, and so he had become entirely responsible for organizing meals and getting his younger siblings to school in the mornings. Another described his family's sitting room, where the television had been thrown out to make space for a rank of PCs, where his parents and older siblings could sit in a row, staring wordlessly at their screens. The next room had a row of beds where the family took turns to catch a few hours' sleep. Sadly, this boy was as "hooked" as the rest of his family and saw school as an unwelcome intrusion. It offered him a world he could not manage. "Computers are more predictable than people", he would say.

There are different problems facing children whose parents have been addicted to sexual excitement. Some children have been exposed to adult sexual activity or pornographic material from an early age, and they come to believe that this *is* the adult world. They then have difficulty with understanding any other form of intimacy. There is then profound confusion between sexual excitement and physical affection or comfort. Attempts by adults to offer physical comfort are misinterpreted. Child psychotherapists have to work with a sexualized transference in their treatment of children where sexual abuse or exposure to sexual activity has been a feature of the child's experience. These child patients are either wary in case their therapist makes a sexual advance, or they become seductive themselves, seeking the kind of contact that is familiar to them. They are determined to be the one in control of the seduction that they believe to be inevitable. Masturbation in sessions often becomes a focus of the work. One 6-year-old boy found it impossible to believe that his female psychotherapist did not want physical contact with him and spent months of his treatment setting up situations in which she had to set very clear boundaries and talk to him directly about what was *not* going to happen between them.

I will illustrate some of the issues explored above in more detail with reference to two clinical cases involving two adolescents in long-term psychotherapeutic treatment. Both had one alcoholic and one absent parent.

Katy

Katy was 17 years of age, and she lived with her alcoholic father in the family home, while her mother lived a short distance away. Katy despised her mother for being selfish, and she adored her troubled, unreliable father. She saw herself as being the one who would have to make sure that he kept his job and therefore their home. She convinced herself that his employers did not know about his drink problem. She spent her time checking the house for bottles, clearing up after him, and driving him to and from his AA meetings. If he went on a binge she would ring to tell his work that he was ill, and she would stay home from school to watch over him and clean up after him. If she suspected him of drinking, she would hide the car keys and sometimes lock him in for fear that he would wander into work and be seen in a drunken state.

When sober, Katy's father would speak of his shame and make promises about the future. When drunk, he would accuse her of holding him prisoner and of ruining his life with her puritanical, "stuck-up" attitudes, which he said were just like her mother's and were the cause of the broken marriage. Katy also chose to blame her mother for everything, so their stories were coherent and had enabled them to go on living like this for some time.

Katy sought help from her family doctor when she was not sleeping and was having difficulty studying for her exams. She wanted antidepressants or sleeping pills. Her GP knew of her father's problems and referred her to her local CAMHS service.

In once-weekly therapy, Katy began to talk, not just about her current situation but about her memories of her childhood. She described an idyllic family life. She and her older brother were loved and wanted. They had a nice home and did not go short of anything. She loved primary school and was thought to be very clever. Her father was so proud of her. He called her "princess", and she felt herself to be just that: his princess. She could remember feeling profoundly jealous of her mother and had uncomfortable memories of triumphant feelings when she managed to get in between them on the sofa or when her father intervened to say that she did not have to eat her vegetables if she did not want to. She described holidays in which she would go out with her father, leaving her mother and brother behind in the caravan.

Over a period of one year, Katy worked hard in her therapy sessions. She was secretive at first and only talked about school and about her ambition to go to university. Over time, she talked about her father and her fear that, if she left him to go to university, he would drink and lose his job. She eventually talked about some emerging obsessional symptoms—rituals she had to go through at bedtime and in the mornings. She described the way in which she told herself that if she kept to all these rules, her father would stay sober. She also thought that if she did not, her mother would have an accident or become very ill—and it would be her fault. Katy was astonished that her therapist seemed to listen to this without laughing at her, and she became braver about describing her dreams and about sharing the ups and downs of hope and disappointment in the external world as her father repeatedly broke his promises.

Katy did not know what had changed, but she thought that she was beginning to see things through slightly less rosy spectacles. A boy was showing interest in her, and she was tempted to respond. She had a few conversations with her mother in which she was able to check her own memories against her mother's version of events. She hardly dared voice the thought to her therapist, but she was beginning to question her father's culpability. He had let her down so many times, and she began to dread the cycle of events which had become all too familiar. One weekend when she discovered him drinking on a Friday night, she went to her mother's flat and asked to be allowed to stay so that she could revise for her exams. When she went back home on the Sunday, a sobered-up father greeted her and told her that she had been right to go. He had felt relieved that she had prioritized her own needs and had given him a bit of space to think. He told her that he wanted her to be his daughter, not his nanny, and that if he made a mess of his life it was his choice. She should go to university and leave him to take care of himself.

In her therapy, Katy began to think about the way in which she had built her relationship with her father on the foundations laid down in the very early years. Instead of moving on from the infantile, oedipal situation, she had held on to her "special" relationship with him. Consciously, she blamed her mother for the divorce, but unconsciously, she believed that she had ousted her from her rightful position as wife and mother. The obsessional rituals had been put in place in an attempt to manage her guilt and hold the fear of retribution at bay.

Katy's relationship with her therapist was interesting. In common with many children of parents with addictions, she kept a "safe" distance. The discussions of her dreams or her obsessional thoughts were conducted at what might be thought to be a somewhat intellectualized level. She had said at the outset that what she would appreciate in a therapist was an entirely neutral and non-judgemental stance. She could not bear the idea that a therapist would criticize her father, nor that she might speak up in defence of her mother. She was terrified of becoming dependent on the sessions, and a particularly intense and challenging session would often be followed by a missed one. After a number of missed sessions, her GP and her therapist combined in a helpful way to get her back. She expressed surprise at the way these two adults had agreed on a strategy—something she thought her parents had never achieved. She began to take risks by verbalizing her new perspective on the family dynamics and, in time, was able to admit that she was interested in the therapist's response.

Matthew

Matthew was just 14 when he came into psychotherapeutic treatment. He was living with foster carers, having reluctantly moved out from the home he had shared with his alcoholic mother. Her alcoholism was chronic, and, after several failed attempts at rehabilitation, her health was seriously compromised. Matthew's father had remarried and did not manage to make much space in his life for his son.

Matthew made a study of alcoholism. He had read all the available information on relevant websites and had his own theories about the nature of the addictive personality and the likelihood or otherwise of traits being hereditary. In sessions, he treated his therapist to lectures on the aetiology of alcoholism. She sometimes felt as if she might as well have gone to sleep or left the room because he seemed only to have come to pontificate and listen to himself doing so. Of course, if her attention did wander, he would notice immediately. He had spent years observing his mother closely for signs of depression or drink, and now he observed his therapist in the same way. On a Monday, he would scan the therapist's face for signs of a "heavy session", and on Fridays his assumption was that she could not wait to get away from work and hit the bottle.

Matthew professed himself to be resolutely opposed to drinking. He said he would never touch alcohol, and he thought his peers ridiculous for being so drink-focused. At the same time, he would appear at his therapy sessions wearing badges with drink-related pictures and slogans, as if he were at the very centre of youth culture. His therapist found herself gazing at the picture of a foaming pint of beer on his lapel, unable to question the link between this and what he was saying about the pathetic behaviour of his friends. Of course, it may have been a ploy to mislead his peers, or a taunt directed at his mother, but his therapist also thought that at an unconscious level it was a communication about just how dominated his mind was by thoughts of alcohol and just how vulnerable he was to becoming a drinker.

Matthew had much in common with Katy. He refused to allow for the possibility that his therapy might become important to him, such was his terror of any kind of dependency. If he felt himself to be in danger of looking forward to a session, he would miss it. For many months, he refused to acknowledge any neediness. It became clear that he could not bear the idea that his therapist might be invested in the success of the work. He tried, as the therapy progressed, to intellectualize his understanding of psychotherapy in the same way as he intellectualized addiction. Again, he trawled the Internet to see how the process was supposed to work. His therapist was working in the NHS, and this enabled him to think of her as simply seeing him to meet her "outcome targets". He suggested that she should move on to the next patient—he did not want her to care about him.

Matthew's relationship with his father was complicated. He could not decide whether he hated him for leaving the family or admired him for having got away when he could. He declared himself to be free, but he really believed that he was trapped forever in the cycle of his mother's drinking—a cycle that would only be broken if she died, which he dreaded she might. He did not dare miss seeing her, because he was sure that if he let her down, she would drink. At the same time, she constantly let him down. He claimed that he did not much care whether or not he saw his father, but it was clear that he cared very much about both parents and was burdened, like Katy, with guilt. Was it his fault? Was he a disappointment to his parents? Could he have prevented any of it? Would their marriage have survived if he had not been born?

Matthew eventually began to be less controlling of the conversations with his therapist. He seemed less compelled to teach her what he had learned from Internet sites and was less critical of her contributions to their discussions. She felt that he was benefiting from the simplicity of the structure of therapy: a set routine with clear appointment times. She did her best to make no unexpected changes. Matthew, on the other hand, took the opportunity to experiment with being unreliable and unpredictable. He would arrive late or miss sessions entirely, sometimes with an apologetic message, sometimes with no warning or explanation. He spent some sessions talking non-stop, others entirely silent. His therapist talked to him about an idea that he was giving her the experience that was so familiar to him: the experience of never knowing whether the other person was going to be there, or whether he was going to be left on his own. When he was in the room with her, she sometimes felt him to be effectively absent, again a feeling she assumed to be familiar to him: to be a child with an unavailable parent.

Like Katy, Matthew came to appreciate the fact that his therapist worked closely with other professionals. His relationship with his foster carers and his attitude to social workers and teachers was characteristically cynical. They were only in it for the money. They were not well enough trained in his view, an idea his therapist was able to take up in the transference in relation to her own qualifications and his doubts that she was really well trained enough to manage him. When she intervened over his sporadic attendance and urged the foster carers to bring him to his sessions, he responded surprisingly well.

Matthew's and Katy's family circumstances were not as dreadful as those of some of the children mentioned earlier in this chapter. Both had a second, non-addicted parent. Both had memories of family life before the addiction took hold, and, in both cases, school was a protective factor. Both had parents who wanted them to be free to live their lives, and in neither case were they being pressurized to join in with the drinking. However, both encountered problems when adolescence required them to revisit the oedipal situation (Waddell, 1998). The "solution" they had both found in earlier childhood proved an unsatisfactory one. They had been in identification with a parent figure: looking after their own parent in the external world but in the process looking after the infantile, unmet need in themselves. In both cases, the relationship with the therapist offered an opportunity to explore these issues in the transference and to make tentative changes in their relationships with their real parents and other adult figures. However, in neither case could the work be said to have been complete. Both Katy and Matthew remain vulnerable to finding their own neediness intolerable. It was by no means clear that either could really acknowledge dependency or manage ambivalent feelings.

The risk for so many children of parents with addictions is that internal neediness goes unrecognized, is denied or hated, such that the individual falls prey to addictive substances or addictive behaviour to avoid or relieve the pain. It is one explanation, perhaps, as to why the children of addicts so often become addicted in their turn. The original deprivation is compounded in the way Williams (1997a) describes in her seminal paper, "Double Deprivation". The internal neediness is hated so profoundly that the individual turns the hatred outwards, projecting it onto those who might offer help, and in so doing deprives him/herself "doubly".

In extreme cases, parents may be culpable in drawing their children into their addictive behaviours. Many addicts have described the way in which they were first given alcohol or drugs by a parent who promised that it would make them feel better. The tragedy of a parent believing that this is the best option for their child is stark. The parent is aware of the emotional pain his or her child is suffering but can only offer the one solution. This is a real cycle of addiction, whatever may or may not be the genetic loading that contributes to the perpetuation of the problem.

CHAPTER THREE

Won't they just grow out of it?
Binge drinking
and the adolescent process

Marion Bower

After a psychology degree, Marion Bower trained as a social worker and then as a psychoanalytic psychotherapist; she currently works at the Tavistock Clinic and in private practice, her experience of young people abusing alcohol coming from both settings.

This chapter moves from a sociological commentary on the developing culture of binge drinking (particularly in young girls) to the central importance of the adolescent process in which the experiences of infancy are revisited. Given that separation from the parents is the prime task of adolescence, pathological experiences of separation in infancy are reawakened; the ensuing anxiety is contained by the pharmacological and psychological powers of alcohol in increasing amounts.

The chapter explores the complex symbolic meanings of alcohol to the young person using Kleinian developmental theory, particularly projective identification and the death instinct, a later component of Freud's thinking. Throughout, the clinical material emphasizes the fear of dependency and the possibility of loss; such closeness is to be avoided at all costs yet it is that trusting relationship which is most needed. Bower stresses the importance of not giving up on the addict despite his or her attacks on the therapy—a theme apparent in many of the chapters in this book.

B inge drinking is increasing dramatically, particularly among young people. By binge drinking I mean the consumption of a large amount of alcohol in one go. The Department of Health (1999, cited in Plant & Plant, 2006) defined a "binge" as consumption of more than 8 units for men and 6 units for women on at least one day a week. The Prime Minister's Strategy Unit (2004, cited in Plant & Plant, 2006) concluded that there were 5,900,000 "binge drinkers" in Britain, and young people between the ages of 14 and 24 were the most likely to binge.

Apart from the sheer size of the problem, one of the most striking aspects of binge drinking figures is the rise of bingeing among women and younger adolescents. In 2004/5 the Office of National Statistics found that 40% of women aged 16–24 had exceeded the daily benchmarks for alcohol at least one day a week (cited in Plant & Plant, 2006). The rise of women drinkers amounts to a social change as well as a numerical one.

> The UK's high level of binge drinking among teenage girls is very unusual. In the great majority of other countries surveyed . . . binge drinking remained more common among boys than girls. [Plant & Plant, 2006, p. 37]

It is not only among older adolescents that these changes are taking place. A number of surveys have shown a rise in drinking among 11–15-year-olds. The average consumption in this age group doubled between 1990 and 2004. As with the older group of adolescents, there was also increase in the proportion of female drinkers (Plant & Plant, 2006).

Binge drinking is often treated as normal in adolescence, a rite of passage; it is rare for an adolescent binge drinker (or an adult one) to feel that he or she has a problem. Yet we know that the physical consequences of heavy drinking are very serious. Much of the newspaper publicity has concentrated on the rise in liver disease among adolescents and young adults; previously this had been the province of middle-aged men. More recently, research has shown that the brain is still developing in adolescence, and the effects of ingesting large quantities of alcohol can do structural damage to parts of the brain.

Not surprisingly, there has been considerable speculation about the reasons for this huge increase in drinking in adolescents and women. The ready availability of cheap alcohol and the production of types of alcohol attractive to young people must be a factor. However, it is not clear which came first, the demand or the product. Is the loosening of social prohibitions also a factor? Although binge drinking is in some ways normalized, it does have the features of an addiction as defined by *DSM–IV* and *DSM–IV-TR* (APA, 1994, 2000) (see also the Introduction) These features include increased tolerance of alcohol: over time more is needed to produce the desired effect. It is often taken in larger quantities over a longer period than intended, and, finally, large amounts of time are given over to obtaining and drinking alcohol. For some adolescents, bingeing has become a major social and recreational activity.

In this chapter I am assuming that binge drinking is an addiction with a significant psychological factor (in addition to its physiological and social aspects). I use psychoanalytic theory to understand the drinkers' relationship to alcohol and how it interacts with their body and their mind. In particular, I focus on a group of young people who start drinking early in adolescence. By the time they reach their late twenties or early thirties, the adolescent process has become chronically unresolved, particularly issues related to dependence and independence. This inevitably affects all their relationships, particularly those with partners and children.

The route to independence

I will start off by describing an ordinary route to independence. This is amusingly illustrated in a cartoon by Posy Simmonds (1982). Jocasta (age about 18) has left home to go to art school. She is living in a grim bedsit. The cartoon opens on a cold night, and Jocasta is returning to her cold and lonely bedsit. She tries to ring her boy-friend, Stefan, and gets his answerphone. She tries to ring her father and stepmother, but they are out and the babysitter is looking after her baby stepbrother. The milk is off, the baked beans are mouldy. Jocasta is feeling desperate, but she has one infallible weapon: a tape recording of her stepmother Trish.

> "Oh Jocasta you poor thing, you're drenched . . . take off those wet things at once. . . . Have a nice drink, there's some medium dry in the drawing room. Your Dad said he'll be a bit late, so we'll start without, OK?. . . . Do pop in and say good night to Willy. . . . God, Jocasta, those jeans look a bit lived in, leave them out tomorrow and I'll shove them in the machine."

With this sympathetic voice in her mind, Jocasta is able to stay alone in her room and tolerate her parents having a life of their own. She does not go out with her friends, and she does not attempt to soften the experience with drink. The glass of sherry offered by Trish is a badge of entry into the adult world, *not a way of blotting out feelings.* It is very important that Jocasta can tolerate her child needs and that Trish is also aware of them, as well as Jocasta's adult self.

"A sense of adulthood which carries deep personal conviction also calls for a relationship in the inner world of one's mind with a figure or figures which could be thought of as a helpful inner couple" (Copley, 1993, p. 84). How does this helpful inner couple develop? Klein (1940) describes a process that begins in the first weeks and months of life. The early ego is fragmented by the workings of the death instinct within. There is an urgent need to internalize good objects to form the core of the ego. The infant splits the experience of the mother into a very good figure and a very bad figure. This is the paranoid-schizoid position, and the leading anxiety is the survival of the self. The leading defence is projective identification, a phantasy that bad experiences or parts of the self can be split off and located elsewhere. The death instinct is projected outwards as a sadistic attack against the mother. The projection of sadism onto the mother leads to the internalization of a very harsh superego.

If all goes well, the infant becomes aware that the mother who is loved is also the mother who is hated. This process leads to feelings of pain and guilt. If the infant can tolerate these or be helped to tolerate them, the depressive position is negotiated, which leads to a more realistic perception of the objects and a modification of the superego, which is internalized as a loved object that loves the self. If depressive anxieties cannot be tolerated, the infant turns to manic defences, which include omnipotence and denial of dependence. This theory places particular importance on the quality of care a child receives:

> Unpleasant experiences and the lack of enjoyable ones, in the young child, especially lack of happy and close contact with loved people, increase ambivalence, diminish trust and hope and confirm anxieties about inner annihilation and external persecution. . . . [Klein, 1940, p. 347]

In many ways the developments of adolescence mirror those of infancy and early childhood, but in adolescence they take on more concrete adult forms. There is the recognition that the mother has a separate life and of the need to come to terms with the parental relationship. Jocasta's father and stepmother are out together. Awareness of the object's separateness can give rise to hate as well as love. However, if the balance on the side of love is enough, there is the internalization of a helpful object who is loved and who loves the self. The device of the tape recorder in the cartoon shows us that Trish is an internal figure in Jocasta's mind. Jocasta can turn to Trish in her mind even though the real Trish is not there. Posy's cartoon shows us another aspect of the internal Trish: her empathy. She recognizes Jocasta's loneliness and feelings of helplessness. Bion (1962) built on Klein's theory of infant development by postulating an aspect of the mother's role, which he called containment. Klein suggests that the infant splits off and projects experiences that are felt to be unbearable. Bion suggests that these projections are received by the mother and processed so that they can be reintrojected by the infant in a more tolerable form. Ultimately the infant will internalize the containing object and have the capacity to process his own emotional states.

What happens to young people who do not have a helpful and containing internal object?

Fears of dependence

All adolescents have some difficulties in tolerating their dependence on parents and significant others. There is the difficulty of accepting that someone who is important to us is not always there and also the awareness of a more "babyish" self at a time when the adolescent wants to be big and powerful. Jocasta can tolerate these experiences because she always has a helpful person in her mind to draw on. Without helpful internal figures, adolescents turn to external figures for support. Paradoxically, they are more dependent on external people, though this is denied.

Young people without a helpful internal object will often turn to external activities such as drugs, crime, promiscuity, where they can obliterate their emotions and feel in control. When young people leave home, the illusion of independence often breaks down, and they may turn to drink. Student drinking is legendary and often given a macho spin in the young person's mind.

Why should the experience of dependence be such a crisis for some young people? I am suggesting in this chapter that there is a lack of a containing internal object coupled with a pathological defensive organization that is profoundly hostile to feelings of need and dependency. Drink is woven into this organization in a way that I describe below.

A narcissistic defence organization

The process of moving back and forth between the paranoid-schizoid and depressive anxieties and defences is part of ordinary development, but if a defensive organization develops using the manic defences I described earlier, the situation becomes stuck. O'Shaughnessy (1981) describes a patient with a weak ego who arrives at the threshold of the depressive position unable to negotiate its pain and guilt. The narcissistic defence prevents the fragmentation of the paranoid-schizoid position but also prevents movement forward. The patient alternates between wanting to know and make contact with his or her objects and retreat to a narcissistic organization. This mode of relating interferes with closeness and intimacy, the resolution of which is one of the tasks of adolescent development.

A narcissistic defence organization combines the idealizing of omnipotent aspects of the self, which are a part of the manic defence, with a denial of dependence on others. Riviere (1937) described a group of patients who presented a "brick wall" to analysis. She suggests that these patients use a complex network of defences to deny the significance of the analyst and evade an underlying depressive state. Riviere stresses the role of manic defences in this organization, with their accompanying omnipotence and contempt. Rosenfeld (1971) describes a pathological defence organization that denies the experience of need and is hostile to needy parts of the self and parental figures. Within the internal world, omnipotent and destructive aspects of the self offer "protection" and freedom from psychological pain to more vulnerable parts of the self. Rosenfeld calls this the Mafia. Within this organization, alcohol functions as an idealized bad object offering freedom from mental pain.

Model Paula Hamilton describes her adolescent drinking in the following way:

> As you get older, you learn that it [alcohol] can take away painful feelings. If the alcohol had not been there I'd have committed suicide as a teenager. It's like being tortured and your mind says "drink or die". [Hamilton, 2006]

What is the torturing pain that Hamilton describes? My hypothesis is that it is the working of the sadistic superego that makes depressive pain so unbearable. The sadistic superego is formed by the projection of the death instinct onto the object, which is then internalized as a sadistic superego. Freud has suggested that there is a risk of suicide when the ego feels hated by the superego. Drink may blot out feelings of pain, but it is also an attack on the internal objects, thus creating a vicious circle.

The price of protection from psychic pain is loyalty to the organization. Those drinkers who want to abstain usually encounter considerable hostility from their fellow drinkers.

An illustration of the organization at work externally is provided by a group of young drinkers, the pressure to join in, the contempt for vulnerability, and the latent or actual violence. Copley

(1993) suggests that the way in which groups of young people take over spaces such as town centres reflects a flight from individual mental life and a forceful intrusion into the more settled population. I would add that menacing or out-of-control behaviour allows the young people to project their own sense of fragility into others. These groups are more accurately described as gangs, as they are gathered together for destructive purposes.

The working of the organization internally is often illustrated by dreams.

> Ms A, age 20, became depressed after splitting up with her violent boyfriend. She started weekly psychotherapy and reduced her intake of drugs and alcohol, despite some mockery from her group of friends. She asked her therapist if she could come twice a week. No sooner had she asked when she had a dream where *she is pursued by a gang of men with knives. One catches up with her and slits her throat. There is no pain.*

> Ms A's therapist suggested that Ms A would rather slit her own throat than allow him to help her. I also think that the "no pain" is an unconscious statement that she would not miss her therapist if she cut off contact with him. Within a short time, Ms A was mocking her therapist as a "sad bastard" and rapidly cut down her sessions and eventually dropped out.

One way the pathological organization defends against experiences of need or separation is through the use of projective identification, a phantasy that part of the personality can be located elsewhere. Acquisitive projective identification is another aspect of projective identification. It is a phantasy that desirable aspects of the object can be appropriated and treated as if they belong to the self. Both these aspects of projective identification deny the reality of the object's separate identity.

> Awareness of separation immediately leads to feelings of dependence on an object and therefore to inevitable frustration. However dependence also stimulates envy when the goodness of the object is recognized. Aggressiveness towards objects seems inevitable when giving up the narcissistic position. [Rosenfeld, 1971, p. 247]

The patient may not give up therapy but may spoil professional success and personal relationships.

> Tim is 19; he suffered from panic attacks. These began when he started university. He was also drinking 10 pints of beer a night on a regular basis. After a period in therapy his panic attacks and drinking both decreased. Tim came back from holiday a day early so as not to miss a session. This drew his attention to his dependence on his therapist. He began to go to the pub after his session and have three or four pints. Not as bad as 10, but enough to affect him and make him late meeting his girlfriend, who naturally complained about the bad effect of his therapy.

> Around this time Tim had a dream. *He and his girlfriend (a non-drinker) are in a car that has stopped in a dark and lonely place. Three or four menacing men approach, he is afraid that he will not be able to defend them both.*

I think that the three or four menacing men are the three or four pints of beer, and his non-drinking girlfriend stands for his vulnerable self as well as his work in giving up drink. Drink is used as part of the narcissistic organization, the menacing men who threaten Tim's attachment to his therapist and his progress. But drink also has a physiological effect. In this way the body is used symbolically and actually as an arena to attack parental figures and the dependent self.

> The attack on the dependent self appears in another of Tim's dreams. Just prior to the dream he had insisted on cutting down his sessions from two to one a week. In the dream he is in a house with another man. *The other man is carrying a nest with two baby birds in it. He follows the other man to the top of the house. The man drops the little birds out the window, and they fall to the ground and die. He is very upset by this.*

> The little birds stand for Tim's dependent self and his two sessions, and the two men are each an aspect of his ambivalence about his therapy and his needs.

So far I have emphasized the attack on dependent needs, but part of the narcissistic organization is also an attack on parental figures;

drink is used concretely to carry out this attack. In adolescence there is an urge to test or push against limits. The binger pushes through the body's limits and floods the liver and kidneys with more than they can cope with. Symbolically, the drinker has overwhelmed a paternal boundary-setting function. I have already described the way in which the mother provides psychological processing or containment for the infant's mental states. I am suggesting that the liver and kidneys that provide physiological processing represent a maternal function. Symbolically and concretely the drinker has attacked the parental figures. The triumph over the parents and the dependent self gives the drinker a high. Over time, more and more alcohol is needed to give the high.

In her work with small children, Klein (1932) discovered that hostility towards the mother or parents can be given expression by fantasies of attack using the infant's own urine or faeces. Fantasies of flooding with urine may be a retaliation for being deprived of milk. This root in urethral sadism is reflected in common terms used to describe drunkenness: "getting pissed", "getting bladdered", "getting hammered", "an old soak". The deprivations inflicted by the mother may be actual, or there may be an intolerance of waiting. Klein found that both children and adults have fantasies of urine as a burning and corroding and poisoning liquid. These attacks lead to fantasies of retaliation and the establishment of a sadistic superego.

All drinkers know the unpleasant effects of alcohol, a hangover, vomiting, and so on. Some drinks are chosen specifically for their burning quality. Yet the body is compelled to continue ingesting drink. Sally Bercow, wife of the Speaker of the House of Commons, puts this very clearly: "I had no stop button" (*Metro* newspaper, 4 December 2009). The body becomes a theatre where sadomasochism is played out. The drinker is both sadist and masochist, attacker and attacked. The attack on the internal parents leads to further depressive anxieties, and these may be blotted out by further drinking. This may be enacted sexually. Sexual attacks on young women drinkers are common. Obviously the attacker cannot be condoned, but the victim can play a part in this too, as part of a sadomasochistic dynamic. Sally Bercow describes deliberately using unlicensed minicabs knowing that she was putting herself at risk. Although there may be no conscious wish to be raped, there may be an unconscious identification with an attacked mother.

> Maria, age 17, drank a series of vodka shots at a party. A group of young men she did not know asked her to go for a walk. Fortunately as they were leaving a male schoolfriend appeared and persuaded her to stay behind with him. Later, when sober, Maria wondered how she could so easily have agreed to put herself in the power of a gang of young men.

Won't they just grow out of it?

Bingeing in adolescence is now so widespread that it is accepted as part of normal adolescence. More research is needed on adolescents who do grow out of it. My own impression is that they are like Jocasta: adolescents with strong and helpful internal objects. However, for many adolescents this is just the starting point of an addiction. The adolescent style of bingeing can carry on beyond 30. What may have started off as an anti-anxiety drug can become an addiction.

In an article, "Nine Drink Diaries", in the *Guardian* newspaper in 2004, Roger Browning, aged 43, reports drinking 61 units during the previous week. He comments:

> I don't consider myself a heavy drinker, though my diary may indicate otherwise: this was a week in which a number of events involving alcohol came together. . . . I grew up in New Zealand; drinking was very much part of the male culture, along with rugby and bad haircuts. I hit my stride with booze as a student, drinking too much, too often. I mostly drink wine or vodka and tonic. Occasionally, I dabble with cocktails. I try not to mix my drinks and generally don't get hangovers. [*Guardian*, 20 November 2004]

In the same article, Steve Hoggett, 32, reports drinking 67 units in the week:

> *Day 1.* Shelve plans to go to the theatre and drink three pints of lager instead. *Day 2.* Go out for dinner, during which I drink three beers. Then on to a bar for a friend's birthday: three pints.

Day 3. Hung over. Can't move without an orange juice. *Day 14.* Drink a pint of Hoegaarden and a glass of white wine with dinner. *Day 5.* Sunny day, so sit in the park and drink three cans of Stella. Cook dinner for a friend and drink a pint of Hoegaarden. Have two pints of Heineken after seeing a show. *Day 6.* Go to a bar and have three pints of lager. *Day 7.* Press night at Soho Theatre, but drink a lot less than I thought, especially as there is free wine: a bottle of Cobra beer and three glasses of wine.

My drinking life

Being a performer requires you to be fit and alert on stage, and touring is decidedly un-rock'n'roll. So, slightly alarmingly, I treat life outside rehearsals and touring as if I'm on holiday. Now my performing role within our company is on the decline, I've joined a gym. But I wouldn't let a gym session get in the way of a healthy beer session the night before. Socialising is almost always in a bar.

As a young boy growing up in Yorkshire, I had a typical introduction to alcohol and did the usual alcoholic development through the early 1980s. My parents always had drink in the house as they had friends around a lot. At university I developed a taste for gin and tonic while others drank Welsh bitter through jockstraps. [*Guardian*, 20 November, 2004]

Both men describe patterns of drinking that became established as adolescents or young adults. Neither of these men seems to have a partner or children. Parents who drink have to face the guilt of its effect on their children. These feelings of guilt are made worse by the severe superego of the drinker and can lead to a vicious circle of more drinking.

The superego of the drinker is very harsh, in line with the sadism of the attack on the internal parents. One way of managing the harsh superego is to project it onto others. Many treatment projects reflect the harshness of the drinker's superego. One of the difficulties of giving up drinking is becoming aware of the damage that drinking can do, both in reality and to one's objects; a harsh superego makes this intolerably painful, and there is a turning to the pathological defence of more drink.

Mrs Z has just begun to be aware of the effect on her children of drinking or taking cannabis when she puts them to bed.

Mrs Z dreamed that she was *in a very high place. She realized that she could get down if she was very careful. As she climbed down, she saw her husband and children in filthy chicken coops. The sight was so awful she climbed higher.*

Mrs Z increased her consumption of cannabis and decreased her consumption of alcohol ("getting higher"). I think the dream shows that Mrs Z feels the damage done to her family goes very deep and she wants to "rise above it".

Growing into it

Recent studies show that British teenagers have among the highest binge-drinking rates in Europe (Plant & Plant, 2006). What is it about Britain that makes this the case? The factors that lead young people to drink are complex and include social policies, social pressures, cheap alcohol, aspects of their own personalities, and their early experiences of care. In this section I would like to look at some early roots, both in the personality and in the environment.

Personality factors

In her seminal paper "Addiction to Near-Death", Betty Joseph (1982) describes a group of patients who inflict physical and psychological torment on themselves in a way that also provides them with masochistic sexual gratification. "I think that they have withdrawn into a secret world of violence where part of the self has been turned against the other part, parts of the body being identified with the offending object, and this violence has been highly sexualized, masturbatory in nature, and often physically expressed" (p. 137). I think the relationship to the body in binge drinking as I described earlier in this chapter is very similar to this group of patients. The sexualized aspect of drinking is reflected in the use of sexualized names for drinks—for example, "screw-driver", "wkd", and so forth. An important aspect of Joseph's paper is that she puts forward some hypotheses about the child-hood experiences of these patients.

> It seems to me that instead of moving forward and using real
> relationships, contact with people or bodies as infants they
> retreated apparently into themselves and lived out their rela-
> tionships in this [pre-oedipal] sexualized way . . . [Joseph, 1988]

Joseph suggests that as infants these patients had a psychologi-cally difficult childhood, such as a lack of warm contact and real understanding. However, she also suggests that these patients had difficulty in waiting or in gaps or with even the simplest type of guilt, so that an approach to the depressive position with its feelings of responsibility and guilt is felt as unbearable tor-ment, and they have taken over inflicting this on themselves. Mrs Z, whom I described earlier, was unable to face the guilt depicted in her own dream.

Environmental factors

In what way do children in our society lack warm contact and real understanding?

Consider this scene: A group of young people screaming, shout-ing, laughing, jumping up and down. There is one boy standing at the edge, silent and depressed. Every so often one of the group gives him a push or a punch.

This is not a group of young bingers, but a group of 2- and 3-year-olds in a residential nursery. They are cared for physically but not emotionally by a constantly changing group of staff. This film was made by James and Joyce Robertson (1969) to illustrate the effects of separation on the very young. The excited gang *do not expect attention from an adult.* They hold themselves together by excitement and activity. The Robertsons' film follows a depressed boy, "John", who has recently been separated from his mother. He seems to have lost her as a good figure, perhaps because she is expecting a baby. John is attacked by the group because he rep-resents something the group is afraid of: feelings of despair and loss. The Robertsons describe the absence of attachment figures. I would add to this the absence of figures who can contain and give expression to the child's emotions. The quarrelling, fighting, and excitement in the group holds the children together in the absence of emotional containment and adult attention.

It seems to me that the gang of nursery children with their absence of helpful internal objects and their turning away from help is a junior version of Rosenfeld's Mafia. I am not suggesting that all children from residential nurseries become bingers. But I do think that certain sorts of care make a young person vulnerable to this when they hit adolescence. Although there are very few residential nurseries, there are many day nurseries where children as young as 3 months may spend a whole day, most days of the year. Many children suffer from what Holmes (1995) has called "fragmented care". By this she means a variety of carers who do not have a long-term role in the child's life. There is no one who really knows the child as a person. Holmes says: "by the age of 3 they have often experienced a range of substitute care and of necessity they have learned to be prematurely independent and to expect little support from adults" (Holmes, 1995, p. 149). Some children will fight for their needs to be met, others will withdraw or get hooked on excitement, like the little gang in the Robertsons' film.

Barnett (1995) found that increased exposure to a nursery led to increased aggression. I think that one reason for this increase is that aggression, which ultimately derives from the death instinct, is not contained and modified by carers, who are emotionally attuned to the children. This aggression can later be turned against the self and the internal parents in the form of adolescent binge drinking.

Social factors

I suggest that the increase in day nurseries and delegated fragmented care of very young children is part of a social trend to deny the importance of the maternal function. I think that it is significant that many day nurseries market themselves as educational establishments. Menzies Lyth (1975) has suggested that this sort of care fosters a premature and fragile independence. Could the lack of value of maternal figures in our society relate to the rise of young women drinkers? Perhaps for young women there is an identification with a debased or damaged figure, leading to a sadomasochistic relationship with the self.

The changing patterns of young people drinking and the changing nature of drinking places themselves may also play into the defences that young people have developed in response to fragmented care. Local pubs in small communities are likely to have representatives of the older generation present, and the young people themselves will be known. This is in contrast to large city pubs, which are anonymous and may have no seats as standing up encourages a rapid rate of drinking. An article in the *Independent* carried the photograph of a young woman drunk and unconscious, her hair covered in vomit and her skirt around her waist. She had no handbag and no friend with her. There is an implication that she has been robbed and is sexually vulnerable.

Binge drinkers in psychotherapy

There are very few accounts, in Britain at least, of binge drinkers in psychotherapy. One reason for this is that most bingers do not think they have a problem. In addition, psychoanalysts and psychotherapists often view binge drinking as a contra-indication for therapy. In practice, drinkers get into therapy for other presenting symptoms: depression, anxiety, and relationship problems. In view of the seriousness of the problem, there is an urgent need for more accounts of working with young drinkers.

My own experience of working in the NHS in the Tavistock Clinic and in a private psychotherapy practice is that many bingers give up or reduce their drinking very quickly once they are in therapy. Psychotherapy provides an externalization of a benign parental couple with structure containment and limits. Most patients give the impression of having been starved of emotional containment for various reasons, including maternal depression, illness, or preoccupation with other siblings. However, there are other specific issues and difficulties that seem common to binge drinkers.

Often the transference mirrors the use of alcohol. Sessions may be flooded with material, often more than the therapist can process. The therapist is not used to give insight but to filter out what is important. Vital information can be omitted or given at the end of the session. In short, the therapy is treated like the patient's liver or kidneys, and the therapy is used as dialysis rather than analysis. In this situation the patient is very dependent on the therapist. Patients often complain that the therapy is addictive. In fact, this is an addictive *use* of the therapy. Awareness of dependence on the therapist often leads to a negative therapeutic reaction. The pathological organization asserts itself, and sessions may be reduced or given up altogether, so it is the therapy rather than the drink that is cut down or given up. This is described in the cases of Tim and Ms A.

As patients emerge from dependence on alcohol, they also have to face the damage that alcohol has caused in phantasy to their internal objects and also to their lives and people around them. As Joseph (1982) says, the sadomasochistic relation to the body can bypass feelings of guilt that are felt to be unbearable. Within the therapy there can be a sadomasochistic relationship established with the therapist .The patient can flood the therapist with words, mirroring the flooding of the liver with alcohol. It can be very difficult not to be either punitive or a martyr. The therapist also can get caught in an addictive relationship to the patient where the intermittent successes of the work produce a determination to cure the patient of drink. Etchegoyen (1991) describes a paper by Sheila Navarro de Lopez on this phenomenon. Skinner's work on operant conditioning with rats (see Ferster & Skinner, 1957) demonstrated that intermittent reinforcement produces the most intense responses: rats who were intermittently rewarded with food for pressing a bar were most persistent. I wonder whether the mothers of drinkers are *tantalizing* objects, containing but only occasionally available, which produces a sort of greedy need that may be assuaged by drink.

The drinkers own superego can be an obstacle to giving up drink.

Mrs Z beat herself up when she slipped off the wagon, and this led her to drink again to escape her savage superego.

This produced a vicious circle. It is very important to be alert to improvements in the patient and to acknowledge these, as this can modify the severity of the drinker's superego.

Conclusions

I have tried to show in this chapter that binge drinking is part of a complex defensive organization. This defence is part of a vicious circle where there is an attack on the dependent self and internal parents. I suggest that this attack has its roots in the hatred of the early maternal object. This hatred arises from the externalization of the death instinct as well as frustrations inflicted by the mother. A crucial factor is whether a containing object is available to be internalized to help process emotional states. Adolescents who are entrenched in a pattern of binge drinking will need help to give it up and be able to depend on relationships with other people.

CHAPTER FOUR

A neglected field

Luis Rodríguez de la Sierra

Luis Rodríguez de la Sierra is a psychoanalyst and psychiatrist who has worked in one of the few NHS clinics to offer psychotherapy to addicts. His chapter focuses on adolescents and young adults. Rodríguez de la Sierra points out that very few addicts ask for psychoanalytic treatment and fewer psychoanalysts are willing to take them on, yet treatment, even when of limited success, offers important insights into the nature of addiction.

This chapter looks at the dynamics that tie the addict to the drug. The drug is seen as strengthening as well as overpowering and weakening. This complex relationship distinguishes the addict from the recreational user. The use of drugs in adolescence is closely connected with failed attempts to deal with intense sexual and aggressive feelings. Rodríguez de la Sierra finds that there is a sadomasochistic relationship between the addict and his internalized objects. This has similarities with the sadomasochistic relationship between the binge drinker and his objects described in Marion Bower's chapter (chapter three).

The risks in treating addicts are made clear in this chapter. One patient makes a serious suicide attempt, and one kills herself after abandoning treatment. Rodríguez de la Sierra suggests that a very careful evaluation needs to be made of the patient's internal and external circumstances, including the severity of the addiction and whether the addict has tried to abandon the habit before. He also suggests an important modification to the treatment, which is to appoint someone to take on a parental role to help keep the addict safe. With adult patients, the presence of a non-addicted partner can be an important ally.

I have been interested in patients with addictions for nearly forty years—namely, for most of my psychiatric and psychoanalytic life. I am sad to realize that, after so many years, this continues to be a neglected and misunderstood group of patients, often dismissed as too difficult and untreatable. I was, and continue to be, concerned about the way in which some people deal with their painful feelings, replacing them with the sensations provoked by virtue of pharmacological intoxication. I have written about the problem in relation to one of the most affected groups—adolescents—but they are not by any means the only ones, and what I say in this chapter applies to both the young and the adult, although many of the clinical vignettes I cite come from my work with young people.

In *Confessions of an English Opium Eater*, Thomas de Quincey (1821) writes:

> I hanker too much after a state of happiness both for myself and others; I cannot face misery, whether my own or not, with an eye of sufficient firmness; and am little capable of surmounting present pain for the sake of any recessionary benefit.

In this statement, we can read the most basic ingredients of the psychopathology of the addict: the incessant search for an ideal existence, not unlike a state of Nirvana; the denial of anything that might interfere with the belief that such a state exists; and an intrinsic ego weakness. We can clearly see the magical thinking connected to the belief that a chemical substance (the magic pill) can make everything right and provide the solution to the most complicated and complex personal problems, including the matter of existing.

The addict functions with a severe split within himself, succeeding in believing that he is calm and unaffected by his surroundings, while at the same time showing that the only way to cope with life (and all the painful effects connected to it) is by creating artificial sensations or by being either asleep or semi-conscious.

In *Three Essays on the Theory of Sexuality* (Freud, 1905d), Freud linked oral eroticism in men with their desire for smoking and drinking, and thus he discovered the most important link in the chain of events underlying drug dependence. The specific action of intoxicants, however, must not be underestimated. In *Civilization and Its Discontents* (1930a), Freud says:

> In the last analysis, all suffering is nothing else than sensation. . . . The crudest but also the most effective among these methods of influence is the chemical one—intoxication. I do not think that anyone completely understands the mechanism; but it is a fact that there are foreign substances which, when present in blood or tissues, directly cause us pleasurable sensation; and they also alter the conditions concerning our sensibility, that we become incapable of receiving unpleasurable impulses. [p. 78]

Freud tells us that in their fight for happiness and to keep misery at bay, this group of people so highly value as a benefit the service rendered by the drug that they have given them an established place in the economics of their libido.

Anna Freud, in *Normality and Pathology in Childhood* (1965), describes the overwhelming craving for sweets in children, who use the satisfaction of the craving as an antidote against anxiety, deprivation, frustration, depression, and so on. She sees a child's love for sweets as a comparatively simple, straightforward expression of a component drive with its roots in unsatisfied or over-stimulated desires of the oral phase, desires that have grown excessive and, by virtue of quantity, dominate the child's libidinal expressions. According to her,

> a true addiction in the adult sense of the term is a more complex structure in which the action of passive–feminine and self-destructive tendencies is added to the oral wishes. For the adult addict, the craved-for substance represents not only an object or matter which is good, helpful, and is strengthening, as a sweet is for the child, but one which is simultaneously also felt to be

injurious, overpowering, weakening, emasculating, castrating, as excessive alcohol or drugs actually are. It is the blending of the two opposing drives, of the desire for strength and weakness, activity and passivity, masculinity and femininity, which ties the adult addict to the object of his habit in a manner which has no parallel with what happens in the more benign and positively directed craving of the child. [p. 11]

Her views on drug addiction help us to distinguish severe drug addiction from the more benign occasional use of recreational drugs such as cannabis, cocaine, and alcohol.

Problems of substance abuse can occur at any level of society and affect all socio-economic groups. It is the interaction of the cultural, environmental, and constitutional elements with the conscious and unconscious forces operating within the addict (or, in other words, the interaction of his internal and external worlds) that mostly contribute to the creation of this condition. The causes of drug addiction and alcoholism are complex. In *The Odyssey*, Homer already sang of a world-famous, mythical adolescent, Helen of Troy, having "drugged the wine with a herb that overcomes all grief and anger and lets forget everything bad". Like her, many of those who use drugs do so because of a powerful psychological need to avoid, regulate, or run away from inner experiences that are painful and distressing. However, the powerful psychological component should not make us forget the question of physical dependency when facing those patients so seriously addicted to drugs that their craving becomes a major priority in their life, which is dominated by their relationship to drugs and alcohol.

Trying to understand the reasons why people abuse drugs is not an easy task. A full metapsychological assessment of such cases would certainly throw a greater light on the subject within the context of possible environmental factors: libidinal and aggressive drive organization with the appropriate phase of development, cathexis of the self and of the objects, ego development (reality testing, internalization of objects), defence organization, superego structure, and so forth. At the same time, it is important to bear in mind the relevance, to the addict, of any changes in self-cathexis, in self-perception, under the effects of the drug. This leads to the question of what changes these people may be trying to achieve. Drugs have different effects on different individuals, and, as I mentioned before, it is very difficult to differentiate between psychological and pharmacological effects. Many people, young and older, use drugs for thrills, to obtain sexual gratification or as a substitute for it, and for them it is the "buzz" that really matters. They may or may not become addicted to the substance they abuse. This substance may be used only occasionally to produce pleasurable sensations and more often when the lack or excess of feelings becomes intolerable to the individual. For intravenous injectors, the use of the needle acquires specific and meaningful importance. Others take drugs for the feeling of Nirvana they provide to ease the despair and misery they experience—for example, some heroin users who, under the influence of the drug and the ensuing physical dependency, no longer care.

The evidence of misuse is probably greatest among adolescents. If it is true that some drug users can be thought of as experimental users and controlled users, adolescence is not characterized as a period of moderation and self-control, and the younger adolescents are, the less likely they are to control the use of drugs once they have become involved. This makes them especially vulnerable.

Some addicts use drugs to increase their self-esteem. Those who have a defect in reality testing or whose egos are weak are indifferent to the dangers of the drugs, which are outweighed by the effect on self-esteem.

Alan, a 19-year-old heroin addict, the only child of an apparently normal family, good-looking, intelligent, and a good athlete, concealed a violent nature under a pleasant and polite façade. Like many of his kind, his self-esteem was rather low. Previous to his drug-taking, he had a history of outbursts of violence in school, manifested in the bullying of other children and, occasionally, gang fights and vandalism. His eccentricities, shyness, and outbursts of violence had made him a rather isolated youth, with no friends at school. He hated his violence and immediately conveyed to me that heroin made him much more peaceful, more at ease with himself, less aggressive and violent. He felt less paranoid and more willing to make friends with others. He felt better liked, particularly by the trendy

youths who were experimenting with soft drugs and also cannabis and even with heroin as something glamorous, attractive, and daring. On one occasion he said to me: "Heroin is a
calming thing. It's the little place you can always turn to and
puts a cloud over everything."

However, in other cases there were no indications that the use of
heroin had any such effect on self-esteem, and it did not function
as a source of narcissistic supplies. In certain cases where there
was an apparent rise in self-esteem, the reasons for this were not
consistent from case to case. In those cases, heroin did not simply
function as a source of narcissistic supplies. There are other ways
in which the use of heroin may appear to enhance self-esteem: the
modification of critical superego functioning, temporary changes
in the defensive organization, redistribution of drive energy, the
approval of other addicts—all these may increase the addict's self-
esteem, at least while the drug is operative.

We are not concerned with a homogeneous group of disorders,
and frequently addicts are very different from each other, hence
the need for a proper assessment and for responding accordingly.
In some heroin addicts, for example, who otherwise would inhibit
their aggressive inclinations, the drug intensifies or even liberates
anger or rage. But in others, heroin may sharply reduce aggressive
behaviour, and that may be the unconscious reason for which the
person uses it. I am not talking here only about destructive aggression, but also about the capacity to use aggression forcefully and
constructively for adaptation and mastery.

Other heroin addicts whose anxieties have been aroused by
their libidinal urges find their libido sufficiently mitigated by the
drug to obviate these anxieties; when sexuality is a source of shame,
the taking of the drug heightens their self-esteem and feelings of
well-being. There is no consistent response in different patients.

For the addict, the drug represents an external object endowed
with positive and negative characteristics, but however harmful it
might be felt to be, it has a necessary function, since the addict feels
there is something bad inside him (anxiety, violence, depression,
guilt, perversion, psychosis, etc.) and uses the drug as if it were a
medicine to anaesthetize or destroy the badness, to "cure" himself.
Drug abusers are "self-medicators" who desperately and vainly try

to deal with powerful, intense, and disturbing inner experiences that threaten to overcome them. Unfortunately, the addict himself is in one way or another in danger of being destroyed.

While many of these patients are thought of as suffering from borderline disorders, the reality is more complex. We can see a much greater variety that goes from the neurotic, to the patient where either alcoholism or drug addiction serves the purpose of keeping a psychosis at bay, to the overtly psychotic individual. There is an unfortunate tendency to see these patients as belonging to one and the same category, and many erroneous generalizations come out of this misconception. One of them is classifying the psychopath and the addict as one and the same. If it is true that addicts may have a fair deal of trouble with the law and become involved in delinquent and criminal acts (in the way that children, as Anna Freud tells us, lie and steal in order to obtain their supplies of sweets), they are not to be confused with the psychopath, with whom they, by definition, cannot be classed. The psychopath experiences no internal conflict and cannot create one. Instead, he establishes a conflict with the outside world and, in so doing, uses alloplastic methods (adaptive responses that alter the environment). The addict does experience an internal conflict and tries to resolve it by a change of endopsychic functioning, which makes their condition an autoplastic one (adaptive responses that alter the self). This difference is an important one and has to be taken into account for the proper comprehension and management of the two conditions, which I illustrate with the following vignettes:

John, a 15-year-old youth, the son of divorced parents, had felt abandoned and rejected by his father, whom he had not seen since the age of 10. Undermined by his mother—who constantly criticized him and who found it difficult to tolerate his presence because it reminded her of her ex-husband—John had very poor self-esteem and had failed disastrously in his studies despite being of superior intelligence. At school, he started mixing with the "bad crowd" and began experimenting with drugs, first with hashish and afterwards with amphetamines, to which he became addicted after experiencing, for the first time in his life, positive feelings of self-esteem. He felt that "speed" gave him a stronger, more powerful personality, which, he thought, helped him to obtain his friends' admiration. In the course of treatment, he was able to acknowledge his "feelings of inferiority" and how he took drugs in order to improve himself and feel "more normal".

Linda, a 19-year-old girl with a long history of antisocial activities, which included shoplifting, handling of stolen goods and vandalism, found herself a patient in an adolescent unit as a result of a probation order. She experienced no remorse over her delinquent activities and was convinced she had been caught only as a result of not being "clever enough". The family history revealed an early life of emotional deprivation, with a sado-masochistic relationship with a mother who had never helped her to master her environment, leaving her with the conviction that she could only conquer the environment by altering it if she had "special powers". Magical thinking permeated her mental life, and she only responded to treatment whenever she felt she was in the presence of a more powerful and clever therapist whose "magic" she could steal.

The implications of the treatment of this kind of patient, young and adult, have been dealt with by other authors (Aichhorn, 1935; Eissler, 1950; Hoffer, 1949). The affect of the addict is usually a troubled and depressed one. There is none of the defiance, self-confidence, and open aggressiveness of the psychopath in them, unless, obviously, under the effect of drugs or alcohol. When the delinquent uses drugs, he does it to increase feelings of omnipotence.

The type of drug used by the person will influence our clinical judgement, since smoking cannabis cannot be equated with injecting heroin. The choice of a specific drug derives from the interaction between the psychodynamic meaning and pharmacogenic effect of the drug and the particular conflicts in a person's psychic structure throughout his development. The choice of drug is certainly not as indiscriminate or capricious as it may appear from superficial observation. The anxious person may use any drug, whereas the psychopath will generally take drugs that will accelerate mental processes. On the other hand, the continuous use of opiates may suggest a psychotic or borderline disturbance with an important

depressive element. Something similar may be said about the persistent use of alcohol, although here it is important to remember
environmental influences in certain cultures. Having said that, it
is important to be aware that the psychic use to which the drug is
put could, in some cases, be more important than the drug itself.

Changes in drug preference may also indicate internal psychodynamic changes. As mentioned earlier, it is extremely difficult, if
not impossible, to distinguish between symptoms resulting from
pharmacotoxic affects and those caused by underlying psychopathology. The conscious and unconscious psychological changes
of adolescence, which are in the process of evolution, are further
obscured by exposure to pharmacotoxic influences. Fears and anxieties accompany the adolescent's curiosity about the functions of
the body and mind; aggression and energy also become confused,
and the adolescent easily adopts the solution of mitigating his confusion with a "downer" rather than trying to deal with it. When
initial experiments to dispose of sexual feelings through casual con-
tacts fail, the adolescent is easily tempted to get rid of the resulting
desolation, despair, and emptiness by means of the instantaneous,
though temporary, relief offered by drugs.

Psychotic anxiety brought out by hallucinogenic substances
such as LSD can be very frightening to the young person, who then
turns to another drug to dispel the previously drug-induced disturbance. As a result, he may find solace in tranquillizers, cannabis, or
amphetamines. The escalation to hard drugs creates a vicious circle
in which the adolescent (as well as the adult addict) is trapped as
he struggles to keep at bay the menace of disintegration.

At the centre of the adolescent's turmoil is the revival of bisexual
conflicts, which the young person often tries to solve through
promiscuity or complete withdrawal. When these attempts fail,
they may look for others in similar circumstances in the hope that
sharing their problem with others might improve their experience.
In such cases, drug abuse is the common link that constitutes the
only possible elective and shared experience.

It has been said that the mildest forms of addiction are largely
reinforcements of unconscious homosexuality. This does not mean
they are easy to treat, particularly in adolescence, for obvious
reasons, and it has deeper implications in the case of the "needle"

addict. The boy in conflict about his sexual identity may be unable to make a fundamental choice between the female within and the female without. The posture he adopts is overtly heterosexual, but his behaviour with drugs seems to negate this. The self-injection and the feeling of well-being that it engenders seem to symbolize and display the unconscious choice, which, however, remains unacceptable. For the girl, the problem has a similar obverse meaning, and the drug abuse has the same quality as the unrestrained promiscuity that often accompanies it. Her relation to drugs progressively replaces object relations until they virtually take over. Masturbation and sexual intercourse are often displaced by the intravenous injection of drugs.

The role of drugs in adolescence has, from a developmental point of view, many different and interesting implications. Sociological factors, trends, peer-group influence, and so on must be taken into account as well as psychodynamic factors when assessing psychopathology, for drug-taking may be part of the normal adolescent's need to experiment, test, or simply rebel against given adult values. This alone would be, of course, a very simplistic explanation. The use of drugs in adolescence is closely connected with failed attempts to deal with intense aggressive and sexual feelings, which the adolescent then tries to relieve by turning to pills or injections that bring deceptive tranquillity to his troubled mind. The analyses of many youngsters and adults reveal a sado-masochistic relationship between the individual and his internalized objects, with its accompanying persecutory anxieties. Glover (1932) describes the symbolic dramatization of the love-and-hate relationship with the parents—namely, the battle with continuous and unresolved problems, which prolong a very disturbed relationship between infant and his mother, towards whom the addict remains highly ambivalent. If to all this we add the depression that we so very often find in adolescence, we can begin to understand the psychodynamic meaning of a drug addiction that began in adolescence and continued into adulthood.

Some people compare over-eating with addictions and alcoholism, but such cases would need to demonstrate, on the instinctual side, the characteristics described for the addict. Besides, there is no additional pharmacological complication in eating disorders.

It is a fact that the number of confirmed addicts asking for psychoanalytic treatment is small. Their impatience and tension intolerance predispose them against the slowness of analysis. The number of analysts and psychotherapists who will accept them is even smaller, and the number of addicts who complete their treatment yet smaller. Those few may benefit, and the work with them may inform us all about the psychodynamics of drug addiction. As in many other areas of psychopathology, there is no psychoanalytic consensus on the treatment and management of these patients. Opinions vary from those who consider these patients absolutely unsuitable for psychoanalysis to those who feel no need for any modifications whatsoever of the usual psychoanalytic approach. As I have mentioned above, this is not a homogeneous group, and this has to be borne in mind when deciding what to offer to the addict. Analysis and psychoanalytically oriented psychotherapy would be the treatment of choice for those interested in understanding themselves. For those who are not, there may well be alternative provisions.

I personally feel that I must respond to the addict who seeks help, but I also like to give careful thought to what sort of help I can offer. This may involve a tricky and long period of assessment, where I must be aware of the possible complications of an incipient transference that must be dealt with, even if a patient is to be referred to somebody else. I believe that some addicts can be treated psychoanalytically, but careful consideration of the patient's individual psychopathology must be accompanied by an even more meticulous evaluation of his personal external circumstances and environment in general (including contact with other agencies, relatives, etc.). Special consideration must be given to facts such as the severity, frequency, and quality of the addiction and whether or not the patient has succeeded in abandoning it before. If I feel that the addiction is such that to start treatment in such a state would endanger the analysis, I suggest that the addict be admitted to an institution and that detoxification be carried out by a colleague with whom I could work closely in the future if appropriate. Referral to a detoxification centre might be necessary again when in the course of treatment the patient relapses in a bad way and the analytic work is threatened by that relapse. If I decide to start treatment outside the clinic or hospital, I make sure that the patient's living conditions are safe, and I make a point of establishing a link or collaboration with someone living with the addict and prepared to take on the parental guiding role without which one finds it difficult to ensure the survival of the treatment or indeed of the patient. Close collaboration with other doctors involved, probation officer, social workers, hostels, and so forth is, in my opinion, a *sine qua non* in these cases.

I also think that in addition to an accurate understanding of the addictive psychopathology and a great deal of empathy on the part of the analyst, one must be prepared to adopt the role of the indestructible object if one is to meet the great challenge that addicts present us with. I do not mean by this that we should believe we are indestructible, but that in our attitude we should convey to the patient that we shall not easily succumb to his destructive attacks. I am not talking here about the so-called emotional corrective experience but about the application of Anna Freud's method of developmental help to areas of the psychopathology related to developmental deficits (often observed in the history of many of these patients) rather than to purely neurotic or psychotic conflicts. Developmental help does not mean that one stops being an analyst, but it implies some departures from classical analytic technique.

Pierre was 24 when we first met. He was an only and adopted child who had witnessed his father's death at the age of 8 and his mother's when he was 11. Both died of a heart attack. He had been brought up by a distant relative up to the age of 15, when they fell out and Pierre started living with girlfriends who were clearly mother substitutes. When we first met, I became immediately aware that he looked and behaved as a much younger boy, forever stuck in perpetual adolescence. He told me that his father had been a doctor and that perhaps it made sense that he should seek help from another doctor. He was good-looking, intelligent, and very articulate. It soon transpired in the analysis that he also had very poor self-esteem and saw himself as useless, stupid, ugly, and "good-for-nothing". Before taking drugs, he used to be extremely shy and completely unable to make any use of aggressive energy. Shortly after his first intravenous injection of heroin, he felt more self-confident and more able to do useful things. He felt more attractive and soon became addicted to the feeling of increased self-esteem and well-being. He used to be brought to his daily analytic sessions by his girlfriend's mother, and he shook hands with me at the beginning of every session, something rather unusual in England. I chose not to comment on it as I soon became aware that he was unconsciously afraid of me and of being rejected by me, being able to make contact with me only through the physical contact offered by the handshakes. One day he was late, apologized, and told me he could not find a taxi. I noted that he had come alone, for the first time. From then on, he continued to come on his own, and I noticed he had stopped shaking hands with me. When I felt that Pierre was ready to hear it, I drew his attention to it and said to him that he had to be brought to his sessions like a child because he was afraid of me and that he had to literally touch me to reassure himself that I was not going to reject him. To have interpreted this to him prematurely would have been experienced by Pierre as a humiliating narcissistic blow and would possibly have created an unnecessary resistance to the analysis.

This way of working contrasts with the corrective emotional experience in which the therapist might actually believe that by playing the role of a parent, he is correcting what went wrong. Developmental help is very close to making a relationship, but it involves meeting the patient at his stage in development. For example, with Pierre, shaking hands enabled him to experience contact, but at a concrete level until he was ready for symbolic contact through interpretation. This is not "correcting" and not offering a new mother or father, but letting patients develop in a slightly different way until they are ready for the more classical psychoanalytic approach. The making of the relationship plays a very important part in the treatment of patients like Pierre who come prepared to be rejected and disliked and to whom the drug represents a replacement of the human relationship they never had or fear they cannot have.

The transference relationship is always an affective one, because the analysis is not an intellectual but an affective process, and for the analysis to proceed we need what we call *rapport*. It is only when we make direct contact with the affects through empathy that we can interpret them intelligently and be certain of how the patient is feeling. Accurate empathy is indispensable to sound analysis, and the wisdom we need is a combination of intelligent insight and emotional understanding. We have to register and interpret affect in instincts and object relations terms, but we also have the further task of analysing the affects themselves. We must have logical theory, but we do not work with theory: we work with living impulses and feelings. This, of course, applies to all patients, but it is of the utmost importance to bear this in mind when treating the addict, who not only deals in a very complex way with his feelings, but is also capable of provoking disconcerting and confusing feelings in the analyst, who may not always be emotionally ready to deal with them. The issue of countertransference is therefore very important with these patients. The therapist's personal values, opinions, and attitudes towards them need to be acknowledged.

The highly ambivalent attitude of the addict towards the drug, first seen as a remedy to his problems and later seen as an enemy, as a persecutor to get rid of, is recreated in the transference, where the analyst becomes identified with the drug. This frequently takes place unconsciously in the mind of the patient who has to miss sessions in order to put a distance between himself and the analyst, by whom he feels persecuted and threatened. The understanding of this phenomenon and the way in which the analyst deals with it will greatly influence the possible outcome of these analyses.

One often observes that the addict craves to be united with an ideal object, and one can say that when the addict develops an intense positive transference reaction when meeting an analyst, it is frequently linked with the unconscious phantasy that this ideal object has finally been found. Sadly, the conflict experienced by the addict is that at the same time he dreads that union with the object and feels persecuted by it. He then becomes addicted to acting out the drama of fantasy introjection and separation from the drug, which is at one and the same time the analyst.

To illustrate some of the difficulties encountered in the treatment of these patients, I would like to return to Pierre, the 24-year-old heroin addict referred to me because of a long-term heroin addiction and a history of emotional and parental deprivation from a very early age.

Shortly before his first analytic holiday, this patient had become rather obsessed with the idea of being admitted to a detoxification centre, although he was not at the time heavily involved with drugs as he had been able to considerably reduce the amount of heroin he took during the course of analysis. For reasons that I cannot explain without betraying confidentiality, I had thought it necessary to let him know of my whereabouts during the holiday, and he had insightfully admitted to fantasies of both being admitted to the drug addiction clinic where I worked at the time and/or going to spend his holiday near me. We were both aware that these fantasies were a response to the anxiety he was feeling as a result of the impending break.

On a Thursday afternoon, Pierre arrived forty minutes late, and as he lay down on the couch I noticed he was sleepy and his speech was slurred. I immediately challenged him and asked him what he had taken, and, after a not very convincing initial denial, he said he had taken "just a little bit of coke". I refused to believe him and asked him to stand up in order to look at his pupils, which he refused to do. I had by then decided to prolong the session as I was anxious and worried about a situation that had never before taken place during our work together. When the time of finishing the session arrived, I felt no clearer as to what had happened.

As Pierre was leaving, he said that he knew I had always been interested in his poetry, and he wanted to leave me a tape that contained not his poems but those of someone who wrote in a very similar style to his. I accepted the tape, and as soon as my patient left, I experienced an urgent impulse to listen to it as I thought he was both very anxious and angry about my holiday, and I feared what he might do. The poem on the tape made references to treacherous foreigners who deserved nothing but death and who had to be abandoned before they could become too dangerous. It was obvious that this was a reference both to his parents, by whom he felt abandoned when they died, and to me, as I was going to leave him to go on holiday. I immediately decided my patient was in very serious danger, and, preferring to take the risk of being an alarmist, I telephoned him. There was no reply. I then remembered that the social worker involved in the case lived near him, and I rang her up and asked her to knock at the door and to call me back immediately if she got no reply. I telephoned for an ambulance. It transpired that my patient had overdosed on heroin, and he was taken immediately to casualty where, by that night, he was out of danger as the overdose had not been massive. He telephoned me the following day saying that he was going to discharge himself and asking me to see him on Saturday, which I did. During that session he suddenly remembered something that he said he had never thought about since he was a child. His father apparently often used to go abroad for lectures, and the little boy always managed to cut himself or have an accident before his father's departure to try to compel him to stay. Pierre broke down in tears and was able to talk with much feeling about the events that were a re-enactment, in the transference, of past events involving his father during his childhood.

Of even greater severity is the case of the confirmed addict characterized by a depressive organization that, when combined with self-destructive and destructive factors, make for an uncertain and poor prognosis.

In this connection, I am reminded of a gifted, talented artist, a young woman with a long history of heroin addiction, depression, and homosexual affairs. To her, the needle, the syringe, and the act of getting a "fix" were as important as the drug itself. She often told me that playing with the injected liquid and her blood, pushing it backwards and forwards, gave her enormous pleasure: "It is like delaying an orgasm: the more I stop it, the more I enjoy it in the end." In common with many addicts, she had appallingly low self-esteem, which convinced her from the start that, in spite of her many attempts to seduce me, I could not possibly even begin to like her. She constantly submitted me to innumerable tests, with the only aim seeming to be to prove her conviction that I disliked her intensely. All these "tests" contained strong self-destructive and destructive elements, which often threatened the viability of the analysis, as when she presented me with a small suitcase (which I initially interpreted, wrongly, as her desire to move in with me and stay near me), which turned out to be full of heroin and would have put her at risk of being stopped by the police if she had taken it away with her. I would have found myself in a similarly difficult situation had she left it with me and had I been found in possession of it on my way home from my consulting room. I said to her that she found herself trapped between the wish to destroy herself, and thus put an end to everything she disliked about herself, and her need to perpetrate an envious attack against me by putting me in an impossible situation. This brought back painful memories of childhood. She spoke of her mother, a prostitute, who constantly brought different men to the house, men who treated her in such a way that she felt dirty and bad. She remembered her shame and her intense rage against her mother, whose death she often desired. I added that I thought she had identified with the denigrated and hated mother, whom she tried to destroy every time she attacked herself. In the transference, I was both the hated mother and the normal, sane object whom she intently envied and wished to destroy. After this, she decided the best way to solve the problem was to flush the heroin down the lavatory, insisting that I should examine the suitcase afterwards to make sure that she had disposed of everything inside the suitcase. I said it was easier to flush the heroin down the toilet than to dispose of all the badness inside her, to get rid of all the rage that she felt unable to contain. In spite of these many difficulties, a certain improvement was obtained. The patient's lover, mistaking this for a definite cure and disobeying my advice not to do so, succeeded in persuading the young woman to stop analysis and move to another country. I was not to hear about the outcome until nearly three years later. The young woman had apparently returned to the city where her mother lived. Their relationship had continued to be rather tempestuous. One evening my ex-patient apparently invited her mother to the theatre. After seeing the play, before they went on to a restaurant, the young woman decided to go back to her flat to change her dress. Once there she went into a rage, insulted her mother, and blamed her for all her problems. She suddenly jumped out of a window, killing herself instantly.

As the analysis of this young woman lasted only seven months, my thoughts about her basic aggressive cathexis of the self can only be speculative. Moral masochism, guilt, and the need for punishment were powerful factors in the various ways in which she attacked herself. She attacked her body as a source of unwanted instinctual urges, but it was also clear that the use of drugs and the self-destructive acts that culminated with her suicide represented a massive punitive attack on the object. The case sadly illustrates the multiple meanings that attack on the self may have for the same patient.

Note

In this chapter, the masculine pronoun has been used throughout for non-specific instances.

CHAPTER FIVE

The deprivation of female drug addicts: a case for specialist treatment

Angela Foster

Angela Foster's training was in social work and psychoanalytic psycho-therapy. Over her professional career she has worked with drug ad-diction as an individual and group therapist and Assistant Director of a residential treatment service, as a supervisor to other workers in the field, and as a consultant to substance misuse services. In this chapter she describes how each of these roles must be based on a profound understanding of the fundamental psychopathology of the addict, focusing particularly on the female addict. Central to her thinking is the concept of the female addict's perverse relationship to her own body, and pivotal to this understanding is the work of Estela Welldon. The account that Foster provides is of the female addict's use of drugs to simultaneously alleviate psychic pain and to destroy the body (and relationships). Splitting and projection of negative affect are everywhere, with the result that the addict alienates the sources of support that she most needs. The chapter describes how this is based on experiencing a fundamental failure of being mothered, which she attempts to repair in her successive attempts at mothering herself, yet which she is compelled to destroy. This dynamic is enacted with the maternal functioning of the therapist and with the institution: for either to survive, the thinking space of supervision is essential.

The image below vividly captures something of the plight of female drug addicts; hence "Mia" is the name I have attributed to my main case example. She is an amalgam of clients whom I have known in treatment and those I have heard about in supervision and consultation over 40 years of work in substance misuse services.

Mia's story

In giving her life story to other residents and staff, Mia vividly described a memory she has of standing in her cot watching her father violently and sexually attack her mother. She thinks she first started to get "out of control" aged 7 as she rebelled against her father's drunken beatings. By age 12 she was drinking, and

Figure 5.1   *"Yasmin admires Mia for always being there for her friends." Mia is a drug addict and prostitute. (From the long-term project "Mia: Living Life Trying" by David Hogsholt. Third prize winner, World Press Awards, 2005.)*

later, when introduced to heroin by older male friends, she found that the beatings no longer hurt. She had a violent boyfriend, left home, and drifted into prostitution as a way of supporting herself financially.

Unsurprisingly, as Mia's time is taken up with procuring the money for her drugs and obtaining her drugs, she fails to take care of herself in any other way. She is physically damaged by her injecting and suffers from abscesses. In addition she cuts herself and appears to have an eating disorder, most likely bulimia—bingeing on her food then vomiting it up, ostensibly as a way of keeping slim, but in fact this, like her other activities, is more evidence of her "addiction" to self-punishment and her inability to believe that she is deserving of any good nourishment or care. She feels a bond with other women in her position and takes on a maternal role with them, which may be as close as she can get to looking after the needy and abused child within herself. She has a child who was taken into care at birth.

Introduction

"Mia" is representative of a significant sub-group of female addicts who are the focus of this chapter: women who are multiply deprived and abused and seem to be addicted to re-enactment of these experiences through self-imposed or self-initiated deprivation and abuse of their bodies. They find relief from pain and anxiety through these processes in which they are always the victim and often the perpetrator. The nature and multiplicity of their addiction(s) has received very little attention, and it is possible that the paucity of writing on female addicts is reflective of a collusion between this client group, those treating them, and society in general to turn a blind eye to their needs and their particular pathology. This may also be reflected in the paucity of specialist treatment models for female clients, and tragically, when they access generic drug treatment services, the sadomasochistic relationships that so often characterize their lives are relived in their experience of what feels like punitive treatment from their care workers when they provoke discharge or discharge themselves for non-compliance with treatment models not designed to meet their needs.

We have come to know these women well essentially because we fail them. Consequently they come to our attention over many years, apparently unable to benefit and move on from the care and treatment we provide. What is it about these women that renders them so resistant to help, why haven't we spotted it, what do they need that they are not getting, and how might we work more effectively with them? I will attempt to answer these questions, hypothesizing about why we have been so slow in addressing the problem and making links to relevant psychoanalytic theory. I imagine workers in this field will be familiar with the biographical details provided, recognize the dynamics described, and, I hope, find my analysis helpful. But first some caveats:

» Early deprivation and abuse doesn't necessarily lead to drug addiction, nor are all those who become addicted to drugs suffering from early deprivation, though many of both genders are.

» Many clients of drug treatment services, both men and women, are able to make good relationships with their workers and recover.

» The particular perverse dynamics I will describe are not true of all female drug addicts, nor are they exclusive to women— though they are much more rare in men, and I will not be covering this here.

» I am not proposing all-female services. This is a different and complex discussion. Male and female drug addicts need to experience healthy relationships with both male and female workers. There is a case for some women-only services for those clients who have histories of severe abuse and who initially need the sanctuary that these services can provide, but the same sado-masochistic dynamics will be present and need addressing.

» Finally, I want to add that my purpose is not to criticize workers in the field, who are, in my experience, highly committed to their clients' care; rather, it is an attempt to analyse the particular difficulties we all face in the treatment of a significant group of women and to offer some thoughts about how these might be overcome.

The most persistent and chaotic drug users are traumatized by failed early relationships, and their drug use is secondary to this, constituting a form of self-medication to ease their pain. Over time the relationship with the drugs becomes primary, as it is felt to be safer and more reliable than human relationships. They are often diagnosed with borderline personality disorders in which recourse to drugs constitutes a form of "psychic retreat" from both depressive and persecutory anxiety, and they have little capacity or desire to take part in a relationship in which their pain would be addressed (Steiner, 1993). As Steiner (though not writing specifically about drug-addicted patients) notes:

> The priority for the patient is to get rid of unwanted mental contents, which he projects into the analyst, and in these states he is able to take very little back into his mind. He does not have the time or the space to think, and he is afraid to examine his own mental processes. [Steiner, 1993, p. 131]

"Psychic retreats" are borderline psychotic positions in which we remain stuck developmentally:

> It is as if the patient has become accustomed even addicted to the state of affairs in the retreat and gains a kind of perverse satisfaction from it. . . . A perverse pseudo-acceptance of reality is one of the factors which makes the retreat so attractive for the patient who can keep sufficient contact with reality to appear "normal" while at the same time evading its most painful aspects. [Steiner, 1993, p. 12]

Another characteristic of the borderline phenomenon is the claustrophobic–agoraphobic dilemma described by Henri Rey (1979), in which any relationship that falls short of a fantasized perfect match between client and worker gives rise to anxieties, described by Britton as those of being trapped by "a deathly container, or, exposure in a shattered world" (1992, p. 111). Britton continues: "faced with these two catastrophic alternatives, incarceration or fragmentation, some people . . . remain paralysed at the frontier, on the threshold" (p. 112).

These dynamics are experienced in client–staff and staff–client interactions through transference and countertransference, and workers are required to form caring relationships with people who are rarely able to reciprocate. We have to manage ourselves and our ambivalent feelings without resorting to projection or retaliation, at the same time managing that which is projected into us by our clients. Our job is to give back a sense of reality and substance to people who through continuous processes of projection feel unreal and empty. We have to be able to judge what the client is able to tolerate and contain at any given time and formulate our interventions accordingly (Foster, 2002).

We became aware of the challenges that this poses for staff when I began work in this field in the early 1970s as Assistant Director of a mixed-gender residential therapeutic community for the treatment and rehabilitation of addicts newly detoxified. We understood the importance of focusing on the nature of interpersonal interactions as a route to gaining an understanding of how clients' early experiences of parenting (internalized object relationship patterns) impacted on their personalities and their lives, and it was through this approach that I became particularly interested in the needs of our female residents, who appeared to be more disturbed and differently deviant from the men. I will identify these early concerns with reference to a client, "Sue", but it was only many years later, when Estela Welldon began writing on female perversion (1988, 1996[1]), that I was able to gain a better understanding, illustrated here in an account of "Mia's journey through treatment".

My focus is on the particular nature of perverse female pathology. In psychoanalytic terminology referring to someone as perverse is not a moral judgement:

> it means simply a dysfunction of the sexual component of personality development . . . [and] . . . The main difference in a male and female perverse action lies in the aim. Whereas in men the act is aimed at an outside part-object, in women it is usually against themselves, either against their bodies or against objects which they see as their own creations: their babies. In both cases bodies and babies are treated as part-objects. [Welldon, 1988, pp. 6, 8]

It is essential that we recognize the difference and different needs of female clients who fit into this category, the importance of providing appropriate treatment models in mixed-gender services, and, by implication, the need for policies that equip and enable staff to engage in sustained longer-term work, to the point where their clients are able to use and can be referred on for further psychotherapeutic help.

Sue

In a mixed residential treatment setting, Sue's behaviour reminded me of the little girl in the nursery rhyme: "When she was good she was very, very good, and when she was bad she was horrid." When she was good she was capable, responsible, and caring of others—a valuable, effective, and apparently successful member of our community; when she was horrid, she was "mad"—shouting, screaming, unable to listen to reason and likely to harm herself as a way of "cutting out" her pain and disturbance. We understood that Sue was able to split off and deny her feelings of being bad, worthless, and undeserving through offering good therapeutic help to others. When she could no longer maintain her defences, she became depressed, angry, and self-destructive. Her behaviour was typical of our female residents.

Contemporary feminist psychoanalytic writing enabled us to begin to shed some light on these differences between our male and female clients. Nancy Chodorow (1978[2]) identifies the mother, or primary carer, as all-powerful in an infant's life, both a giving and a withholding figure, and she argues that one way of avoiding the painful envious feelings this generates is to devalue the envied object by splitting off the good and projecting the bad into it.[3] The devaluation of women is, "in the final analysis, devaluation of mother as a primary object of dependency" (Kernberg, 1972[4]). The boy's penis and masculinity enable him to assert his difference, and this facilitates separation, whereas girls do not have something different and desirable with which to oppose their mothers and are more likely to retain a pre-oedipal stance whereby they are pre-occupied with issues of symbiosis and primary love without a sense of the other person's separateness. This is compounded by the mother's projection and identification through which she conveys her ambivalence about her femininity, her own unmet needs, and her repression of these. Consequently girls learn early in life to put their own dependency needs secondary to those of others and, through identification, to recognize and respond to the needs of others while disowning their aggression.

Our female addicts presented as passive victims of neglectful, abusive, and cruel parent figures and partners, and when their aggression surfaced, it was often more dramatic and violent than that of our male residents and was directed against their own bodies. They were then seen as especially disturbed—"mad"—and therefore to be feared and kept at a distance: marginalized. Welldon notes that men are allowed and encouraged to express anger, whereas women are inhibited from doing so. "They are encouraged and trained to cry and to be sensitive and perceptive about others' needs and predicaments. Revealingly enough, if these 'rules' are transgressed, the penalties are contempt and pejorative comments . . ." (Welldon, 1996, pp. 485–486). It therefore follows that female addicts transgress this social code more violently and damage their social identity more fundamentally than male addicts. In addition, as women are expected to be the mainstay of the family, they suffer greater stigmatization and carry more guilt if they fail to fulfil their responsibilities to husbands and children (see Metherall, 1982). The pain of this guilt then leads to further splitting of the "good" and "bad" parts.

Sue left treatment and went on to be a professionally trained and highly respected race relations worker before killing herself. At this point it seemed clear that none of the treatment she had received had enabled her to internalize a "good-enough" integrated maternal object. Her disturbing behaviour was managed but not properly understood. We failed her because we colluded with her splitting by welcoming and appreciating the care she could offer while turning a blind eye to the disturbance that lay beneath it (see Foster, 1984). One of the big challenges facing workers in this field is to resist being over-hopeful about a client's therapeutic progress by holding the aggressor in mind and daring to address that part of the personality in the belief that this will lead to longer-term gain. Such work requires a great deal of trust on both sides. Workers are understandably reluctant to spoil the good feeling in the present client–worker relationship, and clients, like Sue, will do all they can to maintain the status quo, resisting the deeper work because they are reluctant to relinquish their destructive powers, preferring, instead, to retain these as secret weapons should they need to resort to using them in the future—an attractive but dangerous strategy.

Female drug addicts have needed and used their aggression to survive, and they need to be in touch with it in treatment so that the destructiveness can be faced and the aggression subsequently harnessed in a positive way to enable them to be assertive about their needs in treatment and in pursuing what they want as they work towards their rehabilitation. Without this, their journey through treatment is the journey of a false, compliant self while the needy part is hated, disapproved of, and marginalized—still subject to the murderous part, as both remain hidden and neglected. As Welldon (1996, p. 486) points out: "women at times keep all negative feelings inside, which leads to depression, low self-esteem, self-hatred and consequent withdrawal from all contact with others. It is easy to see how this might end in suicide." Had we persisted in working with Sue's "horrid" side during her "good" periods, things might have turned out differently.

However, the problem is more complex than this analysis would suggest, because we need an understanding of female perversion in order to help our clients integrate this split. Early feminist writing focused on women's oppression; it was many years before we could begin to think about women as perpetrators as well as victims, and if we can't think something, then we can't work with it. Earlier attempts made by female analysts were simply derided. I will now move on to Mia's story to illustrate these dynamics as they emerge in the treatment setting and how we might work more effectively.

Mia's journey through treatment

When Mia spoke her life story (and when it was reported to me second-hand in supervision), the emotional impact of her first memory was considerable. We had all identified with the toddler standing in her cot helplessly witnessing and being invaded by the images of her drunken father's violent sexual assault on her mother. We took in this image with all its horror via a powerful unconscious process of projective identifications, meaning we felt it as an "offer we couldn't refuse". Projective identification takes two forms that need not be mutually exclusive.

> One is to eject violently a state of mind leading to forcibly entering an object, in phantasy, for immediate relief, and often with

> the aim of controlling the object and the other is to introduce into the object a state of mind as a means of communicating with it about this mental state. [Hinshelwood, 1989, p. 184]

We understood, through reflecting on the feelings Mia induced in us, that Mia has internalized both the maternal vulnerable, needy, and abused object and the paternal aggressive and abusing object: the masochistic and the sadistic. Her self-destructiveness is a re-enactment of the murderous intercourse she witnessed. This is in contrast to creative psychic intercourse, which would produce something healthy—such as a new thought or a belief in a way forward.

Deprivation × 1 & 2: inter- and intrapsychic processes

Following the work of Louise Emmanuel (2002) on triple depriva-tion, I am proposing that the abused and deprived little girl—Mia—suffers firstly from the impact of parental failure which was out of her control, then secondly from the narcissistic, self-defeating defences she develops intrapsychically in an attempt to protect herself from the pain of the early environmental deprivation. Mia's life story vividly illustrates how defensive, self-defeating processes of secondary deprivation led to chronic re-enactments of her early deprivation and abuse.

Deprivation × 3: Repetition in the system of care

The third deprivation identified by Emmanuel arises in our sys-tems of care. The defences clients bring to a helping organization mean that staff are subject to powerful projections and are, through transference and countertransference processes, at risk of falling into the trap of re-enacting the experiences of early deprivation by colluding with their clients' need to make them fail.

Having told her story, Mia engaged the empathy of the commu-nity and felt accepted. This is just as it should be. But something else had happened. Through the process of projective identification Mia had effectively transferred her unbearable and unwanted feelings into the staff, and as a result, unburdened and lighter in mood, she was free to become a cheerful, willing, and able participant in the community tasks of cooking (though staff had suspicions that Mia was vomiting up the good food) and cleaning. Shortly afterwards Mia also became particularly attached to Yasmin, a younger woman who, unlike Mia, was clearly suffering from her life experiences. Mia was empathic, supportive, and caring towards Yasmin. Mia was being "very, very good". But was this healthy?

Mia was hindering Yasmin's chances of recovery because through this relationship Yasmin was firmly placed in the role of the tragic one who couldn't be expected to take on too much—not least because she was additionally burdened with Mia's tragic self via projective identification. In addition, Mia was not helping herself because, through this process, she was disconnected from her own distress and unable to make use of the therapy available to work with this.

Yasmin had been a willing recruit into role as a part-object in Mia's psychic world, acting as a container for Mia's pain and vulnerability. Left in the role of the victim—the tragic one who couldn't be expected to take on the challenge of working towards her own recovery—Yasmin appeared to lack any inner resources and remained dependent and hopeless, not least because she had projected all her competency into Mia. But Yasmin was reluctant to challenge this by asserting her strengths because she was afraid of losing (a) the benefits of being relieved of responsibility for tackling her difficulties, and (b) the protection of a "special friend" if she did. In the persecutor–rescuer–victim triangle, a person in the *victim* position cannot tolerate his or her own hostility and anger and is unable to distinguish between destructive hostility and competent assertiveness, whereas a person in *rescuer* position can bear neither vulnerability nor hostility in him/herself. A *persecutor* is therefore sought who can be blamed for all hostility (Hughes & Pengelly, 1997, pp. 100–101).

Team members, not wishing to be identified in the role of perse-cutor, chose not to challenge this developing relationship between Mia and Yasmin (but were sufficiently concerned to bring it to supervision). On reflection it seems that Mia, Yasmin, and the staff had a collective vested interest in being seen as sweet, caring, and well-meaning, even if this also meant being rather ineffective—

a stereotypical image of women. No one wants to own the rage, and all are afraid of inciting it, so the destructiveness remains under wraps.

However, the other residents, who know that being good and helpless is not the true picture of a female addict, are in touch with the aggression disowned by Mia and Yasmin and express this in group sessions by being angry at Mia for not owning her problems and at Yasmin for appearing so helpless, not owning her strengths. This confrontation may well feel persecuting to Mia, and if she is not helped to understand and own her rage, it will become her excuse for leaving treatment, claiming that she is mistreated and misunderstood. In fact, Mia and Yasmin may leave treatment together, preferring to maintain their symbiotic co-dependency—a part-object relationship based on mutual projections—rather than face the pain of being separate, which would involve taking back and owning their own split-off parts.

If the staff and community remain afraid to raise these issues, then a temporary stalemate exists until it becomes increasingly difficult for Mia, as her anxiety level rises, to maintain this split-ting. It is then that (like Sue) she becomes filled with self-loathing and rage until she finds some relief in the "blood-letting" of cut-ting herself, and if she succeeds in goading staff into discharg-ing her, this experience reinforces her defensive belief that she cannot be helped and so change is not an option; she abandons treatment, seeking self-medication, in the form of illegal drugs, to numb her pain. Thus Mia becomes the persecutor, but the victim is her body. When she is bad, she is horrid. With reference to the work of Chasseguet-Smirgel (1985), Stern states that "an addict uses perverse mechanisms to obliterate psychic reality and psy-chic pain" (1996, p. 262).

In returning to drug use, Mia is at risk because she is desperate to take enough drugs to kill off both her long-standing pain and also the fresh pain of seeing herself as failing in life yet again. This can be thought of as Mia's murderous internal object masquerad-ing as self-care, not least because Mia could unintentionally kill herself with an overdose—her tolerance having dropped during the time she has been drug-free. Assuming she overdoses and sur-vives death but suffers a new devastating crisis as a result, Mia, temporarily in touch with a more integrated self—needy, destructive, and remorseful—has the capacity to request that she is taken back into treatment.

How are the staff to respond to such a request?

First, there might be general, often unconscious, relief when Mia and those like her leave treatment, and this adds emotional support to the rational argument that she has broken the rules, so they have no option but to refuse re-admission. They will argue, rightly, that boundaries are important and that staff cannot be seen to reward acting out. They will also assert, again rightly, that Mia was hindering Yasmin's treatment and that they have a duty of care to maintain a non-abusive treatment environment, otherwise it becomes unhealthy for all and therapeutic work becomes impossible. Residential treatment is an expensive resource, to be taken seriously and not abused.

But emphasis on procedures is no guarantee of reflection on the particular presenting problem or thought about the emotional state and needs of individual clients—in fact, "rules" can have the opposite effect.

> Children . . . who have no means of coping with their distress, evacuate them [sic] through their provocative behaviour, leaving their carers feeling devalued and abused. We can understand how easy it would be to react to these constant bombardments by, in turn, rejecting the child, threatening to end the placement, retaliating in ways that simply return the child's unwanted feelings back into him. (Emmanuel, 2008, p. 9)

It is not difficult to imagine how rejection would increase Mia's feelings of hopelessness and despair, lead to further self-destructive acting out, and make any future therapeutic work even harder.

However, there are likely to be splits in the staff group representative of the splits in Mia: between the part (represented above and identified with an internalized harsh father figure and masochistic mother) that considers her to be not only undeserving of help but deserving of punishment; the hopeless part (identified with her internalized helpless and ineffective mother figure), which considers her to be a lost cause (i.e. beyond help); and the part that believes she needs, deserves, and wants further help. Consequently these opposing parts of the team are viewed by each other as either cruel, defeatist, or soft.

There is a real danger that the "cruel" and "defeatist" sub-groups manage to kill off or silence the "soft" sub-group in a re-enactment of the dynamics of Mia's internal world. But a staff team able to use supervision to reflect on the splits in their ranks can take back their projections into each other—the cruel, defeatist, and soft—recognize the ambivalence they all feel about Mia, and begin to understand her as they piece together their experiences. The "soft" group will argue that Mia needs a second chance and that the last thing staff should do is reject her when she is distressed. This argument rests on the belief that if Mia's request is rejected, the danger is that she will experience this as a repetition of her past traumas in relationships in which only her "false self" (Winnicott, 1960) was acceptable, and "being real"—expressing her rage, confusion, and self-hatred—led to rejection. The staff group as a whole can then try to take a true middle road. This is akin to locating the depressive position. When functioning in the depressive position, efforts to maximize the loving aspect of the ambivalent relationship with the damaged "whole object" are mobilized" (Hinshelwood, 1989, p. 138). This involves recognition that these apparently contradictory positions are all real parts of Mia, which need to be held in mind and linked with empathic understanding—that is, contained: "the containment of anxiety by an external object capable of understanding is a beginning of mental stability" (Hinshelwood, 1989, p. 246).

It then becomes possible for a plan to evolve whereby, for example, a member of the team, invested with authority from the others, agrees to keep in contact with Mia, sharing this understanding with her and working out a plan for her return to the treatment setting. This is not a "soft option". The possibility of returning is likely to depend on Mia conforming to boundaries set by the team. She will be expected to become drug-free, stay in touch by attending for testing to ensure that she is drug-free, and make use of counselling sessions provided as a bridge to her return.

I am proposing that this worker should be a woman, because people with histories of substance misuse, functioning in pre-oedipal mode, tend to think concretely—not symbolically (responding to others as part- not whole objects; as gender stereotypes, not unique individuals, as is clear from Mia's story thus far). For women who have histories of inviting and receiving abuse from men, a dedicated female worker may be the only viable option at this stage. However, this is still teamwork as the assigned female worker needs support in order to be effective in her role of providing Mia with experience of effective maternal containment—a prerequisite for psychological development. If the male staff are seen to be supportive of this work, then Mia would have an experience of effective parental containment.

Through this process the workers provide a psychological presence able to hold in mind Mia's fragmented and previously split-off parts, contain her fear that to link her needy (maternal) and destructive (paternal) parts would be deadly, and survive her attacks on both the work and the worker by managing both the transference and the countertransference dynamics. This includes being sensitive to the likelihood that Mia will engage in further acting out if she feels overly exposed, shamed, and afraid (for guidance on how to manage shame in therapeutic relationships see Mollon, 2002). Of course, Mia's key worker, her staff team, and supervisor will not always get it right. Understanding Mia in all her complexity takes time, but if through this process Mia can learn to trust, believing that those working with her are genuinely committed to struggling with her, learning from her, understanding her, and holding her interests in mind, then she will have embarked on the path to recovery. Through empathic engagement with Mia's predicament, workers offer a new and valuable opportunity—the possibility of introjecting a bearable sense of herself as separate, whole, known, and understood—that is, the possibility of negotiating oedipal dynamics, locating within herself a more integrated ego, and embarking on the path to recovery.

On returning to treatment Mia naturally remains ambivalent. She swings constantly between the two views of herself as deserving or undeserving, fearful and courageous or despairing, and this again impacts on the staff, but through understanding gained by both parties and the increased trust between them Mia is able to successfully reach the end of her treatment programme. While it is widely understood that most addicts will relapse in the course of their treatment, even those who make good use of the therapeutic help available can deeply disappoint their workers by relapsing just prior to discharge through fear of not succeeding in a drug-free life. If we can remain mindful of our clients' vulnerability at the point of discharge, we can support those clients who relapse and enable others to avoid this through individually designed discharge plans, a gradual transition, and the provision of aftercare.

Let us imagine that Mia fails to return to her treatment setting either because the staff team choose not to offer it as a possibility or because even when they do, Mia rejects the offer, choosing instead drugs and her old ways of mindlessly getting by. She is more needy and hopeless than before. Drugs will ease the pain, but she is also likely to find a man (whether previously known or not) into whom she can project her own violent, self-hating, and abusive parts and who will abuse and punish her, thereby repeating her mother's and her own experience, as if this is the only remaining solution. She may also find a "Yasmin" into whom she can project her vulnerability. She then becomes pregnant for the second time.

Mia believes that this pregnancy will somehow make her better. She finally has something good inside her and has the chance of giving birth to someone whom she thinks of as an extension of herself (a part-object) into whom she can project both her vulnerability and the ability to see her as lovable and good—another "Yasmin" who will love her. She attends the antenatal service, who are rightly concerned about the welfare of her baby, refer her to a drug-treatment service where she is allocated a specialist female who will see her through her pregnancy, and liaise with social services. Here the danger is that Mia repeats her pattern of being "good", and worker and client are hopeful that this time it will work. Mia becomes drug-free, sees that her man is not good for her, leaves him, is provided with her own accommodation, and begins to plan for her new life as a mother.

> Perverse women can also be mis-diagnosed since, unlike their male counterparts, they perpetrate on their own bodies, or on their body products, namely their children. When they act out with others, perhaps as prostitutes or in sadomasochistic relationships, they are often regarded as having made a conscious choice, or are looked on as victims, and the solution is frequently seen as removing the male leaving the perverse woman untreated. [Lloyd-Owen, 2007, p. 105]

On nearing the time when she will give birth, Mia becomes increasingly afraid that she does not have the necessary inner resources be a "good-enough" mother. So just before her baby is due, Mia returns to drug-taking—which, as we know from her life story, eases her self-doubts, her pain and torment. Suddenly, everyone becomes very concerned, and plans are put in place to remove Mia's child at birth, placing "her" in care. All are both relieved and deeply disappointed. Once again, good work has been destroyed, and a devastated Mia collapses on her drug worker, putting herself at her mercy. Again there is a split in the team. The "rules" state that Mia is no longer entitled to the services of her female worker because she has chosen to return to drugs and because her child is now in safe hands. But what is her worker to do with the painful and desperate feelings of bereavement and increased neediness that Mia has successfully communicated to her via more projective identification? The worker, unlike Mia, can cry about it, but she has no clear remit to maintain her relationship with Mia. It is only through exploring these feelings in the context of the team's work that it is possible for all to face the frightening possibility that if Mia is dropped by her worker, then she is most likely to do what she knows and repeat all the trauma by finding a man who will provide a shoulder to cry on as well as punishing and abusing her. Mia thinks she deserves this and further drug abuse will numb the pain, but, of course, she may well become pregnant again.

> There are people in whose lives the same reactions are perpetually being repeated uncorrected, to their detriment, or others who seem to be pursued by a relentless fate, though closer investigation teaches us that they are unwittingly bringing this fate on themselves. In such cases we attribute a "daemonic" character to the compulsion to repeat. [Freud, 1933a, pp. 106–107]

Deprivation × 4: Repetition through generations

Were Mia to succeed in keeping a baby, the neglect and its accompanying pathology would most likely be passed on to the next generation. Most addicted mothers are neglectful because the care and attention they provide is inconsistent; moreover, those who act perversely towards their own bodies are at risk of being actively cruel and abusive to their children. The baby's needs, demands, and distress would awaken Mia's own unmet needs and her painful, unbearable memories. Mia hates these feelings and, projecting them into her baby, then punishes "her" for this and for facing Mia with her fear and inadequacy as a mother. Motz states that "Reactivation of traumatic memories can lead to violence towards an infant, and dissociation as a psychological defence against pain, can protect the violent mother from fully recognising her actions" (2008, p. 71[5]). She also stresses that this is happening unconsciously. Mia, we know, consciously wants to provide better parenting than she herself received, but, faced with the reality of a needy child and her own unmet needs, she fails to cope. Thus Mia's child grows up with "her" needs both unmet and punished and learns, like Mia, to hate this neediness and punish herself for it. Also, like Mia, this child may well be witness to domestic violence. A male child, though differently identified, would not fare well either.

One addict who killed her daughter has been presented to me over many years. While she is now aware of the danger to children who carry the projections of their mothers (as hers did), she holds on to the fantasy that her next baby will enable her to make reparation. But, of course, she is not allowed to keep any subsequent babies, so further pregnancies and the terrible repeated experiences of dashed hopes, loss, and deprivation continue.

Deprivation × 5: Repetition in societal responses

As a society we, too, appear to have "a compulsion to repeat" the same limited treatment models, seemingly unable, like Mia, to learn from our failures or take into account the enormous cost socially and financially of doing so. It is the idealization of motherhood that causes us to reject and punish women who don't conform.

The impact of parental substance misuse on their children varies depending on the degree of disturbance in the parents and their social and economic situations; however, it is a factor in the majority of child-care cases, and research indicates that the detrimental effects are chronic, not temporary (see Kroll & Taylor, 2003). The services working jointly with Mia during her pregnancy recognize the risks of neglect and physical harm to children of addicted mothers and aim to provide a non-stigmatizing, coordinated response; however, this is not easy. Adult services and those for children have different remits, and mothers with histories of drug addiction, wanting to keep their children, are likely to distrust and conceal the truth about their drug use from child-care services. Additionally, women like Sue and Mia are (as I have shown) seductive and able to keep their perverse pathology hidden until their defences break down. Kroll and Taylor (2003) advocate the provision of family-focused multi-agency interventions as a way of overcoming these difficulties, but if this process ends with the removal of her children, the needs of the mother often remain unaddressed.

A new way forward

The Family Drug and Alcohol Court (FDAC), a recent initiative, is a pilot project that aims to address parental substance misuse and, where possible, keep families together through an intensive, holistic care programme delivered by a multidisciplinary team. An implicit aim is, no doubt, the saving of lives, time, and money. Clients have to choose to enter the tightly structured programme, but there is no requirement that they are drug-free as they will be helped to stabilize their drug use or work towards abstinence. The team consists of drug and alcohol treatment specialists, clinical nurses, social workers, child and adult psychiatrists, a family therapist, and judges. Additional support is available from parent mentors, ex-drug and alcohol abusers with experience of their children being taken into care, and through prompt linking with other community resources—housing, benefits, health, mental health, domestic violence, and nursery/schooling services where necessary.

Once the process has started, there are formal court hearings with the same judge and care team every 2–4 weeks until the final review. The whole process will take around 9–12 months but may be shorter, depending on the progress. It is a process of continuous assessment of needs, interventions, and progress in which some clients are discharged and others discharge themselves, but the majority stay the course. (For detailed information including the interim outcomes of the evaluation research by Brunel University, see FDAC, 2011.)

Unsurprisingly, team members meet all the same transference and countertransference dynamics described earlier. The judge has a key role here in that he (the two current judges are both men) represents an authoritative, engaged, and caring father figure, something most long-term drug users have not experienced previously either in their families or in court hearings and something they do not expect to encounter. New experiences are challenging to people like Mia, who expect and provoke repetition of the old patterns of rejection and abuse; consequently much of the staff time is spent doing the important and essential work of struggling to maintain effective engagement and repairing breaks in this. Many of the clients relapse during the process, and it is a widely held view that relapse is part of recovery, enabling further work to recognize and understand the triggers leading into consideration of strategies for relapse prevention. The team will also continue to work with parents should their children be removed and, importantly, can, once their ego is insufficiently integrated, facilitate access to long-term support and psychotherapeutic help to promote increased self-awareness and self-management (personal communication, Steve Bambrough, General Manager). If Mia were offered and accepted by a service like FDAC and embarked on the process, she may well be one of those who drop out, but, alternatively, she might recognize something that was more appropriate to her needs and allow herself to be held by the team as she embarks on a different journey into new territory.

It is particularly difficult to do effective therapeutic work with someone like Mia, but she is one of many who are known to substance misuse, mental health, and child-care services. Essentially my argument is that we need multiagency cooperation and multidisciplinary teams supported by social policies that will enable staff to provide longer-term interventions, because if we fail (just like Mia) to recognize unmet need and if we respond inadequately to the entrenched perversion in the form of the violence that she, and other women like her, repeatedly inflict on themselves, then we are complicit in perpetuating a very costly cycle of deprivation. Of course Mia, and the others like her, may be too damaged to see such a process through, but until workers in the field are supported by their agencies, through good supervision, to persevere in the struggle with these clients rather than discharge them prematurely, they, too, are left with feelings of guilt and failure.

In conclusion

What I am arguing is that we correct by this recognizing the particular needs of many female addicts through

» finding a way of thinking about the complex, perverse, and disturbing individual and interpersonal dynamics that clients, workers, policymakers, and society often prefer not to think about

» legitimizing and funding longer-term care in which staff will be supported in managing the enormous challenges posed by their female clients

» recognizing the need for psychoanalytically informed supervision to enable workers to process violent and complex projections and survive inevitable attack and rejection from clients without acting on their countertransference desires to retaliate with further rejection

» recognizing that many clients need to test to the limit the caring capacities of their workers before they can trust in them sufficiently to give up drugs and develop the capacity for more mature relationships

» believing in the value of this seeing this process through in the knowledge that no one is guaranteed a successful outcome.

Notes

1. See also the special issue of the *British Journal of Psychotherapy* (BJP, 2009).
2. See also Chasseguet-Smirgel, 1970.

3. Chodorow, 1978, ch. 7 ("Object relations and the female Oedipal configuration"), discusses the work of J. Chasseguet-Smirgel (1964) on feminine guilt.

4. Cited in Chodorow, 1978. Also quoted in chapter entitled "Early origins of envy and devaluation of women: Implications for sex-role stereotypes", in Lerner, Howell, & Bayes, 1981.

5. See also Motz, 2009.

CHAPTER SIX

Flying a kite: psychopathy as a defence against psychosis—observations on dual (and triple) diagnosis

Rob Hale & Rajeev Dhar

Rob Hale is a psychiatrist and psychoanalyst who works at the Portman Clinic. He has many years' experience of consulting to medium- and high-secure units. He was the medical member of the Buchanan Homicide Enquiry. This chapter, which emerged from clinical discussions with Raj Dhar, is based on these experiences.

Hale's chapter focuses on a type of patient who is typically given a triple diagnosis—schizophrenia, drug and/or alcohol addiction, and personality disorder. Hale suggests that it is more useful to consider these categories as a single entity. The underlying cause is a breakdown of the mother–infant relationship, followed by disruptions of care and often abuse. This leads to an underlying psychotic state from which there is no real progression and to which the person will always be vulnerable. In the people on whom Hale focuses here, the defences employed against this are psychopathy and drug and alcohol addiction.

Hale suggests that people like this turn early to drugs and alcohol as self-medication. He suggests that cannabis is the most dangerous. With continuous use and progression to a stronger form of the drug, the ego boundaries dissolve, the psychopathic defences break down, and an active paranoid state emerges. It is in this state of mind that violence potentially occurs.

This model has implications for the type of services that are best placed to meet these patients' needs and also identifies the window of opportunity in which therapy can take place. For treatment to be effective, it may be necessary to remove the patient from the corrupt psychopathic or drug culture that sometimes prevails on secure wards. These can be compared to the pathological organizations described by Marion Bower in chapter three.

Hale's chapter has implications for the way in which diagnosis is approached in forensic services, but the significance of his ideas goes beyond diagnosis: in considering the interrelatedness of these apparently different types of pathology, substance misuse, personality disorder, and psychosis, Hale brings a psychoanalytic perspective to this issue, inviting us to think about the whole person with his or her developmental history and defensive structures.

Within conventional psychiatry, diagnosis is seen as a pivotal function serving to identify a primary illness or disease entity that may wax and wane throughout a lifetime and that serves to organize everything else. This chapter proposes a radical departure, espousing a more psychoanalytic framework for conceptualizing the *dis-ease*. It is seen as manifesting itself in different forms and with different content at different times throughout the life of the individual. Each facet has its own distinctive way of functioning and relates to specific parts of the mind and indeed the brain. Taken overall, however, the fluctuating pattern represents a single entity. Whether this constitutes diagnosis is a different matter.

A shorter version of this chapter was originally published in *Criminal Behaviour and Mental Health* (Hale & Dhar, 2008). After it had been published, I realized why I had written it: in 1992 I was the medical member of the Buchanan Homicide Inquiry, the chair of which was Chris Heginbotham, then Chief Executive of Riverside MH Trust and now Professor of Psychiatry and Philosophy at Lancaster. Michael Buchanan, who has since died, was a young man who had ricocheted between prison, psychiatric hospital, and probation and had been a heavy drug user. His "index offence" was that, while in the community, he killed an off-duty policeman who refused to give him money for drugs. The dilemma we faced was how to conceptualize his disorder(s). There was no doubt that he had a psychopathic personality (although I do not know whether he was given the Hare Psychopathy Check List), he was a heavy user of cannabis and cocaine, and he had psychotic episodes. This chapter is an attempt to explore the relationship between the three. In doing so it draws on various conceptual frameworks—psychiatric, developmental, neuroscientific, genetic, legal, moral, social, and psychoanalytic.

In recent years there has been a recognition that many people who are resident in secure hospitals in the UK (Michael Buchanan was transferred from prison to Broadmoor, where he died) can most appropriately be categorized as falling into at least three diagnostic categories. This usually implies that they have an Axis 1 (*DSM–IV*) diagnosis of schizophrenia, an Axis 1 diagnosis of alcohol and/or illicit drug addiction, and an Axis 2 diagnosis of personality disorder—usually from Cluster B—predominantly antisocial (Blackburn, Logan, Donnelly, & Renwick, 2003; Dolan & Davies, 2006; Taylor et al., 1998). Blackburn and colleagues (2003) comment: "The evidence that Axis1 and Axis2 disorders are more likely to coexist than to occur alone among mentally disordered offenders indicates that multiple psychiatric problems will be the rule rather than the exception" (p. 113). The three diagnoses are often seen as coexisting and largely independent of one another, although co-morbidity is recognized as influencing both behaviour and treatment outcome. In clinical practice there is often argument over which is the "true" diagnosis on the basis that the existence of one excludes the existence of the other.

This brief contribution proposes a different theoretical model: a single entity, which, I think, more accurately makes sense of the observable phenomena. The basis on which it is made is that for the past 12 years I have provided weekly clinical discussion groups for medical, nursing, and psychology staff groups at six medium (and high) secure hospitals. I have thus had presented to me upwards of 2,000 case histories, and I have developed this explanatory model from what I have heard. This has been an iterative process with constant challenge and discussion from the supervision groups, and particularly from Rajeev Dhar. It could not have happened in any other way. An essential part has also been the observation of how the clinical and management teams function as a way of understanding the psychopathology they contain.

As clinical material I have used the life of Michael Buchanan because he exemplifies so much of what I am trying to describe. Virtually all of it has been published in the inquiry report (Heginbotham, Carr, Hale, Walsh, & Warren, 1994). My own contact with him was brief but highly revealing. Were he still alive, I would have sought his permission.

In the report we expressed the view that

> The question of diagnosis is of crucial importance as on this rest many decisions concerning management, treatability (long and short term), detention and the acceptance of responsibility for long term care. If a model is chosen of multiple concurrent diagnoses—schizophrenic illness, personality disorder and drug abuse—then the responsibility for organising long and short term care lies with the local psychiatric services.
>
> If, however, it is accepted that the principal diagnosis is psychopathic personality disorder, leading to drug addiction, in turn leading to psychotic episodes, then the primary responsibility lies not with the psychiatric services but with the probation service, prisons and social services, with the occasional need for psychiatric care. This also raises the issue of the need for long term psychotherapeutic treatment whether provided in a health service based institution or in a custodial setting. [Heginbotham et al., 1994, p. 17]

This chapter takes and develops the second option, which Chris Heginbotham and I preferred, and seeks to provide an explanatory model for what we observed using all of the frameworks described above—to build bridges between theories.

The life of Michael Buchanan was brief, painful, and full of contradictions and splits. From his childhood two stories emerged—one from the children's homes and the other from schools. In adult life, one came from law, probation, and social services, and the other from mental health. From adolescence onward what connected them was his drug use, which served many purposes and was intimately connected with his index offence.

An outline of his life is drawn from the inquiry report:

Born 1964.

Age 1:   Admitted to care on the grounds that his father was unable to care for him and his mother had deserted the family. A foster mother was found, but she was unable to care for him, and he was transferred to a private nursery.

Age 2:   Moved to a residential nursery.

Age 3:   Recorded as being a very aggressive little boy. His mother visited him twice, but he was terrified of her.

Age 4:   Moved to private fostering.

Age 5:   Moved to a residential nursery.

Age 6:   Returned to live with his father but was locked in his room quite often until 11 p.m. while his father was at work. He had already been suspended from infants' school.

Age 7:   Moved to a children's home, as his father was unable to cope with him. He was noted to be "totally deprived and socially immature, unable even to wipe his nose, and had an uncontrollable temper".

Age 7:   Moved to another children's home. Starts at V.H. school.

Age 8:   Moved to reception centre. Assessment by child guidance because of his disturbed behaviour in the residential setting, which was not apparent at V.H. school.

Age 8:   Transferred back to previous children's home. Progress at both home and school but started to steal. Considered dull and backward, with an IQ of 72 (borderline learning disability).

Age 8–11:   A period of relative stability and success, such that he was considered suitable for transfer to normal schooling. However, this did not take place. He was considered by the headmaster of V.H. school to be "a delightful boy who was making progress in his schoolwork and had won the local school's diving championship".

Age 11:   After three years in this children's home, removed at 48 hours' notice as a consequence of an "immoral association with an adult male" who had assaulted him.

Age 12:   Change of children's home.

Age 12:   Application for long-term fostering. No suitable applicant found.

Age 12:   Return to previous children's home.

Age 13:   One year conditional discharge for theft.

Age 13:   Placed in a residential school for maladjusted pupils.

Age 13–16:   Seven further court appearances for theft.

Age 16:   Sentenced to Borstal training for further offences.

Age 17:   Convicted of actual bodily harm.

Age 18:   Detained in Remand Centre and assessed by psychiatrist, who found him to have a psychotic reaction, possibly early-onset schizophrenic illness.

Age 19 :   Referred to Hospital at Crown Court after assault charge.

Age 19:   First hospital admission. Diagnosis on admission—no psychosis/personality problem. It was thought that the psychotic illness may have subsided while he was in prison prior to admission. Violent while in seclusion; discharged after three weeks back into the community into homeless person's accommodation. No follow-up.

Age 20:   Three further Court appearances.

Age 20:   Second hospital admission directly from court. Diagnosed as having schizophrenic psychosis. Discharged after four weeks to probation hostel; no record of follow-up apart from outpatient appointment.

Age 20:   Two-year probation for theft.

Age 20:   Convicted of assault.

Age 21:   Sentenced to 12 months for actual bodily harm.

Age 22:   Third hospital admission; presenting disturbed behaviour, aggression, smoking marijuana, and refusing medication. No diagnosis made; discharged after six days to probation hostel.

Over the following six years this pattern became established; there were a further seven custodial sentences for increasingly violent crimes and seven probation orders for acquisitive crimes. Nearly all the custodial sentences resulted in his transfer to hospital because of bizarre behaviour in prison often with clear psychotic symptomatology. He was also referred by his probation officer. Over this period of time there were a further ten hospital admissions when he was aggressive, violent, and disinhibited. The longest admission was for three months, and the usual diagnosis was schizophrenia, cannabis abuse, and personality disorder.

When he was 28, the index offence occurred: the killing of Mr Graver, an off-duty policeman; the details of this will be explored later. For the moment let us look at the development of what, by any standards, would be regarded as a psychopathic personality structure.

Michael Buchanan's life trajectory is typical of many of those who end up in forensic institutions and can be represented as shown in Figure 6.1.

The starting point for this trajectory must be the genetic endowment of the foetus; there is evidence of a genetically determined predisposition to psychopathy. However, the extent of the influences of environment, both intrauterine and following birth and throughout childhood, and the way in which they interact with the genetic potential is only now becoming established. Conceptually the proposal that "genotype × environment = phenotype" has existed for many years. Recently, work by Suomi with Rhesus monkeys has demonstrated the direct effects of different patterns of maternal care (or lack of it) on genetic expression. Perhaps, surprisingly, it has been established that there is a small proportion of male Rhesus monkeys who exhibit deficits in neurobehavioural functioning in infancy and poor control of aggression, a propensity to take risks, and excessive consumption when offered alcohol; they have a high mortality in adolescence. They also have low levels of the neurotransmitter serotonin; all of these features are typical of humans who are categorized as having a psychopathic personality structure. Suomi established that these characteristics were associated with a specific polymorphism of the serotonin transporter (5-HTT) gene—that is, they have a specific variation of the genetic-endowment-controlling serotonin metabolism. However, Suomi then established that the variations in brain biochemistry—specifically low levels of serotonin and the manifest behaviour—only

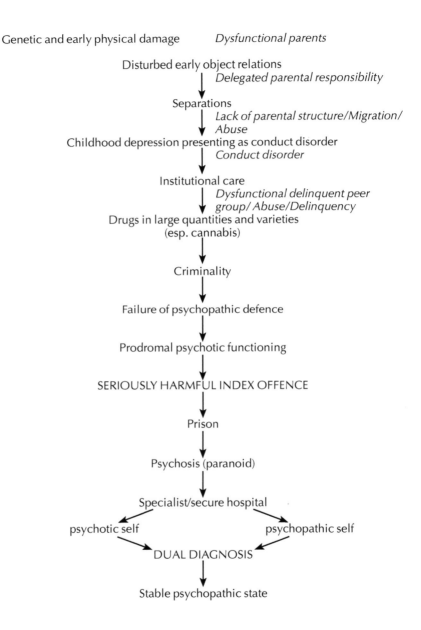

Figure 6.1. *A typical life-course trajectory for people becoming patients in a specialist secure facility.*

occurred when the infant had been separated from the mother and "brought up" by peers and had thus been deprived of consistent maternal care. In colloquial terms this demonstrates that "good mothering can make up for bad genetics". It also suggests that the propensity to become addicted is determined by both genetic and early experiential factors and their interaction.

The starting point is the primary dyadic relationship between mother and child, which in these cases is often characterized by maternal depression or other major psychosocial problems, often resulting in a marked ambivalence towards the child leading to the parents not being equal to the task of caring for the child ("acopia"). Sometimes the child has inherent vulnerabilities, but these are often hard to detect, as such parents may not be accurate observers. Outside agencies often become concerned and involved. Early marital breakdown and separations are common, as is early delegated childcare (in Afro-Caribbean migrants, often to the grandparents). Family migration and dislocation are frequent features, leading to a further feeling of cultural hybridity, alienation, or isolation.

At worst the child is taken into care, sometimes as a result of neglect of the child, sometimes because there is recognition of frank abuse. Being taken into care represents a complete breakdown in the mother–child relationship, whether temporary or permanent. Worse still, this may confirm that such a relationship barely existed in the first place. Symington, writing on psychopathy, comments:

> The psychopath's loss has occurred at the earliest stage, when the infant is still stretching for his object and holding it to himself in a tactile way, and before he can internalize it within the unconscious. The psychopath has suffered a loss when mother and child were still a unit. In Kleinian language, the infant has sustained a loss while in the paranoid-schizoid position. The projective and introjective mechanisms by which the infant separates himself from mother have not yet completed their work. The infant, thus, has not just lost mother but also a part of himself. [Symington, 1980, p. 294]

This failure of physical and psychological containment may be revealed in adult life through the Adult Attachment Interview (AAI), which shows an attachment pattern categorized as either anxious, avoidant, or disorganized (McGauley & Rubitel, 2006).

The discontinuity of experience and lack of coherent explanation of events passively experienced leads to an absence of consistent narrative; memory is scant and, where present, made up of a series of isolated snapshots. All of these are features clearly reflected in their adult relationships and their index offence; these are themes I will expand on further on.

As the child grows older (I am avoiding the word "matures") and enters the stage of latency, behavioural disturbances become apparent, and the child is identified as having a conduct disorder. Significantly, the child may be seen as being disturbed by his or her peers—perhaps the first evidence that psychopathy only becomes evident in a social situation. What the externally visible evidence of disturbance and the capacity to alienate others obscures is the lingering internal suffering of the child and his or her inability to express it in any more acceptable way.

If institutional care is part of their history, patients are likely to report that they were rejected by their peers: they were the outcasts in a group of outcasts, they were part of a dysfunctional peer group. Frequently there is a history of sexual abuse by an older boy or by a member of staff—hardly surprising, given the child's vulnerability and need for affection, sex being the apparent solution. Within the complex nature of sexual abuse is the experience of an exploitative and deceptive relationship in which the child is the victim: a system that his later life actions will constantly aim to reverse and triumph over using the self-same means that made him the victim.

Sometimes, however, as adults, they will in retrospect identify one member of staff in the children's home who showed them particular kindness, consistency (which provides a feeling of being respected), and concern. These people are remembered as beacons in an otherwise dismal and unhappy childhood of misfortune, neglect, corruption, and deception.

Later on in the latency period, bullying and stealing are socially sanctioned and reinforced by being accepted within a seriously delinquent peer group that is already starting to reject and fail in education. The defiance conceals an underlying fear of failure, humiliation, and rejection.

Adolescence is a time of turbulence for all children, but these individuals are not only unusually delinquent but also turn to drugs and alcohol at a very early age. Again the reasons for taking drugs are complex, but one cannot ignore the possibility that they provide a form of pharmacotherapy to control unacknowledged anxiety and depression. They offer a shield from reality and a womb-like cocoon into which the young person can retreat. For the most part, however, internal conflicts are externalized: conscious suffering is avoided and projected into those around him or her. This leads to further rejection and alienation—the last thing the young person needs, but the very thing with which he or she is most familiar. For disturbed adolescents, the "fault" is seen as residing in the outside world around them. Their own confusion is projected into others, as is their anger. Staff in any position of authority or responsibility find themselves indifferent or antagonistic to the patient, tricked and provoked into retaliation in a way that makes them feel ashamed of their response. This then makes them hate the young person all the more.

My own belief is that the defining characteristic of psychopathy is this capacity to bring out the worst in me or in the institution to which I belong. I see psychopathy as a defence mechanism in which individuals hold on to some degree of psychic equilibrium by projecting their feelings and their own experience of badness into others—in this sense, distorting reality to protect their sense of sanity. Current events and problems are described with a disconnected insouciance, without affect, causal relationship, or personal responsibility: again a series of snapshots to protect themselves from facing the reality of who they are and, more importantly, who they are not—an integrated person. It is a psychic survival mechanism, albeit a pathological one because ultimately it is they who suffer and who are the losers.

Drugs and alcohol have already been centrally implicated in the process, but it is cannabis that is, I believe, the most dangerous. Smoking large amounts of cannabis initially, like many substances, is taken to reduce anxiety (and perhaps guilt), buffering the person from external (and internal) anxiety. With continued and excessive use and a progression to more powerful forms of the drug, however, the ego boundaries start to dissolve, and the outside world, which could previously be regarded with disdain, antagonism, and contempt, now takes on an increasingly different complexion.

It is now perceived as powerful, malign, and vengeful. An active paranoid state is starting to establish itself—a prodromal psychotic state. The response is self-medication with yet more cannabis. This is reflected somewhat in the scientific literature, Moore, Zammitt, Lingford-Hughes, Barnes, and Jones (2007) finding that cannabis users are 40% more likely to develop a psychotic illness; however, the authors did not posit a causal link, nor is there evidence that use of cannabis is associated with a long-term diagnosis of schizophrenia—a view confirmed by Crome's (2007) review of the evidence.

What we are observing is the failure of the psychopathic defence to ward off underlying psychotic persecutory anxieties that gradually break through as paranoid delusions. In this psychotic state the individual eventually encounters a situation that to him mirrors his unconscious worst-feared fantasy or complex of fantasies. These will be primitive fantasies based on very early traumatic experiences, such as rejection and alienation, intentional harm, the wish that the person should not exist in the first place, humiliation and self-loathing, thoughts being known and controlled by others, and so on. The current situation mirrors the past for the individual but is only recognized as having current relevance, and the current threat is responded to by physical attack on the persecutory object. Thus the current psychotic state allows and even requires a symbolic attack apparently to rectify the current injustice but really to reverse the traumatic experience of infancy. A wished-for revenge is now made possible by psychotic functioning. The victim, of course, is not the true victim, but the person who happens to fit the bill in the current situation. This, then, is the index offence.

Knowing his history, let us now look at the way in which things in Michael Buchanan's life and mind unfolded, leading to the homicide.

After the index offence, Michael Buchanan was seen by a number of psychiatrists. The reports of two are illustrative. The first, Dr L, was told by Michael Buchanan that he believed that he was unwell at the time of the killing and admitted that he was threatening several people, the reasons for which were not clear to him; he said he was hearing voices at the time of the offences, and on the day of the killing had been smoking £100 worth of cocaine. Prior to attacking Mr Graver, he had visited a friend—although these accounts of events vary. Michael Buchanan said that his friend told him that "the only way you're going to survive is to kill someone"; at other times he said he heard these words from the television when the picture blacked out.

Mr Buchanan told Dr L that he had seen a man, Mr Graver, parking his car and had asked him for a cigarette. He said Mr Graver replied "You shouldn't ask men like me for a cigarette"—which, he felt, had some inference about the difference between their respective social classes. He also described Mr Graver hissing through his teeth and showing some annoyance, which Michael Buchanan took as an insult. He then attacked Mr Graver, hitting him across the back of the head with a plank of wood and seeing him fall to the floor, possibly losing consciousness. He then said he stepped on his head three times "in order to make sure that I could get away". Dr L stated that Mr Buchanan described a sense of realization that he was going to kill the man as he stepped on his face, but this did not stop his actions; after learning that Mr Graver had died, he said he felt shock and was unable to speak for a few minutes. Dr L said it was difficult to ascertain how deeply this remorse was felt.

Dr G reported that Mr Buchanan had told him that he was "kicked out of Shenley" and claimed that he hadn't any medicines or an appointment to see a doctor. Eventually he was "kicked out of the hostel" and said that he was walking the streets and sleeping rough. He told Dr G that he felt very down and out—"I don't know where my Mum is, and my Dad doesn't want to know". He said he attacked a pensioner in order to rob him of his money to buy drugs. He said that on the night of the killing he had watched television with a friend, and the television had said, "the only way you survive is if you kill". He explained, "It was trying to help me, like God when he got inside Jesus and sent him down to die for all our sins."

From these accounts we can surmise that Michael Buchanan unconsciously created his most feared scenario with all its complexities. He rejected and was rejected by a caring maternal presence in the form of the hospital and the hostel. He regresses to a completely paranoid state—"the only way you survive is if you kill". Searching for the means to get drugs that might alleviate this psychic pain, he encounters a man who treats him with disdain and humiliation. Mr G then hisses at him through his teeth, penetrating his final defences. Previously he could intimidate, dominate, and control his objects, but now the position is reversed: it is his objects that have the power to destroy him. His psychopathic defence has failed, and he is the victim of paranoid psychotic forces. With his affective control loosened by the drugs and his perceptions distorted by the psychosis, this man now can and must be eliminated: "The only way you survive is if you kill." At the time of the killing the superego is ablated by triumphant excitement. Only afterwards do both reality and remorse return.

In prison, or indeed a secure environment of any kind, the physical constraints give even less opportunity for psychopathic acting out, and the psychotic state now becomes all the more prominent. Imprisonment/confinement itself is the embodiment of loss of any personal control to a malign force. No one is to be trusted. It is at this point that the psychiatrist enters the scene, encountering a patient who currently fulfils a sufficient number of the criteria (acute rather than chronic/negative) to justify a diagnosis of paranoid schizophrenia. Transfer to a secure hospital ensues.

On the ward the psychotic state continues, and neuroleptic drugs are prescribed by the psychiatrists, often bringing about a rapid improvement; this may be aided if there is an environment relatively free of illicit drugs. At this point the psychopathic state reappears, and it is the nursing staff who bear the brunt. It could be said that psychopathy is a diagnosis in the countertransference and will be made by those with the closest and most constant contact with the patient—the nursing staff. It is not unusual at this point for the nursing staff, overwhelmed by the psychopathy, to question the previous diagnosis of schizophrenia. A compromise is then struck in the classification of dual or multiple diagnoses. As the psychosis recedes, the psychopathic state predominates again, and nursing staff may suggest that the patient was "acting mad" in order to escape the judicial process and advocate that the patient be returned to prison. The patient may respond by advancing a similar description of his previous state of mind or, alternatively, simply collude with the staff view in denying it is psychosis and claiming it was all made up; on the other hand, the dominant psychopathic state may actually drive an attempt to feign psychosis. Thus any diagnostic division between the psychiatrists and the nurses actually represents different parts of the patient's mind: the psychotic and the psychopathic. The patient at this point is likely to side with the nurses, since the psychopathic defence is what, over the years, he has learned to know and to "trust". It is far less frightening than the paranoia of psychosis. Control using the long-established manoeuvres of coercion and corruption is re-established. Allegiance may be given to the corrupting dominant antisocial/ psychopathic or drug culture of the ward. There is a risk that the patient then assumes the role of the "drug baron" or the "toughest psychopath", and he, rather than the ward manager, may end up controlling the ward. The stable psychopathic defence is once again doing its job. Equally, our countertransferential reaction to psychotic as opposed to psychopathic patients is the central theme of Hinshelwood (1999). This characteristic of different staff in an institution to identify with and represent different aspects of the patient's psychopathology is well described by Davies (1996).

When psychosis dominates the clinical picture, there is no opportunity for the establishment of a therapeutic alliance—there is no available ego. Equally, the dominance of psychopathy or the drug culture now precludes such an alliance. Both ensure that the patient remains in institutional care. Paradoxically, should an event occur that necessitates seclusion, a small window of opportunity may appear. The patient is removed from the deviant ward culture and the effects of the illicit drugs but is not caught in the psychotic world. It is at this point that the patient *may* be available for some kind of realistic emotional contact. Sadly, all too often the timing of return to the ward is based solely on the level of "physical" risk, and such emotional contact does not become established. Instead, the psychopathic battle continues back on the ward.

Should the psychotic state continue in hospital, one has to ask the same question as before the index offence: "What is its purpose?" Here Minne (2003) make a very important contribution, proposing that the continuing psychosis protects individuals from experiencing guilt and post-traumatic stress to their own index offence. As the psychosis gradually recedes, a picture of post-traumatic stress disorder emerges—which they would regard as a clear therapeutic advance: a degree of achievement of the "depressive position".

If the observations I am reporting have some validity and give a reasonably accurate account of the whole life trajectory of the young person, how does it affect the diagnosis? My proposal would be that the underlying state is the psychosis of a chaotic infancy from which the person has never really progressed. She or he has, however, constructed a pathological defence—psychopathy—which apparently serves him or her well to an extent, but actually leads to failure to establish any meaningful relationships, to misery, and ultimately to self-destruction in a social and often physical sense. As Cleckley (1964) so accurately describes, it is "the mask of sanity". Relief from the fear that this defensive structure is failing is sought through the use of drugs and alcohol, which paradoxically promote the very breakdown the young person is desperately seeking to avoid.

This is a personal account. It attempts to draw together various conceptual frameworks. It challenges any concept of separate diagnoses, positing instead an underlying primitive psychotic state experienced in infancy from which there is no real progression and to which the person will always vulnerable. The defences employed are psychopathy and drug/alcohol addiction. Each is an apparent and partial solution, but each has within it the capacity to destroy its own function as a defence mechanism. When they fail, frank psychosis ensues.

The overall proposal is, then, of one condition with three elements: psychosis, psychopathy, and substance misuse, all being causally related. Perhaps this requires a paradigm shift in the way we classify mental disorder, but such a shift could allow for more appropriate expectations of a patient's capacities and of change with treatment; it may avert despair. My hope is that others will challenge and develop the ideas I have put forward.

CHAPTER SEVEN

Gambling: addicted to the game

Jessica Yakeley & Richard Taylor

Jessica Yakeley and Richard Taylor, both psychiatrists in NHS practice and one (JY) a psychoanalyst, bring to the subject of gambling a wealth of clinical experience that informs their clinical examples; they bring a broad and inclusive perspective on the cultural aspects of gambling and the range of psychological models of gambling, as well as offering a depth of psychoanalytic understanding of this phenomenon.

They are wary of current diagnostic practice that might artificially dichotomize casual and problematic gamblers, arguing that gambling occurs on a spectrum from everyday to pathological behaviour. For Yakeley and Taylor, as for Freud, gambling is a symptom, and understanding needs to go beyond mere description of the behaviours and accompanying cognitions, to consider the psychodynamic factors that drive the behaviour.

They note that Von Hattinberg's (1914) recognition of the masochism inherent in gambling pre-dates Freud's (1928b) analysis of gambling. The idea that the gambler does not play to win but to lose challenges the popular notion of the gambler as someone hoping to make a fortune. In a very interesting section they describe the object relationship that can prevail in the mind of the gambler, who feels compelled to provoke, seduce, defy, or submit to "Chance", Lady Luck", or "Fate", representatives of omnipotent parental objects.

Is gambling an addiction? They conclude that, psychologically, the behaviour has much in common with addictions, but that gambling is "more" than addiction; in addition to the addictive qualities, gambling is characterized by elements of sexualized and masochistic excitement, though not yet reaching criteria for a perversion. They stress that the "game" to which a person is addicted is not playful but "a sadomasochistic marriage" that excludes real people and becomes "a desperate conflict between life and death".

Yakeley and Taylor note the waning interest in psychoanalytic perspectives on gambling since Greenson's (1947) and Bergler's (1957) important contributions. This chapter demonstrates how much this perspective has to offer to an understanding of gambling, including electronic and online forms of gambling, in the twenty-first century.

Introduction

It was a quarter past ten; I went into the casino with such firm hope and at the same time in a state of excitement such as I had never experienced . . . counting what I had before there was now one thousand and seven hundred gulden—and this in less than five minutes! Yes, in such moments, one forgets all one's previous failures! You see, I had achieved this at the risk of more than my life, I had dared take the risk and—now I was once more among the ranks of men! [Dostoevsky, 1866, pp. 240, 267]

Since primitive times, gambling in its various forms has been a source of entertainment for some but a source of misery for many. Although the odds of winning the jackpot are incredibly slim, the lottery plays on the notion of hope that a big win will allow a dramatic escape from an otherwise unfulfilling, uncertain, or low-paid working life. Dostoevsky's novella *The Gambler* provides one of literature's most compelling accounts of a pathological gambler, a narcissistic and tormented individual whose character is based on that of its author, and who is unable to break free of his gambling addiction despite the misery it causes to himself and others. More recently, Hollywood has capitalized on the fascination that the gambling industry provokes in films such as *Bugsy*, *Casino*, *Owning Mahoney*, and *Leaving Las Vegas*. In this chapter we examine gambling as a problematic behaviour that may in many cases adversely dominate the gambler's life. We will summarize current psychiatric approaches to pathological gambling as a mental disorder but focus on a psychoanalytic approach to understanding gambling. Such an approach has become neglected and even discredited in recent years, but we believe psychoanalytic thinking can offer unique insights into the conceptualization of pathological gambling and in informing its treatment. Although pathological gambling is now predominantly viewed as a behavioural disorder, we do not see the gambling behaviour as a disorder in itself, but as a symptom indicative of underlying disturbance. This symptomatic behaviour is multidetermined and can be seen as the acting out of a fantasy that has unconscious meaning.

The gambling industry and international perspectives

Gambling can be broadly defined as the wager of any type of item or possession of value upon a game or event of uncertain outcome in which chance, of variable degrees, determines such outcome (Bolen & Boyd, 1968). Gambling is an activity that raises many paradoxes and contradictions, and one that occurs in all age groups, cultures, social classes, and historical epochs. Although obtaining money through gambling rather than hard-earned labour is often considered an immoral activity, there is a history of close associations between religion and gambling, with millions of citizens participating in church lotteries and raffles (Greenson, 1947). Many forms of gambling—for example, bingo, raffles, lotteries, and retail store promotions—are often not recognized as such but are thought of as acceptable pursuits. Gambling has historically formed a complex relationship with the law. Dishonesty and fraud pervade the gambling industry, with illegal forms of gambling creating large revenues for organized crime, which has led to the implementation of prohibitive anti-gambling laws in an attempt to control this. At the same time, all countries sanction certain pro-gambling policies and legislation to boost national revenue. Nationalized lottery schemes are now popular with many governments as they generate substantial revenue, but this often leads to increases in mass gambling, with most of the economic loss suffered by the lowest income bracket, which has triggered further anti-gambling restrictions hailed as protective social legislation.

Modern games of chance have developed into a sophisticated global industry, ranging from small stakes wagered on home poker games to elaborate sports-based spread-betting schemes, with the ever-increasing availability of gambling outlets. Casinos, once exclusive clubs reserved for the wealthy and affluent, have proliferated and diversified to cater for the masses. In the United States as recently as 1988, casino gambling was legal in only two States, Nevada and New Jersey. By 1994, casinos were either authorized or operating in 23 States. By the beginning of 1995, legal gambling in the United States (including lotteries) was generating over $37 billion in yearly revenues (Goodman, 1996). Some forms of gambling, such as poker—and, in particular, the variant of the game known as "Texas Holdem", with potentially unlimited pots and a unique combination of luck, skill in calculating odds, and the ability to bluff—have evolved from cult status to a global franchise with million-dollar tournaments (Alvarez, 1996). Robert Goodman, in *The Luck Business* (Goodman, 1996), describes the inexorable rise of the slot-machine industry in which casinos are little more than theme-decorated warehouses designed for mass consumption, which he calls the new "McGambling". Alvarez (1996) notes that it is no longer even necessary to go to a casino to gamble, with slot machines and lottery terminals in bars, restaurants, and stores. Problem and pathological gamblers may be specifically attracted to types of gambling such as slot machines (known as fruit machines in the UK and pokies in Australia) and roulette, as the game is short and the win–lose cycle relentless. The introduction of electronic roulette games to bookmakers in the UK could be seen as a cynical exploitation of an addicted group in much the same way as the drink industry has marketed high-strength beer at a discounted price to target the alcoholic market.

Mr E, the son of a wealthy financier, struggled at school and could not achieve the academic expectations of his parents.

His gambling commenced at age 13 on a seaside trip, when he spent all of his pocket money on slot machines. During his teenage years he increasingly spent all of his free time gambling in this manner. For a brief period he bet on sports events and horse races, but always re-bet his winnings. When he was 18, he discovered electronic roulette machines, and in a single day bet his entire student grant of over £1,000.

Alvarez likens playing the slot machines to an autistic activity "mindless, solitary, and addictive—and its popularity is growing at a terrible speed" (Alvarez, 1996, p. 16). More recently, of course, there is now the opportunity of gambling without leaving one's own home with the introduction of electronic gambling online. The notion of winning big gains on an astute stake has also permeated the financial markets, and the characteristics of the problem gambler, such as chasing losses, can be identified in some high-profile financial disasters such as the collapse of Barings Bank.

Awareness of the damaging effects of gambling on both the individual and society has influenced recent policy-making. In the UK, radical proposals to introduce regional super casinos were shelved following concern about problem gamblers. In Australia, where slot machine gambling is both popular and problematic and is defended as a freedom or right akin to the gun lobby in the United States, the former Prime Minister John Howard, during the pre-election debates of 1996, did not run on an overt anti-gambling ticket but cautiously suggested to the Australian voting public that perhaps Australia had sufficient gambling opportunities.

Problem and pathological gambling: diagnostic controversies

Because of the widespread prevalence of gambling as a human behaviour, it is difficult to delineate the border between gambling that might be considered normal and pathological gambling. Pathological gambling was first included in the *Diagnostic and Statistical Manual of Mental Disorders* in 1980 (*DSM–III*; APA, 1980). Categorizing gambling as a mental disorder, however, encourages a crude bipolar classification of gamblers between "social" gamblers and "pathological" gamblers, rather than viewing the behaviour as existing on a continuum of increasing severity (Dickerson, 1990). Moreover, elevating the observable behaviour to constitute a mental disorder in its own right risks obscuring underlying psychodynamic disturbances of personality, of which gambling may be only one symptom. Current psychiatric classification systems collude in the avoidance of exploring more primary psychopathology in their manifestly categorical, phenomenological, and atheoretical approach, with both the *International Classification of Mental and Behavioural Disorders, Tenth Edition* (ICD–10; WHO, 1992), and the *Diagnostic and Statistical Manual of Mental Disorders* (DSM–IV; APA, 1994) defining mental disorders as descriptive lists or clusters of symptoms and behaviours, regardless of aetiology.

> Ms B was a single socially isolated middle-aged woman who was referred to a forensic outpatient clinic after she had repeatedly harassed public officials with complaints and vexatious litigation in relation to the perceived failings of public services. This compulsive resentful harassment behaviour subsided after she was treated with cognitive behavioural therapy. However, shortly after this treatment terminated, she re-presented to mental health services with severe financial difficulties, having developed compulsive gambling, and was referred to the gambling clinic. Here we can see how current diagnostic conceptualizations support the idea that her obsessive complaining and her compulsive behaviour are different mental disorders warranting different treatments, rather than both behaviours being understood as symptoms of the same underlying psychopathology, which may need to be the target of therapy.

Nosological confusion and controversy are evident in the literature on pathological gambling and persist in attempts to define and categorize the behaviour. As is explored in greater detail further on, psychoanalytic writers were divided as to whether pathological gambling should be viewed as a neurosis or as an addiction or even a perversion indicative of more severe characterological abnormality. Within psychiatry, there is continued debate as to whether problem and pathological gambling is an addiction or whether it is better viewed as an impulse control disorder. The *ICD–10*, which is the diagnostic system used by most British psychiatrists, considers gambling to be a disorder of adult personality and behaviour and categorizes it under "Habit and Impulse Disorders". Such impulse disorders are characterized by repeated acts that the patient cannot control, that have no clear rational motivation, and that generally harm the patient's own interests and those of other people. The *ICD–10* defines pathological or compulsive gambling as

> frequent, repeated episodes of gambling, which dominate the individual's life to the detriment of social, occupational, mate-rial, and family values and commitments. Those who suffer from this disorder may put their jobs at risk, acquire large debts, and lie or break the law to obtain money or evade the payment of debts. They describe an intense urge to gamble, which is difficult to control, together with preoccupation with ideas and images of the act of gambling and the circumstances that sur-round the act. These preoccupations and urges often increase at times when life is stressful. [WHO, 1992, p. 212]

This *ICD–10* definition of pathological gambling specifically excludes gambling as a symptom in people with mania and gam-bling as part of wider dissocial behaviours and personality dis-orders. The *DSM–IV* provides more specific operational criteria for gambling and distinguishes between problem gambling and pathological gambling. *DSM–V*, due out in 2012, is likely to take a more dimensional approach to the diagnosis of mental disorders, which may more accurately reflect pathological gambling as being on a continuum of problematic behaviour and be therefore more compatible with psychoanalytic conceptualization.

Epidemiology

The research literature on the epidemiology and characteristics of the problem gambler has been criticized for its reliance on highly selected samples from treatment settings that do not represent the profile of problem gamblers in the general population (Lamberton & Oei, 1997). Most of these studies included only males, giving a distorted perception about the gender ratio of the disorder. More recent studies suggest that a significant proportion of pathological gamblers are women, who are more likely to engage in online gambling from their homes and so be less easy to detect in epidemiological surveys of the disorder. Female gamblers typically have a later age of onset than their male counterparts and are also more likely to be married to an alcoholic man than are women who are not pathological gamblers (Sadock & Sadock, 2003).

> Mrs L was a childless married woman in her early forties, who had a successful professional career in the City. Her husband, who also worked in the financial industry, was made redundant due to the economic recession. Both Mr and Mrs L had always enjoyed drinking socially, but after becoming unemployed Mr L started drinking much more heavily. Several months later Mrs L presented to her GP with depression. She admitted that she had started to gamble online, initially just to "cheer herself up", but had rapidly almost depleted the couple's retirement savings. She had not felt able to talk to her husband as she did not want to "burden him further", given all that he had recently gone through in losing his job. Mr and Mrs L were referred for couple therapy to address their difficulties in communicating with each other and their pathological ways of coping with stress.

The British Gambling Prevalence Survey 2007 provides an ongoing measure of UK gambling in its totality (Gambling Commission, 2008). This showed that almost 70% of the population participate in some form of gambling, the most common being the National Lottery Draw and scratch cards. The survey revealed that gambling participation varied by a number of socio-demographic, health, and lifestyle characteristics. Gamblers in general were mostly white men in their late thirties or early forties, from a higher socio-economic background, who were separated or divorced. Problem gambling was defined as "gambling to a degree that compromises, disrupts or damages family, personal or recreational pursuits" and was found to be present in over a quarter of a million problem gamblers in Britain. The survey found a significant association between problem gambling and being male and having a parent who gambled regularly, especially if the parent had a gambling problem. Other factors associated with problem gambling included poor health, being single, being from an ethnic minority, being separated or divorced, having fewer educational qualifications, and being younger than 55. There is considerable global variation in pathological gambling, which is linked to the differing degrees of state control of gambling. The prevalence of problem gambling is relatively low in Britain compared with that found in other countries—for example, Australia, a country where there are much higher levels of access to legalized gambling, particularly slot machines, which are more likely to attract pathological gamblers because of the very quick win–lose cycle.

Pathological gambling is associated with a host of complex personal and social problems. These can include co-morbid psychiatric conditions—for example, alcohol or substance misuse, depression, anxiety, and obsessive-compulsive disorder, and personality disorders, especially of the antisocial and borderline types (Petry & Armentano, 1999). Gamblers also have an increased risk of self-harm and suicide, with suicidal thoughts present in up to 70% of pathological gamblers (Lesieur & Anderson, 1995; Thompson, Gazel, & Rickman, 1996), of whom up to 20% make suicide attempts (Frank, Lester, & Wexler, 1991). Family difficulties associated with pathological gambling include marital breakdown, domestic abuse, children with behavioural problems, and psychological disturbance in the partners of problem gamblers (Lamberton & Oei, 1997). The problem gambler is more likely to suffer a variety of physical complaints, including headaches, high blood pressure, breathing difficulties, obesity, alcoholism, and impotence (Lorenz & Yaffee, 1988; Taber, 1985; Taber & Chaplin, 1988). The social, economic, and criminal costs of pathological gambling are considerable. The pathological gambler may incur huge occupational costs due to functioning at well below his or her productivity, as well as large legal costs in lawsuits. Large gambling debts are commonly accrued, and the gambler may turn to other sources of money such as theft and fraud, or the sale of drugs, under pressure from bookies or loan sharks who provide the capital to gamble with.

Prognosis

Pathological gambling tends to be a chronic condition that waxes and wanes in its severity. Four phases have been identified in the typical course of the disorder, which can evolve over many years (Sadock & Sadock, 2003). The first is the "winning phase", in which the person wins a large sum of money and is then hooked. This is followed by the "progressive-loss phase", in which the pathological gambler structures his life around gambling, progressively takes more risks, and makes ill-thought-through decisions. The third phase is described as "desperate" as the person increasingly gambles large sums of money, accumulates debts that he cannot pay back, and may become involved with loan sharks and illegal activities such as embezzling. The final stage is deemed the "hopeless phase", when the gambler accepts that losses can never be recovered but continues to gamble anyway, due to addiction to the associated arousal and excitement. At this stage the mental state of the pathological gambler can deteriorate rapidly, and he is most likely to seek treatment.

> Mr L, a 24-year-old junior mortgage clerk, started betting heavily on horse races after a big gambling win of £5,000. He opened an online gambling account with a book-maker. While at work, he would use his computer to transfer funds from his personal account to his betting account, so that he could place bets during the working day. His work involved crediting client mortgage accounts with lump-sum payments, and he discovered that he could transfer sums from his clients' accounts to his own account after experimenting with a tiny one-penny transfer. This escalated to the point where he would transfer £5,000 of his clients' money to bet on a single horse at a time. Six months later a routine audit discovered that he had embezzled over a quarter of a million pounds. Psychiatric assessment at the time of his trial, requested by Mr L's defence lawyers, revealed that he was suffering from a severe depressive episode with suicidal ideation.

Aetiology of pathological gambling

Models of causation of mental disorder in general have proliferated in the last quarter-century. Rosenthal's comprehensive review of the literature of pathological gambling in 1987 identified two other theoretical models used to understand the pathological gambler in addition to the prevailing psychodynamic model of the time—these were the behavioural model and the physiological model or model of arousal (Rosenthal, 1987b). A review of problem gambling a decade later (Lamberton & Oei, 1997) delineates no fewer than nine different aetiological theories offering explanations for the genesis of pathological gambling—namely the affective, behavioural, arousal, cognitive, general addiction, physiological, normative, psychoanalytic, and socio-cultural theories, respectively—many of which claim to be backed up by considerable empirical research within gambling populations. More recently, and not surprisingly in the current era of neurobiology and genetic determinism, genetic factors have been added to the mix of putative causative agents implicated in pathological gambling (Beaver et al., 2010).

This plethora of theoretical approaches may be more reflective of the general trends of current scientific research and contemporary cultural interests rather than the particularities of gambling as a disorder and may obscure the choice of the most appropriate explanatory model for the complex phenomena and dynamics specific to pathological gambling. Although the psychoanalytic or psychodynamic model has become unfashionable due in part to its lack of supporting empirical research evidence base, in these authors' views it retains value in its developmental perspective and consideration of the underlying personality factors and psychodynamic mechanisms that give rise to the more overt gambling behaviours. However, before examining the psychoanalytic literature on gambling in detail, it is worth summarizing the other main models used to understand pathological gambling, models that overlap in their theories and which may not be incompatible with a psychoanalytic approach.

The most popular paradigm used to understand gambling as a pathological behaviour is the cognitive behavioural one. Behaviour theorists view pathological gambling as a learnt behaviour, where placing a bet becomes classically conditioned to a state of arousal

and operant conditioning occurs in the gambling behaviour, providing an escape from this state of anxiety by offering promises of
fortune and happiness. Cognitive theory develops the behavioural
model by viewing the gambler as holding a set of false beliefs that
he will continue to win despite the odds, giving him the illusion
of control (Walker, 1992). "Chasing" is an example of such an irra-
tional belief (Dickerson, 1990), in which the gambler thinks that as
he has lost so many times, it must be his turn soon for a win, and
that he will eventually recoup his losses.

> One man that we have assessed, following a large win on a sin-
> gle roulette number, would repeatedly bet on the same number
> during a gambling session until all his available funds had gone,
> because of an irrational belief that this was his lucky number.

A more sophisticated cognitive behavioural model suggests that
the gambler has low self-esteem and limited coping mechanisms
(Harris, 1989) and uses gambling as an activity to combat painful
feelings of conflict, anxiety, and depression. Such a hypothesis
concurs with the basic premise of affective theory, which is that
pathological gamblers gamble more frequently when reality is
more painful (Custer, 1982). Here, gambling is viewed as a strategy
for escaping into a state of emotional numbing or dissociation to
protect the person from painful occurrences in his present or past
life. This explanation may be compatible with a psychoanalytic
perspective, in which the gambler seeks a manic solution to his
difficulties by employing primitive ego defence mechanisms such
as omnipotence and denial to protect him from primitive anxieties,
both internal and external. Arousal theory (Brown, 1987) goes one
step further in suggesting that this manic defence, which leads to a
state of arousal, is the major reinforcer of the gambling behaviour
and that the gambler becomes addicted to the feelings of excitement or "high".

This leads to understanding problem gambling via an addiction
model, which has its roots in formal treatment programmes, such
as the 12-Step model, that were developed for people with alcohol
and drug addictions. Here, pathological gambling is viewed as a
progressive medical illness that may be halted through total abstinence (Blaszczynski, McConaghy, & Frankova, 1991). The addiction model for pathological gambling has been criticized in that,

unlike with alcohol and drug addiction, gambling does not involve the ingestion of a toxic substance to be physiologically addicted to (Rachlin, 1990). However, physiological theory puts forward a biological basis for pathological gambling, with evidence of various abnormalities in neurotransmitters found in pathological gamblers suggesting that they may suffer from an addiction similar to a chemical addiction. It has been found that some pathological gamblers have lower levels of noradrenalin than normal gamblers, and it has therefore been suggested that as noradrenalin is secreted under stress, arousal, or thrill, pathological gamblers gamble to make up for their under-dosage (Roy et al., 1988). Abnormalities in the serotonergic and endorphin systems (Blaszczynski & McConaghy, 1989) have also been implicated in the aetiology of problem gambling.

Normative theory uses models of probability to explore the behavioural strategies and decision processes of the problem gambler. Unlike normal gamblers, pathological gamblers are less likely to be motivated by the long-term pay-offs, as they usually run out of money before these can be realized; they are, rather, more susceptible to random variations that result in short-term losses (Lopes, 1983). Socio-cultural theory takes into account factors intrinsic to the gambling environment, demographic variables and societal factors that may influence the development and maintenance of problem gambling (Ocean & Smith, 1993). Thus, the feelings of belonging, sense of camaraderie, and high status afforded amongst fellow gamblers may accentuate the conflicts that the pathological gambler often experiences in relation to mainstream societal mores and attitudes, keeping him in the insulated sub-cultural world of gambling to avoid facing the social isolation and occupational and relationship difficulties that he typically experiences in the external world.

A psychoanalytic understanding
of pathological gambling

Psychoanalytic theory incorporates and develops many of the themes highlighted in the aforementioned theories, to offer a richer and more meaningful account of the aetiology of gambling. Psychoanalysis is interested in the exploration of the intrapsychic phenomena, the complex constellations of affect, object relations, and unconscious phantasy that underpin the more obvious behavioural manifestations of mental disturbance and psychopathological conditions such as gambling. But these unconscious processes of the mind that are the focus of the psychoanalyst will, of course, have their cognitive, neuroanatomical, and chemical correlates in the brain. Thus, a psychoanalytic approach does not aim to replace cognitive or biological theories of causation but may be used to complement and expand such accounts.

The first psychoanalytic reports of gambling date from the early twentieth century. Von Hattingberg, in 1914, set the scene by delineating three themes that he hypothesized were central to the psychodynamics of gambling—these were the sexualization of anxiety, anality, and masochism (Von Hattingberg, 1914). He believed that the tensions and anxieties in gambling had been erotized, that these anxieties arose from an early anal stage of infantile development, and that the gambler derived pleasure from this anxiety—in other words, masochism was a core feature of the pathological gambler's personality. Von Hattingberg's insights foreshadowed many of the contributions of later psychoanalytic writers, including Freud. Simmel, in 1920, provided the first account of the psychoanalytic treatment of a pathological gambler (Simmel, 1920). In his brief report, Simmel highlights the role of a very active pre-genital anal-sadistic libido, and he believed that gambling behaviour was an overdetermined symptom containing multiple meanings. Simmel identified a core unconscious auto-erotic fantasy of omnipotent independence in which the patient gave anal birth to himself, thus triumphing over mother and father, negating feelings of smallness and dependency, and where ejaculation, defecation, and castration were interchangeable and the patient's own excrement provided endless nurturance. Simmel proposes that the gambling behaviour represents a compromise formed of "man and woman—active and passive—sadism and masochism—and finally the unsettled decision between genital and anal libido . . ." (Simmel, 1920, p. 353). It is notable how similar Simmel's understanding of the fantasy world of the gambler is to much later psychoanalytic conceptualizations of perversion as a defence against acknowledging generational and sexual difference, as proposed by Money-Kyrle (1971) in his "facts of life" and by Chasseguet-Smirgel (1985) in her description of the pervert's "anal-sadistic universe", in which penis, faeces, and child are all equal and interchangeable.

Freud addressed the psychodynamics of gambling in his essay "Dostoevsky and Parricide" (1928b), in which he analyses Dostoevsky's novella *The Gambler* (1866). While Freud's paper has been criticized in its treatment of Dostoevsky, it makes several important points in relation to the psychoanalytic understanding of gambling (Rosenthal, 1987b). Freud saw pathological gambling as an addiction, and he proposed that all addictions, including alcoholism and drug abuse, were symptoms of a primary underlying childhood addiction to masturbation. Freud linked the activity of the hands in both the "play" of games of chance and auto-erotic "playing". Masturbation and its accompanying fantasies are sources of guilt and fears of castration due to oedipal incestuous fantasies towards the mother and murderous impulses towards the father. Freud emphasized the feelings of guilt experienced by pathological gamblers such as Dostoevsky, who compulsively played until he had lost everything and would only be able to resume creative writing after he had rid himself of his guilt. The gambler therefore does not play to win but to lose, motivated by a sense of masturbatory and patricidal guilt that is atoned through his gambling losses and accompanying masochistic self-punishment. Freud's insights resonate with our observations of contemporary gamblers, who anecdotally speak of how the need to "stay in the game" is more important than winning. Freud proposed that the gambler's relationship between his superego and ego is a sadomasochistic one in which the former represents the sadistic father and the latter the masochistic mother or feminine identification. Later psychoanalytic writers have also studied Dostoevsky's gambling and built on Freud's insights into the psychogenesis of gambling (e.g. Geha, 1970; Rosenthal, 1987a).

Fenichel (1945b) agreed with Freud in viewing gambling as a displaced expression of conflicts around infantile sexuality, specifically masturbation. He proposed that the various stages of the game corresponded to different phases of the sexual act—thus the excitement of gambling equated with sexual excitement, winning with orgasm, and losing with punishment by castration. Fenichel believed that the gambler was fixated at the oral and anal stages, as evidenced through his oral obsessions about getting "supplies" and his anal preoccupation with money. Diagnostically, Fenichel placed gambling firmly under the category of "perversions and impulse neuroses", emphasizing not only the addictive nature of the disorder but also its underlying perverse sexual origins. We will develop these diagnostic insights later in the chapter. Like Freud, Fenichel also highlighted the severe superego of the gambler, the demands of which will only be satisfied when the gambler's compulsive behaviour has driven him to ruin. Fenichel analysed the meaning of "fate" for the gambler, proposing that gambling is an unconscious provocation and fight with fate, which represents an authority figure, originally the father, now internalized as a harsh superego. "Luck" represents a promise of protection and narcissistic supplies.

> Mr E, the young man introduced above who failed to follow his father in a successful professional career, continued to gamble whatever money he obtained and started to accrue substantial credit-card debts. His father finally realized that he was a compulsive gambler, bailed him out financially, and paid for him to go on a gamblers' treatment programme. After achieving a few months of abstinence, he started to gamble again, and soon a pattern emerged in which he would drift away from the educational and training opportunities paid for by his father, to surreptitiously gamble his allowance. He was finally arrested after being discovered committing credit-card fraud to finance his gambling habit, having made little effort to disguise his criminal activities. Here, we can understand Mr E's gambling and fraudulent activities as both an identification with and an attack on an overbearing and critical father, who has become internalized to form a harsh superego that Mr E has to continually defy. Unable to legitimately follow his father in his successful financial career, Mr E deals in money like his father (identification with his father), but via gambling and fraud (provocation of a paternal figure). These activities

can only be stopped by unconsciously submitting to a higher authority figure—the law—which promises both punishment and protection.

Bergler (1935, 1943, 1957) was the only psychoanalyst who made a career of specializing in the study and treatment of pathological gambling and is best known for his work on masochism and his book *The Psychology of Gambling* (1957). Bergler assessed and treated over two hundred gamblers, and his views were widely popularized in the media at that time. He expanded Freud's view of the gambler being motivated by an unconscious sense of guilt and seeking to lose. However, such guilt is not solely based on castration anxieties but is linked to earlier infantile oral and aggressive instincts that form what he called a "bedrock" of psychic masochism, and consequent unconscious craving for defeat, humiliation, and rejection that is enacted in the gambling arena. Bergler believed that gambling reactivated feelings of both infantile omnipotence and unconscious aggression against the parents, particularly the rejecting mother, who forced the child to abandon his omnipotence and face reality. The aggression is turned against the self and converted to psychic masochism, guilt feelings, and the need for punishment. The adult gambler, under the sway of the repetition compulsion, endlessly re-enacts situations of refusal and masochistic misery by provoking "Fate" and "Lady Luck", who are thinly disguised parental figures. This is well illustrated in the film *Owning Mahoney*, based on a true story recounted in the book by Ross (2002), in which a Canadian banker embezzled millions of dollars to gamble at casinos. In a poignant scene, he rejects the offer of a female escort from the casino, as part of their covert strategy to keep gamblers who are winning at the table, saying that the only woman he wants is "Lady Luck".

In an illuminating and stimulating paper, Greenson (1947) expanded the contributions of his predecessors, basing his formulations on the psychoanalysis of five gambling patients, as well as his own experiences and observations as a gambler. Like Bergler, Greenson believed that "Chance", "Luck", and "Fate" represented a father-figure, or a powerful mother-figure, both of whom needed to be seduced, challenged, defied, or submitted to, according to the oedipal constellation of the specific gambler. Winning means being re-united with the nurturing mother, losing represents being rejected by her. These unconscious oedipal phantasies are inevitably accompanied by guilt, which cannot be assuaged by either winning or losing—hence the gambler's need to compulsively continue to play as there is no satisfactory outcome. However, while Greenson proposed that oedipal influences were prominent, he did not believe they were the only aetiological factors but thought that pathological gambling had multiple determinants from all stages of psychosexual development, and thus satisfied oral, anal, masturbatory, masochistic, and aggressive tendencies. Greenson emphasized the regressive nature of gambling in general, and how it was a culturally acceptable way to discharge pre-genital, phallic, and aggressive drives. Greenson highlighted the pre-genital nature of the behavioural habits, rituals, and vocabulary of the poker players and crap-shooters that he observed. For example, he noted that the vocabulary of gamblers tended to be profane and aggressive, but not sexual. Winning is referred to as "making a killing" and losing as "being cleaned out". Unconscious anal-sadistic strivings are evident in scatological phrases such as "falling into a barrel of shit" for the lucky player, "squeezing out a hand" for looking at one's hand slowly, and dice being referred to as "craps". Greenson also observed anal-sadistic derivatives in the gambler's appearance and behaviours: either extreme neatness or sloppiness of dress, sorting and piling of chips, and even a ritual expelling of gas that some poker players indulge in. Oral tendencies are reflected in the large amount of eating, drinking, and smoking that occur around the gambling tables. Magical thinking is evident in the prevalence of superstitions and magical rituals such as good-luck charms on the table, looking at cards in a certain order, changing seats or walking round chairs, and rubbing cards and dice on particular parts of the body.

The few psychoanalytic papers on gambling that have been written since Greenson are based on the authors' experience of single case studies (Galdston, 1960; Harris, 1964; M. Laufer, 1966; Lindner, 1950; Niederland, 1967) and expand some of the themes introduced by their predecessors, but they add little to an overall theoretical understanding. Following this, there are a few papers on pathological gambling published in psychiatric journals (e.g.

Bolen & Boyd, 1968; Moran, 1970) that continue to refer to a psycho-analytic framework, but since the 1980s this is largely abandoned in the burgeoning literature on pathological gambling, with its emphasis on behavioural and biological determinants (Rosenthal, 1987b, being a notable exception). We suspect that one of the rea-sons for the disappearance of a psychoanalytic perspective from the thinking about gambling may be due not simply to the wane of the popularity of psychoanalysis as a theory and treatment in mental health in general, but that alternative models of psychopathology such as the cognitive behavioural or addictive model offer a simpler approach to understanding gambling, focusing on manifest behav-iours and conscious thought processes and not addressing the more complex underlying psychodynamics that may include negative emotions such as aggression, and shameful unconscious phantasies that the problem gambler does not wish to acknowledge.

It may be useful at this point to summarize the psychoanalytic contributions to the understanding of pathological gambling and to revisit diagnostic considerations. Although Freud and other early psychoanalytic writers on gambling saw gambling as a masturba-tory substitute and emphasized oedipal conflicts in its psycho-genesis, we can see that later analysts highlighted the regression inherent in the pathological gambler, who is seen to be struggling with pre-oedipal disturbances and narcissistic psychopathology. Gambling may be seen to represent an unconscious guilt-provoking activity (Bolen & Boyd, 1968) or crime (Rosenthal, 1987b), which involves the transgression of boundaries and consequent need for punishment. This crime may be oedipal, involving conflicting feelings towards both parents of hatred and competition on the one hand, and feelings of dependency and the wish to be loved on the other, unconscious conflicts that are passionately enacted with symbolic parental surrogates personified as "Fate" and "Lady Luck". However, the transgressions may have pre-oedipal origins, involving oral and anal-sadistic fantasies of aggression towards a powerful pre-oedipal mother who may be experienced as both intrusive and rejecting. Primitive defence mechanisms such as projection, denial, and identification predominate in the gambler's mind. The gambler's omnipotence may be seen as a global attack on reality, a manic defence against loss and death, or the denial of the fundamental differences between the self and others, genders, and generations. Feelings of guilt are dealt with in complex ways, including self-punishment by losing, but also covert satisfaction in the eternal re-enactment of the crime and the erotization of aggression towards the self, so that losing becomes a vehicle for perverse masochistic fantasies.

Diagnostic re-evaluation

In her discussion of the compulsive use of virtual sex, including Internet pornography, Wood (2007) asks whether this behaviour should be viewed as an addiction or a perversion. We may ask a similar question in relation to the diagnosis and categorization of compulsive gambling behaviours. Wood notes similarities between addictive and perverse behaviours. In both, the person experiences a "manic high" that can be physiologically explained by the chemical effects on the brain of a drug, or by the endorphins produced during orgasm. At a psychological level, this subjective feeling of elation or omnipotence can be seen as a manic defence against underlying feelings of dependence and vulnerability. As described above, some of the very early classical psychoanalytic writers on gambling, such as Simmel (1920), noted how the excitement of winning involved an unconscious auto-erotic fantasy of independence that triumphed over parental objects, a conceptualization that is remarkably similar to Segal's (1975) and other post-Kleinian descriptions of the use of manic defences where control, triumph, and contempt replace feelings of dependence on the object. This manic state of mind is, however, transitory and precarious, and the addictive or perverse act needs to be endlessly repeated to recreate the sense of excitement and control, clearly seen in the gambler's determination to continue to place bets despite heavy losses. Wood also notes a similar pattern of disturbed object relationships in people who suffer from addictions and those who enact perverse behaviours. In both, a mutually intimate relationship with another person who is recognized as separate and independent is replaced by a narcissistic engagement with a depersonalized other, who may be controlled and used as the vehicle of projections and internalized object relations. Thus the drug user's preoccupying relationship is towards the drug rather than any real partner he may have, who is only used to procure drugs. In the same fashion, the pervert gains gratification from his sexual fantasies and perverse behaviour that he demands his partner to collude with, rather than experience him or her as a person in their own right. Gambling serves the same function in becoming an all-consuming activity for the gambler that erodes any personal relationships he may have with others in his orbit, who now only retain his interest if they can further his chances of winning or losing.

Wood notes, however, that the addictive model may be used defensively, by both patients and clinicians, to turn a blind eye to the meaning of the problematic behaviours and, specifically, the perverse aspects of these behaviours. Although she is describing the compulsive use of virtual sex, we can see how classifying gambling as an addiction may also conveniently remove the need to acknowledge and explore more uncomfortable underlying motivations and meanings of the behaviour. Wood highlights the over-determined nature of the perverse act or pornographic scenario, which may have multiple meanings relating to the person's history. In Freud's (1895d, 1900a) fundamental concept of over-determination, formations of the unconscious, including symptoms and dreams, have a plurality of determining factors, which may be different causes or a multiplicity of unconscious elements organized in different meaningful sequences, but each containing specific coherence as a particular level of interpretation (Rosenthal, 1987b). As we have seen, many of the psychoanalytic writers viewed gambling as an over-determined symptom containing multiple and sometimes conflicting meanings and serving multiple defensive functions. Wood also emphasizes how the addictive model ignores the aggression, including the sadism, that is inherent in the perverse act but disguised by the widespread use of sexualization. While gambling as a behaviour does not involve overt sexualization in that it does not involve conscious sexual fantasies or behaviours necessary to achieve orgasm as in the perversions or paraphilias, it may involve the psychic erotization of aggression as a defence. This may be erotization of aggression directed towards the self, exhibited in the

masochistic gambling behaviour of persistent losing or self-recrim-
inations, or the erotization of aggression towards real and internalized objects, resulting in sadistic object relationships, including the
gambler's relationship with his own superego.

Mr S sought treatment for his compulsive use of pornography
and was referred for individual psychoanalytic psychotherapy.
Mr S revealed that prior to using pornography, he was for many
years "addicted" to gambling on slot machines, through which
he lost large sums of money, which contributed to the breakdown of his marriage. His mother, who had never commented
on this behaviour, finally expressed her overt disapproval,
which according to Mr S enabled him to miraculously give
up the gambling almost overnight. However, a new addiction
surfaced, the pornography, which quickly came to dominate
his life in the way that gambling had previously. In therapy,
Mr S was able to explore how both the gambling and looking at pornography represented a rebellion and triumph over
his moralistic disapproving parents, to whom he had always
felt a disappointment. His compulsive behaviours can be seen
as compromise symptomatic formations that defended against
underlying feelings of dependence and vulnerability and associated anger and aggression towards both his mother for her
intrusive and neglectful attitude towards him, and his father,
whom he experienced as emotionally absent and preoccupied
with his successful career. As Mr S began to feel able to lessen his
reliance on these activities as an escape from feelings of impotence in his work and relationships, he was able to acknowledge
feelings of dependence on others and express more manifest
feelings of anger both in his external life and also towards the
therapist—especially around breaks in treatment—who was
experienced transferentially as a withholding maternal object
more concerned with her own needs than with those of Mr S.
In both of his "addictive" behaviours perverse mechanisms are
at play, and Mr S's symptomatic progression from gambling to
Internet pornography can be understood as resulting from a
consolidation of perverse intrapsychic defences against aggression, from the erotization of aggression resulting in gambling,

to the more overt sexualization exhibited in his compulsive use of pornography.

Thus we would argue, following Fenichel (1945b), that pathological gambling should be viewed as more than an addiction—perhaps not as a fully-fledged enacted perversion, but as part of a narcissistic character disorder in which perverse psychic mechanisms are prominent. What is notably absent in the pathological gambler is any room for growth and creativity, that the "game" to which he is addicted is not playful but a desperate conflict between psychic life and death in which there is no transitional space to play with a fantasy of the object (Winnicott, 1951), nor the possibility of a third perspective (Britton, 1989) that could facilitate more healthy object relationships. The gambler remains trapped in a sadomasochistic marriage to his game and, despite the many different models of intervention that are available today, as detailed in the next section, attempts to divorce him from his obsession may prove very difficult.

Treatments for pathological gambling

The multitude of treatments for pathological gambling that have appeared in the last few decades reflect the diversity of theoretical approaches that have been utilized to explain the psychopathology of gambling. Treatment programmes for pathological gambling often employ an eclectic mixture of theoretical models, and many are not standardized or have little empirical evidence for their efficacy. The majority of research treatment outcome studies have been conducted within the behavioural, cognitive, and cognitive behavioural spectrum, with cognitive behavioural interventions showing the largest effect size (Pallesen, Mitsem, Kvale, Johnsen, & Molde, 2005). The emphasis on evidence-based practice has contributed to the discrediting of psychoanalysis or psychoanalytic psychotherapy as a first-line treatment for pathological gambling, due to the methodological difficulties in conducting psychoanalytic outcome trials in general. Most of the psychoanalytic literature on gambling is based on single case studies, with the notable exception of Bergler, who assessed over 200, of whom 60 engaged in therapy. However, Bergler's treatment technique has been questioned as to whether it was really psychoanalytic, as he would engage his patients in argument and challenge their beliefs (Rosenthal, 1987b). Although psychoanalytic therapy is today not routinely available for pathological gambling, psychotherapy of various modalities is frequently used in combination with other, often group-based, interventions. Many of the multi-modal or eclectic treatments offered for pathological gambling are based on drug and alcohol addiction programmes (National Research Council, 1999).

Gamblers Anonymous (GA), a self-help group-therapy treatment approach based on the addiction model, is the most long-standing and arguably still the most popular intervention for pathological gambling. Originally founded in 1957, GA uses a 12-Step programme adapted from Alcoholics Anonymous and places an emphasis on peer support to help the gambler acquire coping mechanisms. In many jurisdictions services are free or subsidized by government agencies. Telephone counselling services are also available in many countries—for example, GamCare in the UK and Gambler's Help in Australia. However, there is evidence that GA may not be very effective, with retrospective studies showing that 70–90% of GA attendees drop out (Brown, 1985; Lester, 1980; Stewart and Brown, 1988), and only 8% achieve a year or more of abstinence (Brown, 1985). Individual and group psychotherapy, when coupled with Gamblers Anonymous, may improve outcome (Lesieur & Blume, 1991; Taber, McCormick, & Ramirez, 1987). Couple and family treatments have also been attempted, including Gam-Anon, which is the spousal equivalent of the Al-Anon approach in alcoholics (Gamblers Anonymous, 1989). Treatment, such as Gam-A-Teen, for the children of pathological gambling families, has also been advocated due to the high levels of addictions and behavioural disturbance seen in many of these children (Steinberg, 1993).

Behavioural therapy has been used for pathological gamblers, with limited success (Greenberg & Rankin, 1982). Techniques include the use of a diary to record gambling behaviour, limit-setting, enlisting the help of significant others, and planning incompatible behaviours in controlling the frequency of gambling sessions (Dickerson, 1990). Behavioural modification techniques such as aversive conditioning and imaginal desensitization have also been tried (Greenberg & Marks, 1982; McConaghy, Armstrong, Blaszczynski, & Allcock, 1983, 1988; McConaghy, Blaszczynski, & Frankova, 1991). Other behavioural treatment approaches include abstinence or controlled gambling, and restitution of gambling debts as treatment goals (Schwarz & Lindner, 1992). However, these programmes have been criticized in using abstinence as the sole criterion of success, as it ignores other indices of improvement, such as reduced frequency and intensity of the urge to gamble, and relapses can lead patients to feel despondent and lower their motivation for future change (Blaszczynski, McConaghy, & Frankova, 1991).

Cognitive behavioural therapy (CBT) has been shown to reduce symptoms and gambling-related urges (Ladoucer et al., 2003; Wulfurt, Blanchard, & Martell, 2003). CBT focuses on the identification of gambling-related thought processes, mood, and cognitive distortions that may trigger compulsive gambling behaviour. CBT approaches for pathological gambling also utilize social skills training, relapse prevention, assertiveness, gambling refusal, and problem solving. Motivational interviewing has also been used as a therapeutic intervention to achieve incentive to change amongst heavy gamblers (Hodgins, Currie, el Guabaly, & Peden, 2004).

A growing method of treatment is peer support. With the advancement of Internet gambling, many problem gamblers now use various online peer-support groups to aid their recovery. The popularity of this treatment approach may be due to its ability to retain anonymity for the gambler who may not wish his family or associates to know of his difficulties. Self-help workbooks, with or without telephone support, have also been advocated as an effective treatment (Hodgins, Currie, & el Guabaly, 2001).

Although many pathological gamblers express a wish for medication to help with their difficulties (Bellaire & Caspari, 1992), as yet there are no drugs specifically approved by the US Food and Drug Administration for the treatment of pathological gambling. Various mood stabilizers such as carbamazepine (Haller & Hinterhuber, 1994) and lithium (Moskowitz, 1980), and SSRI antidepressant medications such as clomipramine (Hollander, Frenkel, DeCaria, Trungold, & Stein, 1992), fluvoxamine (Hollander et al., 1998), and paroxetine (Kim, Grant, Adson, Shin, & Zaninelli, 2002) have been used in the treatment of pathological gambling, with varying degrees of efficacy. Opiate antagonists such as naltrexone (Kim, 1998) have also been trialled with apparent success for the treatment of compulsive gambling. Appropriate psychotropic medication is recommended if the pathological gambler suffers from a concurrent major mental disorder such as bipolar disorder, major depression, or schizophrenia (Bellaire & Caspari, 1992).

Conclusion

Should we abandon psychoanalysis as a paradigm for understanding pathological gambling and informing its treatment? We have argued in this chapter to the contrary: that the psychoanalytic model retains value in its complexity and focus on the intrapsychic dynamic processes that are hidden beneath the overt behaviour, which, we propose, is a multidetermined symptom of deeper psychopathology. Although few treatment programmes or services for gambling may today include psychoanalytic therapy as a mode of treatment, patients with gambling problems may find their way to psychoanalysis or psychotherapy via other routes, perhaps seeking help for less shameful psychological difficulties such as anxiety and depression, and only later will they admit to their problematic gambling behaviours. In others, the gambling behaviour may apparently resolve, only to be replaced by another distressing or compulsive behaviour.

The psychoanalytic method may raise uncomfortable insights into the unconscious motivations underlying problematic behaviours such as pathological gambling—behaviours that already cause much distress to the individual concerned and to those around him. A therapeutic approach, however, that facilitates such insights being acknowledged, tolerated, and explored may enable the gambler to begin to free himself from his self-inflicted torment, shifting his pathological defences and leading to more long-lasting intrapsychic change.

CHAPTER EIGHT

The nature of the addiction
in "sex addiction" and paraphilias

Heather Wood

Having qualified as a clinical psychologist, Heather Wood trained as a psychoanalytic psychotherapist and has worked at the Portman Clinic in London for the past ten years.

This is an outpatient psychotherapy clinic, founded 75 years ago, which treats people with a history of violence or sexual perversion. The range of perversions is wide, and the clinical knowledge is derived from long-term therapy of people who seek treatment voluntarily.

While some of the chapters in this book explore the perverse component of addictions, this chapter examines the addictive qualities of perversions. The fantasies that drive this sexual behaviour are complex and often mutually contradictory and will often be more explicit than those that drive drug or alcohol addiction. The underlying defensive purpose is often very similar, but the childhood trauma is often more clearly linked to the adult psychopathology.

Wood poses the question "Why is insight not enough to enable someone to gain self-control?" and later suggests that for this change to take place, there must be the experience within the therapy of the underlying terror and the experience that it can be contained and made bearable. It is not an intellectual process. Implicit in this is the assumption that the central sexual fantasy may not change, but its power to dominate the person's life may be attenuated.

A man in his early forties is referred for psychotherapy. (To protect confidentiality, fictionalized composites of patients have been used as illustrations throughout the chapter; these should be thought of as prototypical rather than actual cases.) Mr A has a successful career in the media. He comes for help because he is unable to resist casual sexual encounters with men. If he catches the eye of any man in the street, in a supermarket, or a bar, he is willing to go and have sex with him. This happens several times each week. If it does not, he arranges casual sexual encounters via the Internet. He feels preoccupied with sex all the time; he feels in a constant state of anxiety and guilt, and it casts a shadow over his life. An enterprising man, he has tried every self-management strategy he can think of: he has been indulgent with himself in the hope that pursuing his every wish will leave him fulfilled and satisfied: it does not. He has tried being strict and punitive with himself in the hope that he can thereby exercise self-control: actually this only leads to him becoming more defiant and determined to be self-indulgent. He is very concerned that his behaviour will jeopardize his career and his long-term relationship.

Mr A is quite self-aware. He can see his compulsive behaviour as a way of trying to get control of intimacy and desire, so that he is never caught off guard by loss and betrayal, as he had been as a child. He describes a split between a constructive part of himself that is very motivated and has overcome adversity and a destructive part of himself, and he conveys a constant feeling of agitation about the conflict between these two. He also refers to the possibility that if he stopped what he was doing, he would be exposed to depression. Yet none of these insights has made any difference to his behaviour; indeed, they are recounted with the same sense of mounting panic and powerlessness as are his other disclosures.

Mr A feels himself to be in the grip of a powerful force or drive within himself that he feels unable to resist; he describes an urge to repeat a behaviour that seems, at best, futile and, at worst, destructive to health, career, relationships and to his sense of self and well-being. What is this quality of compulsion associated with paraphilias and other sexual behaviours? Why is insight not enough to enable someone to gain self-control? And how can it happen that a behaviour that is so patently a source of harm and distress also seems to promise irresistible pleasures?

The paraphilias are a group of mental health disorders distinguished by recurrent, intense sexually arousing fantasies, sexual urges or behaviours involving nonhuman objects, and the suffering or humiliation of oneself or one's partner, or children, or other non-consenting persons (*DSM–IV*; APA, 1994, 2000). Some people who habitually engage in such behaviours will experience the behaviour as ego-syntonic—that is, in harmony with, or at least not in conflict with, their sense of themselves; these people are unlikely to seek help to address these behaviours unless it causes difficulties for a partner or an other, or if the behaviour is illegal and brings the person into conflict with the law. The people who seek help from psychotherapists and other mental health practitioners with such behaviours or impulses are more likely to be those who experience these impulses as ego-dystonic and a source of conflict and distress.

There is considerable overlap between the mental health diagnosis of a paraphilia and those behaviours implied by the psychoanalytic term "perversions", but "perversions", in the psychoanalytic sense, are defined in terms of the dynamic function of the behaviour, not on the basis of the characteristics of the behaviour per se. Psychoanalytic definitions of perversions vary, but a recurrent theme is that perverse behaviours are distinguished by the use of sexualization as a defence to manage anxiety, particularly those anxieties that are aroused in intimate relationships, such as anxieties about loss of control and castration (Freud, 1927e), anxieties raised by confrontation with the "facts of life" such as generational and gender difference (Limentani, 1989), or claustro-agoraphobic anxieties about loss of self or abandonment—Glasser's core complex (1979). Central to most theories of perversion is the notion that what is sexualized is aggression, so that the perversion represents a fusion of sexual and aggressive forces; thus a behaviour ostensibly concerned with sexual expression is primarily driven by aggression rather than by libido (see Stoller, 1975). The psycho-analytic notion of "perversion" therefore encompasses behaviours that might seem culturally acceptable and non-paraphilic (such as repeated casual sexual liaisons, or use of legal pornography), which may nevertheless serve a "perverse" function within the mind. On a continuum with behaviours that are explicitly paraphilic or per-verse are those sexual behaviours that would not meet any of the criteria for paraphilias, nor would the individual recognize them as perverse, yet the behaviour is experienced as compulsive. Thus there is considerable overlap between the behaviours denoted by the terms "paraphilias", "perversions", and "compulsive sexual behaviours", and these terms will be used fairly interchangeably, though there are subtle differences of emphasis between them.

A striking quality of paraphilias, perversions, and compulsive sexual behaviours is the resemblance they bear to addictions. At a subjective level, patients with both paraphilias and substance dependence report feelings of compulsion, difficulty countering the urge to enact, and a perceived inability to limit behaviours that may be harmful to themselves or another. At a behavioural level both addictions and paraphilias are characterized by repetitive behaviours often conforming to rigid or fixed "scripts". At an affec-tive level the desired behaviour is felt to evoke a sensory "high". Both paraphilias and addictions may show signs of progression or escalation, where increasing doses of the desired substance or increasingly extreme stimuli are required to effect the same eleva-tion in mood.

Of the criteria for dependence on psychoactive drugs listed in *ICD–10* (WHO, 1992), only one, a physiological withdrawal state, cannot automatically be applied to behavioural addictions. The others (persistent desire or compulsion, lack of self-control, toler-ance, progressive neglect of alternative pleasures, and persistence despite harmful consequences) would be recognized by many peo-ple in the grip of a paraphilia to be applicable to them. Ragan and Martin (2000) propose that "If one substitutes sexual behaviours for substance use in the [*DSM–IV*: APA, 1994] criteria for substance dependence, it appears to accurately describe the syndrome of sexual addiction" (pp. 161–162). From a psychological perspective Griffiths (2004) notes key components of an addiction: salience, mood modification, tolerance, withdrawal, relapse, and conflict within the self and with others regarding the behaviour. All of these can be seen to apply to chemical addictions and behavioural addictions such as gambling, as well as to "sex addiction".

In the United States sex addiction is a recognized problem, though not yet included in major classificatory systems. The term "sex addiction" is used to refer to "paraphilic or nonparaphilic sexual behaviours, where there is a loss of control over sex and a persistence in sexual behaviours despite adverse social, psychological and biological consequences" (Ragan & Martin, 2000, p. 161). The breadth of this definition is useful as it encompasses both explicitly paraphilic behaviours and newly emerging phenomena such as compulsive use of Internet pornography and virtual sex which may not meet somewhat out-of-date definitions of paraphilic behaviours in *DSM–IV* and *ICD–10*, yet have much in common with these other behaviours.

Describing paraphilias as an "addiction" captures the subjective experience of compulsion: sufferers may feel themselves to be unable to resist the allure of this particular stimulus, and clinicians may find treatment approaches that draw on methods developed in addiction services to be useful with these problems of sexual behaviour (see, for example, Delmonico, Griffin, & Carnes, 2002). However, the notion of an addiction can serve a defensive function (see Wood, 2007), drawing attention away from the meaning of the behaviour. The notion that "it is just an addiction" deflects attention away from the content and symbolism of the behaviour, and particularly away from aggressive and perverse aspects of the behaviour. The addiction model is also sometimes associated with an assumption that the individual is powerless in the face of an irresistible force, a framework that has proved useful in 12-Step-based models of addiction counselling, but which may foster a sense of passivity that is not conducive to work in psychotherapy.

A further problem with the belief that sexually compulsive behaviours are akin to or reducible to behavioural addictions is that there can be kudos for the patient in seeming to have an addiction. Drug and alcohol treatment programmes have to contend with the status that may accrue to the person seen as the toughest addict with the worst problem; there can be a perverse idealization of risk-taking and dicing with danger and death. Having an addiction is a badge that is often worn with pride and can shore up feelings of omnipotence and grandiosity that potentially impede psychotherapy.

In psychotherapeutic practice, the notion that someone with a paraphilia or sexually compulsive behaviours has an addiction may therefore at times be an unhelpful rather than a helpful one. Nevertheless, sexually compulsive behaviours have strong parallels with addictions, patients talk about the experience of feeling themselves to be in the grip of an addiction, and theories of addiction and psychoanalytic theories of perversion may usefully inform each other. Thus it may be fruitful to try to unravel what is meant by saying that compulsive sexual behaviours and paraphilias have an "addictive quality".

Both addictions and perversions have in common the manic high that is engendered by intoxication or sexual arousal and orgasm; both involve the illusion of a relationship to an other (the sexual partner, the partner in procuring drugs), when what usually prevails is a relationship to a narcissistic object, the drug, or the fantasized sexual other that is used to fulfil a pre-existing internal "script". There are also important differences: while in both perversions and addictions there may be ritualized behaviours, in perversions there is the creation of an explicitly sexual scenario that is experienced as compelling; while both addictions and perversions may have an erotic or libidinal charge or meaning, in perversions there is explicit sexualization and the sexualization of aggression. (For a fuller account of the similarities and differences between addictions and perversion, see Wood, 2007.)

The underlying unconscious phantasy in addictions and perversions may also differ: in addictions the unconscious phantasy may be of an ever-present breast that can be omnipotently controlled and that will provide unending supplies of comfort and the sensation of well-being without incurring the risk of dependence on an other; as such, the unconscious phantasy in addictions involves a denial of the dependence on the maternal breast. In perversions the unconscious phantasy involves a repudiation of the oedipal couple; the individual regresses to pre-genital forms of sexuality, in which generational differences, gender differences, or developmental stages may be blurred or obliterated.

There are two further features that compulsive sexual behaviours share with addictions that are considered here: the first is that there is frequent repetition of the behaviour—indeed, repetition beyond what might be expected in order to accomplish any particular aim. A second quality is what Griffiths (2004) refers to as "tolerance", which is accompanied by a progressive increase in the dosage that is required of addictive substances in order to achieve the desired effect. With sexual addictions this seems to be evident in increasing frequency of the behaviour, but also in the individual seeking out ever more extreme stimuli or engaging in increasingly extreme acts. While this search for novel and more extreme stimuli may be underpinned by biochemical and neurophysiological processes, I will use the term "escalation" to emphasize that there are also psychological processes occurring and to distinguish this from a biochemical tolerance that may occur in relation to addictive substances. Repetition and escalation will be considered in turn.

The use of Internet-accessed, online sexual materials is reported with increasing frequency by patients with compulsive sexual behaviours. Specific attributes of the Internet may act as a catalyst, amplifying and exacerbating problematic sexual behaviours and so making Internet sex seem particularly "addictive". Particular qualities of the Internet and Internet sex that might lead to acceleration in repetition and escalation will therefore also be considered.

The urge to repeat and possible explanations

What is it about these sexual behaviours that means that they are often repeated compulsively and with increasing frequency? Griffiths (2004) cites a study reported in the *Guardian* newspaper (Brooks, 1999), which found that people surfing the Internet typically click once or twice and then get out of a website. Huberman (from Xerox's Palo Alto Research Center) found that some people clicked up to 200 times on a site, and virtually all of these were people accessing sex sites. Clinicians working in the United States with people compulsively using Internet sex found that those who engaged in more than 11 hours per week of online sexual behaviours suffered significantly more adverse consequences, and so suggested a cut-off of 11 hours a week, plus evidence of sexual compulsivity, to distinguish between so-called recreational use and problematic or compulsive use (Cooper, Delmonico, & Burg, 2000). Within this framework, up to an hour and a half per day of masturbating online may thus be considered non-problematic or recreational, and it is only when the behaviour is more sustained than this that it is seen as problematic. There is evidence here of substantial repetition.

At the most superficial level of analysis this might be attributable to what we would call "habit"; a second-level analysis might address libido or pleasure and unpleasure, and a third possible level of analysis relates to object relations.

Habit

"Habit" refers to a behavioural pattern, perhaps underpinned by a neurobiological pathway, that is so established and ingrained that it is the default option, the easiest path to follow. The behaviours may be comfortingly familiar and predictable and used to soothe or ease anxiety. Repetitive sexual behaviours might seem "habitual", and yet, unlike mere behavioural habits, the urge to enact them can be highly variable. The man who seemed to be in the grip of a compulsive sex addiction can have a realization about himself, or be arrested by the police, or meet someone who makes an impact on him, and the compulsion he seemed to be locked into can apparently evaporate or diminish instantly. At other times the degree of subjective pressure to enact a particular behaviour is so intense that the individual feels helpless in the face of this urge. Perhaps what determines whether this "habit" is seemingly immutable, or easily overridden, is the degree of unconscious pressure to enact.

Mr B, for example, had been compulsively using telephone chatlines and Internet chat rooms for years; he had run up huge debts doing so. After four years of therapy the behaviour had abated, and he had explored many of the issues underlying his compulsive behaviour. However, something happened that then re-ignited the compulsion: he was in contact with his only living relative of his parents' generation and discovered that this relative was terminally ill. We may suppose that this re-stimulated unconscious rage and grief about the loss of functioning parental figures to which he was exposed in childhood, with an apparently wayward father and a mother whom he barely knew. All he was consciously aware of was that he took off into a frenzy of chatlines and chat rooms, stayed up all night, and for seven days barely did anything else when he was not at work. On the seventh day he thought, "It's just a habit." This instantly enabled him to stop. What does this "It's just a habit" mean? I think for him it means that it was not going to bring him any lasting satisfaction, it was not going to solve his problems, it was not going to resolve his grief. Internet sex certainly was the default option for him when faced with apparently intolerable or conflicting emotions, but a "habit" can be broken and can cease as suddenly as it may reappear. It can be stopped without withdrawal symptoms. The behaviour is not driven solely by a well-learned mechanical pattern but is influenced by unconscious pressures to defend against feelings or thoughts that are experienced as intolerable.

Pleasure and unpleasure

To understand the compulsive repetition of a particular act, it may be necessary to look at the underlying fantasies or unconscious drivers for that act. A patient coming for psychoanalytic psychotherapy who had been through Sex Offender Treatment Programmes in prison commented: "I know all the strategies, but I can't trust myself to use them." The self that cannot be trusted here is the unconscious self that is unlikely to be reached by a psycho-educational approach. Mr A may know that he is trying to master profound anxieties within himself, but if he has not had an experience of that terror being contained and made bearable, this insight is not enough to defuse the charge that this compulsion has for him.

If we look beyond the observable behaviour, there are a number of possible reasons why someone might compulsively repeat a specific sexual act. The first is that it is very *gratifying*, and they want more of this gratification; the second is that it is *disappointing*, and actually they never quite reach a state of satisfaction, but keep repeating the behaviour in the hope of being satisfied; the third might be that it is *gratifyingly frustrating*—that is, there is a pleasure in being thwarted; we might think of this as the masochistic element. Compulsive sexual behaviours may potentially fulfil all of these, though perhaps in different proportions in different people.

When talking about compulsive sexual behaviours, the most obvious reason why someone might repeat what they are doing is that it is a source of pleasure, that the gratification derived from sexual arousal and orgasm is such that they cannot wait to repeat the experience. This might be a contributory factor, but it is not very convincing as a total explanation for compulsive behaviours. Usually behaviours that bring pleasure bring satisfaction and satiation, and there is a recovery period when the person is less likely to repeat the behaviour.

It is hard to think of a paraphilia that is solely frustrating because the presence of sexual arousal ensures a sense of excitement and pleasure; however, the combination of gratification and frustration, even a masochistic pleasure in frustration, is commonplace.

Exhibitionism is one of those behaviours that is often repeated regularly over years if not decades, with low levels of arrest and conviction. Patients may come for treatment because they have been arrested for the first time, having been exposing themselves for 20 or 30 years. In the person's mind there is usually a specific scenario that is sought after, which is sometimes realized occasionally, and sometimes almost never. A man may be seeking a particular look on the victim's face—for example, of pleasure, excitement, and collusion—and may strive to ignore any signs that the victim is frightened or alarmed by his behaviour. One man I saw specifically fantasized that a woman who saw him would be aroused and would desire him, yet he chose to expose himself in an area of woodland known for casual homosexual encounters, where the likelihood of being observed by a woman was very small, let alone by a woman who would be sexually aroused by his behaviour. Thus disappointment and frustration were integral to this ritual.

How could something be gratifying and frustrating at the same time? It seems no coincidence that it was in writing about perversions that Freud first postulated the idea of a split in the ego. In his paper on "Fetishism", Freud (1927e) suggests that we can know something in one part of our mind and hold a contradictory idea in another part of our mind. In this paper, Freud suggests that it is the knowledge of the mother's lack of a penis that the young boy finds intolerable. If she has no penis, he assumes she must have had one and lost it, and if that can happen to her, he, too, may be at risk of castration. Freud therefore suggests that the boy becomes fixated on a substitute, whatever it was that he glimpsed in the moments before becoming aware of the mother's castration, which now has the power to excite him. The fetish object, the shoe, or the fur standing for pubic hair, or the woman's stockings or underwear, thus block out knowledge of and anxiety about the mother's lack of penis and replace it with sexual excitement. In one part of his mind he knows that the mother does not have a penis; in another, perverse part of his mind, he wipes out this knowledge.

This notion of a split in the ego is invaluable when working with perversions. Someone can know that they are anatomically male, yet believe themselves to be taking on the identity of a woman as they cross-dress. A person may commit an act, such as a sexual assault on a child, which in one part of their mind they know will do harm, while in another part of their mind believing that they are bestowing an experience of love. This notion of a split in the ego also enables one to consider the apparent juxtaposition of pleasure and unpleasure. Someone can "know" in one part of their mind that the pleasure of enacting a paraphilia is short-lived and often followed by guilt and self-disgust, yet in the moment, they can believe fervently that this will offer fulfilment and satisfaction of their deepest cravings and that nothing should stand in the way of them having the sought-after experience.

Rosenfeld's seminal paper on drug addiction (1960) provides a particularly useful articulation of the splitting that may prevail in addictions from a Kleinian perspective. He describes how the drug can represent both the idealized breast, which the individual feels to be under his omnipotent control; as the drug is ingested, there is the fantasy of having control of the idealized breast; in the mind of the addict, the desired situation is one where there is a constant supply, so that he is never exposed to an experience of loss or wanting. Simultaneously the drug can symbolize a "dead or ill object", a bad part of the self, which is projected out into the drug and then taken back into the self, gratifying a suicidal or destructive wish. Compulsive sexual behaviours can have similar qualities: in one part of the mind the individual believes that the behaviour promises extreme pleasure and gratification; yet simultaneously the behaviour may gratify a masochistic desire to subject the self to something demeaning, dangerous, or painful. One man drifted from looking at legal pornographic images on the Internet to looking at images that were ambiguous in terms of legality. He described two parallel states of mind while engaged in this activity: in one he imagined himself connected to a limitless source of arousal and gratification, like an umbilical connection to a font of sensory pleasure; in the other state of mind he was enacting his punitive loathing for himself. Far from idealizing or putting a gloss of denial on his actions, he chose passwords to access websites that expressed his extreme self-disgust as though enacting his hatred of himself and courting the condemnation of a punitive superego.

In a similar vein, Mr C would phone telephone sex chatlines and would scroll through voices for an hour or more until he found the voice that had the right quality of abusiveness and sadism. At one level he was seeking sexual stimulation and gratification, the sensory and physical pleasure that could be had at will as if under his complete control, but simultaneously he was seeking a repetition of an emotionally aversive experience of painful and demeaning abuse, familiar from his childhood.

So why repeat something that is unpleasurable or endlessly frustrating? Freud, in *Beyond the Pleasure Principle* (1920g), suggested that people sometimes repeat aversive or traumatic experiences that have been passively endured in an attempt to gain active mastery of the situation. Where there has been a traumatic experience that cannot be fully metabolized or processed, repetition of the experience in a symbolic or coded form represents an attempt by the ego to gain mastery of something that could not previously be managed. An illustration of this would be where someone had experienced a traumatic situation, such as being abused, and kept finding themselves in abusive relationships, essentially "revisiting" this situation, as if struggling to find a way to manage it. While this may be one element driving repetition compulsion, the repetitive behaviours evident in addictions and perversions do not usually accomplish developmental aims. There is rarely evidence of progression and resolution. The repetition much more commonly has the quality of an echo—nothing is added or altered to symbolically develop and master the underlying trauma or conflict.

Mr D, a man in his fifties presenting with exhibitionism, almost certainly experienced a depressed and unresponsive mother in childhood and seems to have grown up feeling that he lacked any capacity to arouse feelings of intense engagement in his mother. In early adolescence, while walking through a town, he stopped to urinate against a wall and realized he was being watched by a woman. He reports that, with no words exchanged, he and she repeated this scenario in the same place at the same time on a number of further occasions. His display found a willing partner in her voyeurism, and this experience of arousing interest and excitement in another became compelling for him. Mr D repeatedly wandered urban streets looking for women on their own to whom he might expose himself, often by pretending to urinate. Crucially, these women had to seem lively and energetic, presumably in his search for the antidote to the enduring trauma of the depressed internal mother. The tragedy of his predicament was, of course, that even if he evoked fleeting amusement in the woman, this transient response never filled the internal chasm. Lacking any awareness of what his behaviour represented, Mr D repeated this ritualized behaviour over decades.

For Mr D, repetition of the scenario in which he attempted to engage an unavailable woman rarely led to satisfaction; if he did have an experience that satisfied him sexually, the effects were not sustained, and he was soon searching out a similar situation again; but despite the evident frustrations of this behaviour, it was not relinquished. Perhaps one reason why the behaviour is neither satisfying nor can it be relinquished is due to the nature of symbolism involved. At this point it is necessary to shift from explanations in terms of libido theory to object relations theory.

Object relations

We commonly think of people with perversions as being particularly concrete in their thinking, and this would certainly apply to Mr D. Just when I thought we had made some headway in exploring the meaning of his behaviour, he would revert to insisting that his exhibitionism was just about needing a sexual outlet, and in this respect, he insisted, he was no different to anyone else.

Segal's (1957) ideas about symbol formation are particularly useful here. Segal distinguishes between the very early use of symbols characteristic of the paranoid-schizoid position, and the later use of symbols in the depressive position. The earliest use of symbols, in the paranoid-schizoid position, occurs when objects in the external world are taken to represent aspects of the internal world. Because differentiation between self and other is incomplete at this stage, the early symbols "are not felt by the ego to be symbols or substitutes, but to be the original object itself" (1957/1988, p. 164). Thus in this early stage, the thumb that is sucked is felt to be the comforting breast. Segal proposes that this "symbolic equation" between the original object and the symbol in the internal and external world underpins the concrete thinking of the schizophrenic. It seems possible that it is this type of symbolic equation that makes the sexual fantasy underlying perverse behaviour so compelling. It is as though, if only Mr D can engage the woman's attention, he will have engaged his mother once and for all. In that moment this is so urgently desired that he will throw caution to the wind and will disregard the risk of arrest, the possible breakdown of his marriage, and the shame of a conviction. Yet disappointment and disillusion is inevitable, because the woman is not his mother, and even if she does smile, it will never be his mother's smile. Thus even if there is sufficient excitement for him to become sexually aroused and satiated, he is never emotionally satisfied.

Segal contrasts this with the use of symbols in the depressive position; where the object is recognized as a whole with both good and bad aspects, there can be an experience of separation from and loss of the object, and symbols are created to displace aggression from the object and to restore the original object within the self. At this stage there is an awareness of loss; the symbol is used to re-create the experience of the original object in its absence. At this stage the symbol is known to have been created by the ego and to represent, but be different from, the original object. If he were functioning at this level, Mr D might have recognized and mourned the disappointments of his relationship with his mother. This might have freed him to turn to a relationship with a woman that he knew was not his mother, but who could provide maternal comforts that he could value and use. Paradoxically, where there is true symbolism and the symbol is known only to represent the thing that has been lost, there is the possibility of symbolic satisfaction; when there is a symbolic equation, there is only the risk of disappointment. Thus it is precisely the fact that perversions do not meet the underlying need or wish that leads to them being repeated endlessly.

An object relations approach also draws attention to the way in which the urge to repeat reflects a constant need to evacuate particular feelings or parts of the self into another. There may be a particular part of the self that cannot be tolerated under any circumstances, and so the individual constantly needs to recreate a situation in fantasy where someone else is made the receptacle of whatever it is that is intolerable; or it may be that it is only at certain times—for example, when the individual is vulnerable, or the feeling is amplified for some reason—that it cannot be tolerated and has to be evacuated. Mr E felt himself to be the feminized daughter of his mother, her companion and confidant, and while he experienced this as a privileged role, at some level he felt enraged that he was, in effect, emasculated by her. His sense of this humiliation was at its most acute when he was 8 years old, when difficulties in relation to parents, peers, and his physical health all coincided; at this age he remembered attending a family function with his parents when he felt particularly constrained and depressed. His sexual fantasies, enacted on the Internet, reflected a search to see an 8-year-old girl, similarly powerless and constrained. Thus the girl becomes, in his mind, the container for all the "feminine" and childlike passivity, helplessness, frustration, and rage that he could not bear within himself.

The urge to project or evacuate becomes suddenly more acute in particular circumstances. Mr B, described earlier, whose chatline "habit" was switched on with a vengeance after the contact with his terminally ill relative, was, most of the time, after four years of therapy, able to bear a degree of depression, loss, and anger about his past. He had understood in therapy how having a string of women on the Internet who he imagined were eager to meet him created a situation where, in his mind, he was wanted and desired and never had to be alone. Mr B's mother disappeared in mysterious circumstances when he was very young. In therapy we slowly came to understand how having a queue of women wanting to know him counteracted the appalling feeling of loss and abandonment that he must have experienced. Most of the time this had become bearable, but the knowledge that his relative was about to die aroused a level of distress about loss, helplessness, and abandonment that he was unable to bear. Then the women on the chatlines or the Internet had to be seduced and made to experience all the desire, so that he could rid himself of feeling unwanted and abandoned and could bask in an illusion that an endless string of women were longing to know him.

If we are to do justice to the compulsion to repeat, an object relations model that recognizes the powerful urge to evacuate and project intolerable experiences seems to be required. Until the person finds a way to increase his capacity to contain and metabolize acutely painful experiences, these will need to be repeatedly projected into others, either through enactment with an actual other person or through a fantasized relationship.

A real-life relationship can function as a screen or a container for such projections, but in real-life relationships the individual will inevitably encounter the other's subjectivity, and real others do not always comply with the role assigned to them. The Internet, with vast amounts of sexual material in which the people may be stripped of personal qualities or portrayed only as body parts, has a lack of human definition that can have a particularly powerful role in eliciting such projections. While the Internet is far from "blank" and has a surfeit of content, the volume and impersonal nature of the content means that it can act as a "blank screen", inviting and providing a receptacle for projections. If the individual encounters information that contradicts his projected fantasy, he can simply switch off or move on, enabling the fantasy to be sustained or developed.

The conscious sexual fantasy and escalation

Sexually compulsive behaviours and paraphilias are usually distinguished by a consistency in the sexual scenario that is sought. Where there is a degree of variation in the person's preferred sexual activities, it rare to find real flexibility in the preferred scenario; indeed, DSM–IV (APA, 1994, 2000) stipulates that, to warrant a diagnosis of paraphilia, the preferred scenario becomes fixed and repetitive. It is possible to think of the external scenario that is sought, either in reality or in the virtual world of the Internet, as an external realization of the conscious sexual fantasy.

For some people, there may be shifts over time in the specific sexual activity they seek to enact or observe, often in the direction of the activity becoming more "extreme". Addiction theories might suggest that this progression or escalation reflects increasing tolerance to the stimulus, or "habituation", so that increasing "doses" of the stimulus are required to achieve the same effect. From a psychoanalytic perspective, such accounts have little explanatory power but merely serve to describe the phenomenon. They are unable to explain why the escalation that occurs takes the particular course that it does. It is notable that escalation is almost always in the direction of looking at younger rather than older models or actors, and towards more violent rather than less violent imagery, and towards the increased blurring of sexual activity with non-sexual functions such as excretion.

To understand why escalation takes the course that it does, it is useful to consider the origins of the core sexual fantasy. A psychoanalytic view would consider that adult sexual fantasy is rooted in earliest experience, in the sensory experiences, unconscious phantasies, and object relations of early childhood. Children's understanding of bodies, relationships, and intimacy will be shaped by their level of psycho-emotional development. These early fantasies and theories about the sexual relations may therefore seem concrete or bizarre (see Horne, 2001) but will be modified as the child's development passes through the various lenses of the oedipal stage (Gillespie, 1956), latency, and puberty, depending on what he or she encounters at these stages.

The adult sexual fantasy also undergoes modification under the influence of another process, which is akin to the process of censorship and disguise by which what Freud calls "dream thoughts", are transformed into the manifest dream content. In *The Interpretation of Dreams*, Freud (1900a) describes how dream thoughts or the latent content of the dream contains elements that, were they to be allowed into consciousness, would disturb the dreamer and disturb sleep. This would include childhood memories, unconscious wishes, and allusions to the transference. Through the process of the dream work a compromise is reached, so that these elements may find expression, but in disguised form. Key mechanisms of disguise are displacement, where the significance or emotional charge of one person or thing is detached from it and displaced onto another person or thing, and condensation, where a number of different ideas are represented by a single idea or image. These transforming mechanisms can be observed at work in symptoms as well as dreams. A phobia of big dogs, for example, might reflect a displacement of anxiety from a ferocious father to a ferocious dog, or a condensation of a fear of being eaten and a fear of castration into a phobia of a snarling dog that encapsulates both threats. To be understood, the symptom needs to be "unpacked" and traced back to the underlying themes or drivers.

In the same way, a conscious sexual fantasy of an adult represents the expression of primitive object relationships and fears, sexual theories, and phantasies and will be shaped by formative sexual experiences of both a disturbing and an exciting nature. However, the conscious sexual fantasy, like the symptom or the dream, is a coded version of these underlying elements, and it is usually only in the course of therapy that the underlying elements are unearthed. The particular scenario depicted in the adult sexual fantasy will contain echoes of the unconscious experiences of childhood and adolescence, but those earlier experiences, often too disturbing to be allowed unmodified into consciousness, will be present in a disguised form. This disguise often involves a reversal of the original experience, so the man who felt himself to be powerless in childhood will now take pleasure in seeing someone else rendered powerless while he feels himself to be in control.

To take an example, Mr F presents for help because he is addicted to sadomasochistic sexual imagery with young-looking models in pornographic magazines. The conscious adult sexual fantasy relates to young adult women being subjected to sadomasochistic sexual acts. The second of two children with a much older brother, when Mr F was about 5 his mother became very friendly with a man in the neighbourhood, and Mr F now wonders whether she was having an affair. He felt that he was included in the mystery and excitement of this relationship, that he was special to his mother, and that it was his father and brother who were excluded. However, his mother's annexing of him was double-edged: he also felt smothered by her and that, in using him as a confidante, she was treating him like a daughter. At an unconscious level he harboured rage towards her, which occasionally erupted in irritability. At 13, on the cusp of puberty, he discovered his father's collection of pornography, which included in it images that alluded to an interest in under-age girls. Thus amongst the underlying, and largely unconscious elements that might shape his sexuality were a fantasy of oedipal triumph and an incestuous relationship with his mother; rage towards his mother for her castrating behaviour towards him and his father; and an identification with a father whose mind, he imagined, contained paedophilic fantasies. The adaptation that Mr F found in adult life to this difficult constellation was that he established a long-term relationship with a woman who had been sexually abused as a child. Ostensibly he responded to her vulnerability and felt protective towards her. He supplemented their sexual relationship by masturbating to pornography in which young-looking models were debased.

Thus the conscious sexual fantasy of young-looking models being treated sadistically is a distilled or cryptic version of the underlying dynamic elements. The young women may represent his mother, whom he wants to see punished for her castrating behaviour; they may represent the mother who is seductive and by whom he feels tricked and manipulated; they may represent the part of himself that he despises, the feminized "girl/daughter"; the young women may also represent the objects of the father's desire, which he wishes to take as his own. Thus both condensation and displacement may be at work. In savouring the sadistic treatment of the women, he allows himself, through projective identification, to take pleasure in seeing another demeaned and controlled, so that he can rid himself of these feelings and locate them in another.

The impact of Internet sex on the mind

Escalation of the sexual fantasy is particularly evident with people accessing Internet pornography and various forms of virtual sex. When the use of the Internet appears to lead to an escalation of people's sexual fantasies, what we might be witnessing is a stripping away of the layers of censorship and disguise, so that what is laid bare are the much more primitive, previously unconscious phantasies that may have underpinned the adult sexual fantasy. These almost inevitably refer to sexual thoughts that are more raw, more infantile, and more taboo. In Mr F's case, exposure to the Internet means that within a relatively short time he is looking not at "barely legal" late teenagers but at 5-year-old girls; the incestuous fantasies become evident in that he starts to look at scenes of frank sexual abuse of young children; the rage captured in his previous sexual fantasies of consensual sadomasochism is no longer contained as he starts to pursue scenes of rape.

There may be a range of sexual stimuli that can have this effect, but Internet pornography and Internet sex seem to have a particularly powerful capacity to foster regression, so that layers of censorship and striving towards developmental integration are undermined and the underlying infantile sexuality, primitive phantasies, and unmodified wishes are revealed in a much more raw form (Wood, 2011). There seem to be a number of ways in which the Internet effects such regression. First, use of the Internet can fuel manic defences, so that the person becomes cut off from the grounding effect of depressive, grey, ambivalent reality. If you wanted to design something that would fuel manic fantasies and defences, it would surely look something like the Internet. Individuals using the Internet have access to extraordinary amounts of information with negligible intellectual and physical effort. They can pass themselves off as whosoever or whatever they like, so they are not constrained by the reality and limitations of their physical self. They can be handsome, beautiful, potent, exciting, a different age, a different gender. At the very least, many people use fake names on chatlines or in chat rooms, as if slipping into another persona. If a person dislikes what is happening, he does not have to face or deal with the other person but can terminate the episode with the click of a mouse. There is an illusion of being invisible and that there are no witnesses. However obscure the individual's sexual fantasy, the chances are that he can find some realization of this on the Internet. All of these can amplify a sense of omnipotence and triumph.

Second, the Internet invites a regression to a childlike state of sexual curiosity. Everyone has within them a sexually curious child, the oedipal child who wonders what goes on behind the door of the parental bedroom. It is as if the Internet plays on people's sexual curiosity, symbolically beckoning the "child" into the parental bedroom with the promise of satisfying their sexual curiosity. Just as the reality of exposure to the primal scene may be profoundly disturbing to a child, so many people report seeing imagery on the Internet to which they subsequently wish they had not been exposed.

Third, the Internet can potentially undermine or corrupt the superego functioning of the adult. The Internet is like a parent who never says "no". Elaborate systems of drop-down menus and pop-ups exist to tempt the user to remain online, to visit additional websites, or to scan more extreme imagery. The pornographic imagery, or the expressed sexual preference, appear to bear the stamp of social approval or endorsement, because there are clearly other people who share this fantasy and have posted the image or information on the Internet. Chat rooms, where it is possible to exchange views with others with socially proscribed sexual interests, appear to normalize the specific sexual interest and create a sense that this is representative of a sub-set of society and hence not "deviant", thus allowing the triumph of a corrupt superego over ordinary social mores. The possibility of breaking the law and then deleting all evidence of the crime may further fuel the sense that the Internet works in the service of a corrupt authority and lends itself to acts of triumph over a watchful conscience.

In a range of ways, the Internet subtly undermines or erodes the integrated, regulated, depressive-position functioning of the mature adult and invites a kind of breakdown to a more regressed and primitive level of functioning. Thus the processes at work go far beyond mere physiological "tolerance" or "habituation" and involve a more complex process whereby disturbed and primitive currents within the psyche are unearthed and crystallize around specific sexual fantasies or scenarios.

Concluding remarks

How may we think about the "addictiveness" of paraphilic behaviours? I think the weakest explanations, though they may have something to contribute, are that the behaviour has become habitual or that it is source of sexual pleasure. It seems unlikely that these behaviours are repeated solely in an effort to master some trauma; if that is what they are intended to do, they are usually very unsuccessful. Usually the trauma is not consciously recognized and understood; there is a heavy symbolism but a lack of symbolization, and development does not occur.

Fundamentally these behaviours create scenarios in the person's mind, with actors and dramas, and those scenarios function as a means of evacuating intolerable feelings, enacting punishments on the self and others either in fantasy or in reality, avoiding the perils of genuine intimacy with another, and filling unbearable empty spaces in the person's emotional world with excitement. The drive to repeat occurs when there has been no resolution of the underlying difficulties and the play must be re-run again and again. An optimistic view would be that it is repeated in the hope of one day finding an object or other who will understand and unpack the symbolic communication; a more pessimistic view is that it is repeated to be rid of whatever it is that cannot be thought about and contained.

The Internet is a remarkable phenomenon, but in this domain its impact seems to be potentially pernicious in that it fuels unconscious phantasies of omnipotence, it fuels regressive sexual curiosity, and it appears to undermine and corrupt superego functioning and the integrating and censoring functions of the ego. The Internet, per se, is just a vehicle for the dissemination of information and a means of communication. But what it makes possible is the combination of instant access to explicit and unlimited sexual materials, apparently without consequence, and the absence of any obligation to engage with the mind of a sentient other. The invitation to narcissistic, manic, part-object, or pre-genital functioning means that Internet sex can have a disturbing effect on psychological functioning, in some ways analogous to the impact of a psycho-active substance such as drugs or alcohol. Clinically we are seeing a marked increase in people presenting with these apparently addictive sexual behaviours, and there is every reason to think this will become more of a problem rather than less as use of the Internet and online sexual materials become more widespread.

CHAPTER NINE

Anorexia nervosa:
addiction or not an addiction?

Susannah Rose

Susannah Rose is a psychotherapist working in an inpatient unit for patients with eating disorders. The unit offers a variety of treatments, as well as individual and group psychotherapy. Whatever treatment is offered, staff have to cope with the pain and anxiety of seeing young people with great potential who have turned themselves into living skeletons. Rose points out the high morbidity of anorexics, and many of the patients recover only to relapse. This has similarities to the patients in Angela Foster's chapter (chapter five) and draws attention to how difficult these patients are to treat.

The chapter initially discusses anorexia as an addiction, with the characteristic illusion of being in control and not needing relationships. Rose describes the anorexic's sadomasochistic relationship to a tyrannical "anorexic object", which she links to Rosenfeld's concept of pathological organizations. This tyrannical object is similar to the superego of the binge drinker described in Marion Bower's chapter (chapter three). Although the anorexic starves herself of food and the binge drinker ingests as much as possible, the distinction is more apparent than real. What links these different addictions is the submission to a tyrannical superego, which compels the addict to cross boundaries or limits in what is, in effect, an assault on the self. The anorexic girl cannot be thin enough, the gamblers described in Jessica Yakeley and Richard Taylor's chapter (chapter seven) cannot be poor enough and feel they cannot stop gambling until they have lost everything.

The second part of Rose's chapter looks at ways of getting alongside patients to talk about their omnipotence, destructiveness, and contempt without alienating them. This approach of getting alongside the addict is also described in the chapters by Vanessa Crawford (chapter one) and Angela Foster (chapter five).

Rose draws on the work of Tustin, Mitrani, and Bick. Mitrani suggests that a pathological organization can have a second skin function in the sense described by Bick. It then acts as a defence against states of disintegration. This is manifested in the addict's wish for a firm, hard body. The therapist's task is to provide a "digesting mind" in the sense described by Bion, to begin the process of converting somatized sensations back into thoughts and emotions that can be held in the mind.

Anorexia nervosa: an extreme illness

The experience of spending time with a severely anorexic patient is of being with someone profoundly caught up in a desperate, destructive internal battle—a battle between life and death. It is a battle that some patients will lose, as anorexia[1] is extremely difficult to recover from and carries the highest rate of mortality[2] of any mental illness. Working as a psychotherapist on an 18-bed inpatient unit for women with severe eating disorders, this is a fight I am engaged in every day, as the multidisciplinary team and I work to keep our patients alive.

The patients' internal battle of anorexia is most evident to observers in the dining room (Bowyer, 2009). Some patients may not be able to accept any feeding orally, and there will be no choice but to feed them through a naso-gastric tube. Others may start off on a milk-based food supplement drink before being able to manage even minimal amounts of solid food. Patients who are willing to eat solid food will usually display a plethora of "food behaviours": cutting food into tiny pieces and eating one at a time; hiding food in napkins; hiding food in the mouth or even the throat, to be brought up and spat out later; separating foods into its component parts; covering food in salt, pepper, or vinegar; even regurgitating food quickly during the meal. Sometimes patients cover their hands with their sleeves so as not to see that they are, in fact, feeding themselves.

Other anorexic behaviours are less evident to observers as they may not take place specifically at mealtimes—such as vomiting following meals and inappropriate use of laxatives. Patients with anorexia can be driven to take drastic measures in order to maintain their starved anorexic state, frequently taking dangerous risks in order to deceive staff or loved ones and keep them from knowing the true state of their illness. To this aim, some patients "water-load", filling themselves with large quantities of water in order to make their weight reading higher when they are weighed. On the unit patients are not allowed access to water without supervision, but may spend huge amounts of time and energy finding ways to get the water they need to falsify their weight reading. Some patients are so experienced in this that they know the exact amount to drink to achieve a specific desired weight reading. Excessive water loading can have serious physical consequences, leading to organ failure, fitting, and even death. I have heard recovered anorexic patients describe the agony of keeping their bladders filled with water in order to be prepared for "spot-weighing"[3] at all times.

Another mechanism for managing weight is exercise. Patients who are compelled to exercise excessively outside the unit but are prevented from doing so on the unit sometimes feel forced by their "illness" to pace for many hours on the unit. It is impossible for staff on the unit to physically force patients to sit down and stop pacing (although we are often tempted to take this approach!). Additionally, we are aware that should we attempt to meet their forcefulness with our own, the internal disturbance within the patient becomes relocated to an external fight between patient and staff—an unconscious manoeuvre, that although welcomed by the patient, does not help with her recovery. Again, I have heard recovered anorexic patients looking back at their pacing, describing their utter exhaustion brought on by the relentless self-enforced regime, where they were virtually asleep on their feet but unable to stop until reaching the required pacing goal. This goal was determined by how many calories they had been "forced" to eat by staff and therefore how many calories needed to be burned, with any momentary distraction during their pacing having to be made up at the end with the addition of another minute or two for each moment lost.

Patients with anorexia aim to remain physically empty at all times, but their minds are constantly active and full, often with repetitive and circular thoughts on which they ruminate for long periods of time—for instance, counting calories, or focusing on their last meal, or their next meal, or other minutiae related to food, eating, or body image. Some patients make very detailed lists—of calories, or things "to do", or any manner of subjects. Many anorexic patients also suffer from obsessive compulsive disorder (OCD), and much of their "mind" and time are taken up with performing secret "rituals"; these may involve straightening objects, checking that plugs and light-switches are turned off or are facing in the "right" direction, writing/saying things a certain number of times etc., and often go along the lines of ". . . if I don't say/do this, something bad will happen to my family". Other feelings patients may have include spending many hours each day "worrying" about what people are thinking of them, and this forms their main activity; they may make a list of their view of others' thoughts about them. We have patients who may spend the entire day watching other patients' every move. This might be to gauge someone else's "behaviour" in a competitive way in order to incorporate it into their own armoury of behaviours. Sometimes it forms part of a projective process where the watched patient is deemed to be "very anorexic" for using behaviours, while the watcher— filled up with feelings of superiority—is free of awareness of being unwell. At times a patient may spend many hours fretting about the "extra" calories they were given at a meal because the size of their portion was experienced as being larger than everyone else's. Often a patient will spend extended periods of time focusing on a specific part of their body that they don't like, perhaps looking in the mirror for a long time as well.

Anorexia is for the most part utterly incomprehensible to friends and family of patients, who are left at a loss, unable to understand how their loved one could actually be starving herself to death by refusing to eat. I often hear the desperate question: "Why don't you just eat!" Anorexic patients convey the sense of being held in the sway of a powerful, deeply malevolent and tyrannical internal object, enmeshed in a repetitive, destructive relationship with this "anorexic object", which they are compelled to perpetuate, and from which they are entirely unable to free themselves. This is reminiscent of Freud's notion of the death instinct. In *Beyond the Pleasure Principle* (1920g) Freud first used the term "death instinct". Noticing patients' compulsion to repeat unpleasurable experiences, he remarked:

> Patients repeat all of these unwanted situations and painful emotions in the transference and revive them with the greatest ingenuity. They seek to bring about the interruption of the treatment while it is still incomplete; they contrive once more to feel themselves scorned, to oblige the physician to speak severely to them and treat them coldly; they discover appropriate objects for their jealousy. . . . The impression they give is of being pursued by a malignant fate or possessed by some "daemonic" power. [1920g, p. 21]

Working with anorexic patients, it often feels that one is invited to "speak severely" to them—to become the cruel and forceful blaming figure who wants to control them and tell them off—and they certainly convey the sense of being pursued and possessed by some "'daemonic' power".

Anorexia: an addiction

Working on the unit, staff members experience a mass of different feelings and emotions throughout each day, many of which through projective processes help identify the character of these malignant internal relationships taking place in the patients' inner worlds. We can feel helpless, passive, and "victimized" by the patients, despairing about how any of them will ever recover. At times we have sadistic and violent feelings towards the patients, wanting intrusively to "make" them eat and "force" them not to exercise. Sometimes we feel no engagement at all with a particular patient and are desperately tempted to give up on her—pulled by the appeal of the anorexic solution of turning away from wanting contact. The work can be intensely distressing, as we are forced passively to witness the self-inflicted near destruction of clever and attractive young women who have turned themselves into virtual skeletons. Often the team will be divided between two opposing sets of feelings, some carrying the hope and care for a patient, others the hatred and outrage. Most of us have one experience in common, however: when we discuss patients in detail, we are frequently left feeling physically starving, "dying" for our next coffee break, when we pounce on the biscuits with relief and greed.

While members of staff are constantly attempting to process these feelings of sadism, masochism, greed, hunger, and despair within themselves, our patients seem to remain free of such awareness of these feelings, as their days and minds are filled with the repetitive thoughts already described. This is reminiscent of Joseph's (1982) description of "chuntering" in her paper "Addiction to Near-Death":

> These patients pick up very readily something that has been going on in their minds or in an external relationship and start to use it over and over again in some circular type of mental activity, in which they get completely caught up, so that they go over and over with very little variation the same actual or anticipated issue. . . . Patients who get so caught up in these activities, chuntering, tend to believe that they are thinking at such times, but of course they are living out experiences which becomes the complete antithesis of thought. [pp. 451–452]

It is hard to think of a better description of anorexia than "addiction to near-death". Patients with anorexia present as being unconsciously addicted to the self-destructive and perverse use of their bodies and the excitement of the perverse worlds they have created, to the masochistic and submissive relationship to the deadly tyrannical internal object that promises protection, to the feeling of living outside ordinary life, hovering just above death.

As with addictions to substances, anorexia provides feelings of omnipotence and absolute control over internal and external objects: in spite of the deep dependence to the craved substance or state of mind, the phantasy is of having transcended dependency, of being able to conjure up your object when needed, only to send it away when not needed. (This is a situation that is sometimes in danger of being enacted on the unit, where parents are summoned to visit, only to be dismissed for some small misdemeanour when they arrive.) With the omnipotence comes the phantasy of superiority and invincibility: nothing and no one is needed to be relied upon. Anorexics appear to be addicted to sadistic projective processes where it is the other who is force-fed feelings of being small, useless, and helpless—for instance, the family members who are unable to visit after all, or the staff member who has to stand by and watch as the patient scornfully and determinedly paces round her room from 10 p.m. until 3 a.m. regardless of all entreaties to stop.

In the anorexic state patients are free of the need for food; free of feelings, emotions, responsibilities; free of hunger; free of the constraints and boundaries of existential reality that weigh down the rest of us (such as "I will die if I do not eat"). They can maintain for long periods at a time the illusion that they are free of all desires. Through their illness they have created a "retreat" (Steiner, 1993) where they can remain cut off from the outside world, from the impingement of relationships and emotional connectedness, and often from physical intimacy as well. Their retreat can provide a way of remaining cut off from their inside world too: from knowledge of what exists in their minds outside the narrow constraints of the restricted anorexic state (Rose, 2009). The cost of this addictive relationship to the protecting internal anorexic object that provides these so-called freedoms is very high indeed.

I am reminded of the image of the Pied Piper used by Sohn (1985) when describing his theory of the "identificate" that takes over the personality. His description is very apt for describing the internal processes at work in anorexia:

> It is as if a Pied-Piper process is at hand, with the dependent parts of the personality constantly being led away to disappearance, leaving the personality like the crippled boy who survived in the story. Simultaneously the same crippling is directed against the analytic work. [p. 279]
>
> To me it appears that in the narcissistic organization, an identification by projective identification has taken place; the process of identification starts the narcissistic organization: that is to say, by becoming the object, which is then felt to be within the possession of the self. It is this that produces the feeling

which we call omnipotence. . . . It is, however, done destructively and can never be used constructively—the destruction being to the state of the ego, and to the object which is consequently devalued. [p. 292]

Others have made valuable theoretical contributions along these lines, with various ways of describing the internal destructive object or organization that seduces the patient away from libidinal relationships. To mention three:

1.   Rosenfeld:
      it is as if one were dealing with a powerful gang dominated by a leader, who controls all the members of the gang to see that they support one another in making the criminal destructive work more effective and powerful. [1971/1988, p. 249]

2.   Meltzer:
      This destructive part prevented him from admiring or respecting anyone by its slander, its omniscient propaganda. [1968/1988, p. 236]

3.   O'Shaughnessy:
      His pathological superego is a culture of the death instinct; we see its chilling tricks and its installing of repeated cycles of cruelty and punishment. . . . It is full of hate and prejudice, sceptical of all renaissance; its aim is to destroy links within the self and between the self and its objects. It generates enormous anxiety in the patient, being the manifestation of the Death Instinct within, an immoral sweeper downhill to destruction, and a punishing incessant beater" (1999, pp. 865–868).

Clinical example

This brief clinical example of this type of internal destructive relationship is from my clinical practice on the inpatient unit where I work.

Sophie[4] is a 22-year-old woman who suffers from anorexia. Last year her elder sister died following a prolonged illness. Sophie is a member of the twice-weekly psychotherapy group that I co-facilitate with another psychotherapist. During her first four groups, Sophie hardly says a word. She sits hunched in her chair, her head bowed, keeping very still. After a while I notice that although she appears to be still, she is actually picking aggressively at the thumb of one hand with the nails of her other hand. As well, I become aware that she seems to be chewing the inside of her cheeks with a forceful and repetitive motion, while holding her feet just above the ground so that her legs, back, and abdominal muscles are being exercised as she sits. When Sophie does speak in the group, it is in a virtually inaudible and noticeably childish voice. Her contributions to the group are all practically identical and are along these lines: "I'm afraid to speak because I'll probably say the wrong thing, then no one will like me; I'll make everyone angry, they won't like me. What's the point of me speaking anyway, because even if I try and recover and put more weight on, it'll still be me, and I always spoil everything."

As the weeks have gone by, Sophie has been able to say more in the groups. This has given me a chance to notice that although the amount of words has increased, the content of what she is saying never varies. What does seem to happen, though, is that as she says more, the intensity of the self-hating increases until she has worked herself up into a fever pitch of crying and despair. An example of this took place in Sophie's ninth week in the group. Another group member comments (not unkindly) on a "food behaviour" that Sophie uses at the dining table, and which the other patient finds difficult and annoying (cutting food up into tiny pieces and taking a very long time to eat each one). Sophie becomes pale and anxious when challenged in this way. She says: "I'm sorry. I'm sorry I made you angry. I always make people angry, it's just me. It's my fault, I shouldn't have done it. It's just me, that's what I'm like, I always get everything wrong, whatever I do. I shouldn't be here at all, I'm to blame, everything goes wrong around me. Everything's gone wrong in my life, everything, and it's my fault; like my sister's death, it's my fault she died." This goes on for several moments. She is crying, wringing her hands, her voice getting increasingly shrill, excited, and louder in volume. It is clear that Sophie is entirely unable to "think" about or reflect in any way on what has been said to her, in the service of developing greater understanding either of herself or of her relationship with the other patient.

Although Sophie is understandably profoundly disturbed by the death of her sister, this does not seem to be a sufficient explanation for the behaviour that I have described. There is a powerful sense when Sophie is speaking and acting in this way that she is engaged in a masochistic activity that appears to be rather gratifying to her on a level. When Sophie is speaking—and even when she's silent—I often find myself in the countertransference feeling provoked and irritated by her. Sometimes I want to tell her harshly to "speak more loudly", to "stop it!" in relation to her "picking" (both the physical picking of her thumb, and the psychic picking away at her mind with the self-hatred and blame). These countertransference feelings seem to lend weight to the idea that Sophie is engaged in an internal relationship with a cruel and harsh figure, as it seems that in the transference relationship I am being invited to become the cruel figure in relation to her, sadistically picking at her and getting at her.

It seems Sophie lives in a masochistic world where aggressive feelings are projected into her objects, where she then evokes feelings of dislike in the other, subsequently becoming identified with their denigrated view of her—agreeing that she is a terrible person whom no one could like. This can make it hard for me to take up directly what I feel is going on. Perhaps I am intended to feel quite helpless—as is the rest of the group—unable to have meaningful contact with Sophie as she masochistically picks away at her mind. It seems that Sophie's own feelings of helplessness have been located in others in this way. I believe that any contact or insight offered by me, the other facilitator, or the group is not experienced by Sophie as nourishing food that could lead to development; instead, it is used as further fuel for her self-blaming activities. No good experience is allowed to develop between her and her objects. Perhaps this feels a great deal safer to Sophie than allowing a good relationship to develop with someone whom, she imagines, she could kill with her aggressive and hostile feelings. In her masochistic world, she has nothing more to lose.

Anorexia: further considerations

In spite of the profoundly addictive nature of the internal relationships involved in anorexia, and "medical model" classifications of anorexia as an addiction, viewing it as an addiction can be problematic. Perhaps surprisingly, bearing in mind the previous section of this chapter, on my unit we do not consider anorexia to be an addiction and do not treat it as an addiction.[5] This is in contrast to other eating disorders, such as bulimia nervosa and binge eating disorder, which are more likely to be thought of as "addictions" by the team. From my perspective there are two main reasons to avoid placing anorexia in the category of addiction.

The first is the treatment modality. Addiction treatments usually involve a behavioural or abstinence approach to treatment and recovery: for instance, an alcoholic will be asked to change her behaviour by abstaining from her "addictive substance"—alcohol—for life. For anorexic patients it is not possible to abstain from their feared substance as their feared substance is food, which they have already chosen to abstain from, and which they cannot avoid for the rest of their lives. If they choose to abstain from so-called "difficult" foods, like puddings, they will be maintaining the "anorexic relationship" to food even if they manage to eat some foods. They could be encouraged behaviourally to abstain from their "addictive behaviours"—food restriction, "food behaviours", over-exercise; but asking them to cease using behaviours solely through introducing further control can be counterproductive. Anorexia involves exercising absolute control over your surroundings/your body/your food intake; abstention and control are the very things anorexic patients are addicted to—not just in relation to food, but in their thinking and their relationships as well. Tempting them with the idea of recovery through even greater control runs the risk of reinforcing the anorexic will rather than helping to diminish it.[6]

With bulimia and binge-eating disorders, the underlying relationship to the illness is equally critical, but it does seem more possible to help patients give up their "feared substance"—that is, quantities of food for bingeing, or purging behaviours such as vomiting—through controlling their behaviour. Perhaps this is possible because these illnesses are less about staying in absolute omnipotent control of the body, and more about a negotiation of control between self and others, between internal and external. Exploring this further is outside the remit of this chapter, but as several authors have considered the differences between anorexic and bulimia/binge eating disorders, I offer a few of their thoughts as possible contributing factors. Waller et al. (2007) describe how restrictive anorexia is considered to be "primary avoidance of emotion (p. 100)" (where primary avoidance of emotion serves to avoid affect arising in the first place), whereas eating disorders where the focus is not only restrictive (binge eating and bulimic disorders) are considered to be "primary and secondary avoidance of emotion (p. 100)" in emotion regulation terms, where secondary avoidance involves the reduction of affect once it is triggered. Williams (1997b) has described the way in which anorexic patients develop an entire "no entry system of defences" (p. 927) in order to keep out unwanted parental projections, in contrast to bulimic patients, who are able to remain "porous" (p. 927) and can take in some projections—and are therefore less completely cut off from others. Farrell (1995) highlights the use of the bulimic ritual as a way "of creating, finding or refinding some kind of a transitional experience" (p. 5), while the anorexic patient is not functioning at a level of transitional experience at all.

This is not to suggest that we do not draw on behavioural and abstinence concepts in the day-to-day management and education of our anorexic patients—but the behavioural approach operates hand in hand with an awareness of the importance of understanding the meaning of the patients' anorexia and encouraging them to become more aware of this themselves. At the dining table patients are expected to change their anorexic behaviour by being helped repeatedly to do things differently—for instance, to eat—regardless of the internal meaning their illness has to them. This is a function provided mainly by the nursing staff. Similarly, much of the group programme is psycho-educational and focuses on finding strategies to challenge and manage feelings and behaviours, regardless of their significance. However, this work is firmly underpinned by a belief in the need to understand the unconscious meaning and significance of the patients' symptoms. Although we are not a therapeutic community (patients are not involved in the day-to-day running of the unit), we do operate as a therapeutic milieu run along psychosocial nursing principles (see, for example, Barnes, 1968), with much of the multidisciplinary team involved in constantly encouraging the anorexic patients (and patients with all types of eating disorders) to develop a greater connection between their physical symptoms and their emotional experiences. Equally, associated co-morbidities such as OCD may well be treated with a behavioural approach.

There are units treating anorexia nervosa that do think of it as an addiction and treat it as such. This is particularly the case with units working to a 12-Step abstinence model of recovery. The 12-Step model for anorexia varies according to different units and is not, strictly speaking, "one approach". It may involve the patient abstaining from problematic foods—such as fatty foods and white sugar—in order to be able at least to eat some foods; it may involve the patient being expected to eat all foods, but being asked to abstain from their addictive behaviour of restricting food intake. Abstinence treatments in these contexts may be successful: although the patient will not have addressed her underlying relationship to food and eating, she may be helped to increase her weight and day-to-day functioning enough to manage a much fuller life—clearly a huge improvement in itself. Additionally, encouraging an anorexic patient to gain the sense of a kindly "higher power" external to herself (part of the 12-Step approach) could be extremely helpful to a person who prefers to shun all dependency. The main difficulty with this approach is that patients are not accepted on to the treatment unless they are motivated to change. Most frequently, patients on my unit come for treatment only at the insistence of their families, schools, places of work, or, ultimately, under a Section of the Mental Health Act. It is very rare for patients to arrive for treatment with any awareness of motivation, as the internal tyrannical "anorexic object" does not tolerate desire for change.

The second difficulty with thinking of anorexia as an addiction also centres around treatment—not just the treatment modality, but how we actually behave towards a person caught in the grip of this terrifying illness. Much has been written about the necessity of talking to anorexic patients in "pastel" words rather than "primary colour" words (Williams, 1997b, p. 928) or swimming alongside them like a "dolphin" rather than chasing them like a "rhinoceros" (Crane, Smith, & Treasure, 2007, pp. 26–27). The great importance of attempting to work in a collaborative way, as both Williams and Treasure emphasize, certainly matches the experiences of the team on my unit. I have already indicated the importance of not getting caught up in a battle of control with anorexic patients and of attempting to prevent the constant re-enactment whereby team members are invited to become increasingly prescriptive and proscriptive in relation to the patients.

Presenting a non-confrontational stance can be problematic when talking to patients of traits associated with addiction—such as control, power, avoidance, compulsion, and dependence—as these subjects have a tendency to alienate and distance the patients. At the same time, we do need to help them gain a sense of their own omnipotence, destruction, and contempt. This presents an interesting technical difficulty, as clinicians struggle to find a way of speaking to the patients about their destructive inner worlds and internal relationships without pushing them further into their anorexia.

In this respect, it is helpful to draw on Mitrani's (2007) thoughts about the nature of the internal destructive narcissistic organization. Rather than focusing on the destructive and envious elements, she compares the function provided by the internal organization to that of a "second skin" (Bick, 1968):

> . . . such defensive organizations are not solely a manifestation of the death instinct but, paradoxically, may be an expression of the baby's hyperbolic striving to preserve life and to protect against unmanageable states of unintegration and disintegration—of non-being and madness equated with the fear of breakdown. [p. 14]

Mitrani's views match my experience of working with anorexic patients. Although the addictive, sadomasochistic elements are certainly evident, what is predominant is their desperate attempt to keep hold of some sense of control, and some order to their otherwise chaotic minds and lives.

Bick's (1968) thesis about second skin functioning is that:

> in its most primitive form the parts of the personality are felt to have no binding force amongst themselves and must therefore be held together in a way that is experienced by them passively, by the skin functioning as a boundary. [p. 484]

She explains that this internal function of containment depends initially on the "introjection of an external object, experienced as capable of fulfilling this function" (p. 484).

> Disturbance in the primal skin function can lead to a development of a "second skin" formation through which dependence on the object is replaced by a pseudo-independence, by the inappropriate use of certain mental functions, or perhaps innate talents, for the purpose of creating a substitute for this skin container function. [p. 484]

She adds that the "second skin" phenomenon that replaces first skin integration manifests itself as either a partial or total type of muscular shell or a corresponding verbal muscularity. Bick notes that when there is a disturbance in the introjection of the containing object, "the concept of a space within the self cannot arise" (p. 484). Bick's "verbal muscularity" as a second skin is a helpful alternative to Joseph's notion of "chuntering" in understanding the constant thinking and worrying of the patients.

It is also helpful to think of anorexia along the lines of M. Eglé Laufer's (1996) notion of "repetitive compelling behaviour". She describes this behaviour as being identifiable by its "repetitive, addictive quality", which "however self-destructive, cannot be given up because of its function as a means of dealing with intense anxiety" (p. 350–351). "Repetitive compelling behaviour" seems to be a useful way of keeping in mind the elements of compulsion and addiction at the same time as the underlying deeply felt anxieties—and the one as a way of dealing with the other.

The anorexic patient is compelled to use her body as the arena in which to play out her emotional world, as her abilities to use her mind to symbolize and to metabolize experience are limited. The use of her body in this way, combined with the addictive sense of control and omnipotence this gives her, is what needs to be understood. What we are attempting to provide is a "digesting mind" (Bion, 1962, pp. 95–96) to begin the process of converting somatized sensations back into psychical experience. If emotions and feelings can become digestible, less like actual concrete chunks, the contents of the patient's mind are felt to be less terrifying and out of control—less "mad". The need for the comforting anorexic figure, the purified retreat, is diminished. In my view this is achieved through gaining an understanding of the "feel" of the patients' symptoms—that is, initially to focus less on the addictive aspects of anorexia (even though they are undoubtedly present), and concentrating instead more on the physical sensations of the patients' somatized experiences as a way of learning about their corresponding emotional experiences and helping them to discover and tolerate the contents of their own minds. We would hope that once patients have a greater ability to bear their own emotional worlds, the addictive appeal of omnipotent self-destruction will lessen.

Returning to the example of pacing, or of excessive exercise and "exercise addiction" more generally, I will illustrate a way of viewing this behaviour that is an alternative to the sadomasochistic, addiction-based model discussed above. I will illustrate the importance of physical sensations to the patient with anorexia. When an anorexic patient presents with an exercise addiction—something that is very common—it would be understandable to imagine the exercise as a way of burning calories, controlling the size of the body, getting rid of feelings through the sense of control, superiority, and invincibility. We might also wonder about the formation of a strong, rigid external muscular "shell" as an attempt to shield the patient from unwanted intrusions and projections into her mental space. These observations would most likely be accurate. However, they also miss important elements of exercise addiction that we frequently observe. Many patients cannot stand the physical sensation of "flab" on their bodies. This is not just the "fear of fat". What cannot be tolerated is the feeling of the undefined boundaries of their body—which to the patient feel "messy", "chaotic", and "out of control": boundary-less. The horror associated with the physical sensation of mess and chaos with no external border equates to a terror of the messiness and confusion of their thoughts, feelings, and emotions, which, if experienced psychically, can make them feel totally out of control and "mad". They need everything around them to be defined and rigid, including the physical sensations of their own body, in order to protect themselves from a state of unintegration—again, similar to Bick's (1968) "second skin", where the physical sensations of the body are used as a pseudo psychic skin.

To ask a patient to stop exercising through willpower alone is to encourage the internal omnipotent anorexic object; to talk to her about her fear of being out of control may not register at all as she does not recognize this fear. What she does "feel" is "flabby", or "splodgy" (these are words patients have used), related to cata-strophic internal anxieties associated with this unintegrated state. At other times she may feel "empty", "full", "fat", "flat", "rigid", "cold", "hot", "itchy", "prickly", "bumpy", "lumpy" (again, all words patients have used to describe how they feel)—all of which have a mental counterpart. The somatizing anorexic patient is experiencing the contents of her psychic world as "concrete" sen-sations in her physical body, and relating to them in that place. It is in this area that staff involved with the care of the patients need to be focusing.

The fear of confusion and chaos and the desperate need to find a way of staving off messy feelings can be seen in many other eating disorder behaviours as well as over-exercise. One way is through a hyper-vigilance over planning: everything must be planned, and the illusion of "certainty" maintained—as feelings of uncertainty or ambiguity are unbearable. Equally, patients cannot eat foods that "run together", such as coleslaw, on the same plate as baked beans, or sandwiches where the filling "soaks into the bread". Many patients cannot bear to have a meal that "collapses" on the plate—and some would even rather have a higher-calorie meal that is "tidy" on the plate than a "messy" lower-calorie meal. Some patients would even prefer naso-gastric tube feeding to solid food as it offers absolute certainty of content (exact amounts and calo-rie content), as opposed to the hated uncertainty of food—which, however it is weighed or measured, can never be an absolute certainty. Separating out of the individual components of a food is extremely common: sweet corn from tuna; peppers, onion, and mushrooms from lasagne; peas and carrots in distinct piles on the plate (patients are not allowed to continue these behaviours once they begin treatment). We often speak about this in terms of the patients' "attacks on linking" (Bion, 1959) or their difficulty with triadic relationships (Lawrence, 2001). Again, these lines of think-ing are accurate and valuable. However, the desperate attempt to keep their emotional worlds in some sort of order and to hold on to a sense of self—however limited—cannot be underestimated. What they are struggling to provide for themselves is an outline, definition, a "skin". If the therapist can recognize the patient on this physical, corporal level, then the patient may feel truly understood rather than feeling forced to lose themselves further to the perceived idea of who they should be, not who they are.

Tustin (1972) wrote about anorexia as a defence against catastrophic anxiety, stressing the "barrier" that keeps at bay the "nameless dread" (Bion, 1962) "that they could liquefy and drain away" (p. 204). Tustin (1986) writes of an anorexic patient, Jean, speaking to her of her feeling that she is a waterfall that, ". . . if spilled into bottomless nothingness, nothing would be left; she would be a no-body, a non-entity" (p. 198). Many authors have subsequently commented on the connection between the use of the body to provide a sense of solidity, and anorexia (Anzieu, 1989; Bick, 1968; Grotstein, 1980; Innes-Smith, 1987; Kadish, 2011; Meltzer, 1975; Mitrani, 2007; Nissen, 2008; Ogden, 1989; Reilly, 2004; Rhode, 2003; Rosenfeld, 1988; Tustin, 1958, 1981, 1986; Willner, 2002). Much of this work focuses on Winnicott's (1960) and, subsequently, Tustin's work on the experiences in infancy of traumatic separation from the mother/nipple—resulting in a catastrophic sensation of losing a part of their body—and patients' experience of spilling and falling away into nothingness—as well as Bick's thoughts on second skin phenomena. Pines (1980) expands on the notion of the skin as a barrier to the outside world in relation to infantile eczema, as does Barrows (1999) in her work with a bulimic patient and the patient's need to protect herself from parental internal objects.

Judith Mitrani (1992, 1993, 1995, 2008) has written widely about the link between the use of the body to stave off unmentalized psychic experiences in anorexia and other pathologies. Following on from Bion's, Winnicott's, and Tustin's work, Mitrani (1993) extends the thinking around failures in the container/contained and the resulting "holes, gaps, or faults through which the nascent self can slip, spill or diffuse". She believes that the infant's mental unmetabolized experiences remain within the body and are evaded or evacuated psychosomatically. In 2007 she focused specifically on an anorexic patient and on the role of the body in adolescence. Like Moses and Eglé Laufer, she notes the re-emergence of earlier difficulties at the time of adolescence.

Clinical example

This clinical example shows a more "second skin" and less "addiction-based" approach to understanding an anorexic patient:

> Matilda is a 16-year-old girl[7] admitted to my inpatient unit due to her low weight following weight loss associated with anorexia nervosa. This was her fourth hospital admission since the age of 11. Matilda had never allowed herself to have individual psychotherapy at any of her previous hospitals, or as an outpatient between admissions. It is part of my job to allocate patients to therapy, and consequently I met with Matilda to discuss the options. She agreed to meet with me for a "one-off", making it clear that this would not be the beginning of therapy and that she would not agree to therapy with any therapist. During this one-off meeting, I agreed with Matilda that she didn't have to have therapy as she felt so strongly that she didn't want to, and I suggested that she and I could have intermittent "review sessions" instead, to check that she was ok and that she hadn't changed her mind about therapy. Surprisingly, Matilda agreed to this.
>
> Initially Matilda and I met monthly, although this was quickly increased to fortnightly as I told Matilda, quite truthfully, that I couldn't keep up with how she was when seeing her so infrequently. I was aware that the need and desire for contact between us was located in me, but I felt that bearing in mind the cut-off anorexic state she had been in for several years, perhaps that was most appropriate at this stage. During the first six months of our meetings, Matilda paced around my office for the entire session. As we were conducting a review rather than a psychotherapy session, we made an agreement that we would review where she was, rather than focusing on where others would like her to be—that is, different from how she is now, "better" than how she is now—and pacing was part of where she was at this stage. As she paced around the room, I reviewed with her each main area of her life (life on the unit, family visits, etc.) without probing into anything about her inner world or how she was "feeling". I was aware of possibly colluding with the anorexic object which says it is acceptable to pace, and

that no one should get in the way of this. Equally, I felt it was appropriate to meet such a "concrete" thinking patient at the concrete level of where she was currently functioning. Matilda had been unequivocal in her statement that "I won't ever talk about feelings", and this was our starting point.

As my meetings with Matilda continued, an interesting phenomenon took place. Matilda became interested in the physical sensations created within me by her physical pacing (watching someone pace does induce feelings of dizziness and can be quite uncomfortable). After a while it became clear that she felt anxious about whether I could bear to be in the room with her, as I might feel too dizzy and disoriented. I wondered to myself about her worry that the wish for contact—which up until now had been located solely in me—may have been lost; I also imagined how disoriented Matilda might feel inside if she were to stop the emotional buffer created by her constant movement. Matilda's anxieties were, not surprisingly, located in the arena of the physical and concrete, and that is where I took them up. I said to Matilda that I wondered whether she thought her pacing and constant movement might be too much for me to manage, and I might not want to see her.

Through these tentative communications, Matilda and I found a way to speak to each other about things other than "reviewing" her day-to-day life on the ward. Over many weeks she began to tell me about the physical sensations she experienced when pacing. Her legs hurt. She feels the "flab" on them moving when she moves and wants to get to a time when there is no movement at all . . . pacing makes her dizzy, but she doesn't mind, because she can't stop. Particularly after a meal she mustn't stop. I felt that Matilda was describing a desperate wish that her "muscular shell" (Bick, 1968) could protect her from the dizzy-making chaotic movement of her internal thoughts and feelings.

After some time, Matilda's communications helped me to understand how difficult her internal world was for her to manage—even to begin to conceptualize it in her mind, let alone telling someone else about it. During another session she told me again how she mustn't stop pacing, particularly after a meal. Not just because of the calories, like you might think, but because she doesn't like to have food in her stomach, she doesn't like the way it feels inside her stomach—she doesn't like it when her stomach sticks out and people can see that she has something inside her. Very gradually, Matilda began to acknowledge that as well as having food inside her, which she doesn't like and doesn't want anyone to know about, she also has thoughts inside her—which she doesn't like people to see and to know about—and that they can be difficult and upsetting thoughts that disturb and frighten her sometimes. This was the beginning of our sessions moving away from the concrete safety of the physical sensations of her body to the uncharted feelings and sensations of her emotional world.

It would have been possible for me to focus on Matilda's pacing along the lines outlined in the section about anorexia as an addiction above—the addiction to the demanding internal organization, the way of filling up every waking moment and every part of her mind so that few thoughts crept into her awareness, a way of projecting feelings of impotence into me and of controlling me in relation to her. I do not believe, though, that Matilda and I would have made the progress that we have. Matilda is now firmly engaged in weekly therapy with me, which she openly looks forward to, making steady progress, and talking freely about her feelings, her dreams and nightmares, her thoughts about how she would like her life to be. She is back at school, has made good friendships, and is seeing her first boyfriend.

Concluding remarks

Anorexic patients are deeply involved in an addictive relationship with internal, destructive narcissistic objects—often formed into internal organizations—which demand (and promise) perfection at all times, which pour scorn on feelings of need, dependency, and warmth. They are addicted to the sense of omnipotence and to the perverse excitement of the masochistic world they inhabit. However, this is only part of the picture. In my view, focusing on the "repetitive-compelling behaviour" (M. E. Laufer, 1996) as a way of managing intense internal anxiety, of conceptualizing the internal organization and external symptoms and behaviours as a possible attempt at a psychic "second skin" (Bick, 1968), is a more fruitful way of working with the illness and with the patients. When working with anorexic patients, I am drawn to an approach based less on traditional symbolic meaning and more on an exploration of the use of body sensations and physical surroundings as a means of managing psychic experience. I am often reminded of Alvarez's (1993) comments about an angry autistic child, that "it was a waste of time talking about *why* he was so distraught and angry. He needed to be shown that I understood just *how* upset he was. The 'what' has to precede the 'why' when the patient cannot think" (p. 119).

Notes

1. For clarity, I would note that the terms "anorexia" and "anorexic" refer simply to loss of appetite, in contrast to the terms "anorexia nervosa" and "anorectic", both of which refer to the illness associated with severe weight loss due to restriction of food intake. These terms are often used interchangeably, and for simplicity in this chapter I refer to the illness anorexia nervosa as anorexia and the state of mind associated with the illness as anorexic. Similarly, I refer to patients as "her", as the majority of my eating-disordered patients are female.

2. Between 10% and 15% of people with anorexia nervosa will die from the condition, making it the most lethal of all mental disorders (APA, 2000).

3. Patients on the unit where I work are weighed twice a week on set days at set times. They may be "spot-weighed" at any time, particularly if the team feels they have been manipulating their weight by water loading, exercise, vomiting, etc.

4. This example is from a composite of patients made up of "typical" experiences with patients on the unit. It is not representative of any one patient in particular.

5. While I have attempted to provide a balanced overview of the culture and philosophy of the unit where I work, this chapter represents my own perceptions, and other members of the team may have different perspectives.

6. The lack of evidence supporting a behavioural approach to the treatment of anorexia is reflected in the National Institute for Health and Clinical Excel-

lence guidelines for eating disorders (NICE, 2004). In these guidelines over 100 recommendations were made regarding treatment options for eating disorders, with ratings from A (strong empirical support from randomized control trials) to C (expert opinion without strong empirical data). For bulimia nervosa, Cognitive Behavioural Therapy (CBT) was recommended at a Grade A rating, and antidepressants were recommended at a Grade B rating. For anorexia nervosa no specific treatment recommendations were made.

7. Again, this example is from a composite of patients made up of "typical" experiences with patients beginning psychotherapy on the unit. It is not representative of any one patient in particular.

CHAPTER TEN

In search of a reliable container: staff supervision at a drug dependency unit

Rob Hale

Rob Hale, a psychiatrist as well as a psychoanalyst, describes thirteen years as a consultant to staff at a drug dependency unit. The unit he describes is a prescribing one, and methadone is prescribed to heroin addicts. The clinic walks a tightrope between an unrealistic expectation that patients will become clean and a more realistic awareness that for many of their patients this will not be the outcome. Some patients use the clinic in a corrupt way, buying and selling their methadone scripts.

This chapter describes some of the difficult emotions engendered by the work: frustration, hopelessness, and despair. This is similar to that described by Susannah Rose in her chapter (chapter nine) on working on an eating disorders unit. Rose describes the pain of seeing attractive, intelligent young people who have reduced themselves to skin and bone.

Hale uses Glasser's theory of the core complex to understand the addict's terror of relationships. He suggests that there is a parallel between the perverse person's need of his perversion and the addict's need of his drug. If perversion fails as a defence, the individual may resort to violence—suicide or murder—to protect himself from psychic disintegration. In an earlier chapter (chapter six), Hale took us into the mind of a murderer.

What does the drug dependency unit have to offer the patients instead of their drugs? The answer is that it needs to offer what Hale offers the unit—emotional containment, in the sense described by Bion. This theory describes how mothers help babies cope with overwhelming feelings. These feelings are projected into the mother, who processes them in her own mind and returns them to the baby in a more digestible form. For containment to take place, the mother or worker needs to be disturbed or unsettled by what is experienced, but then to be able to process this disturbance. Hale only visited for an hour a week, but the workers started to pick up psychoanalytic ideas. These ideas have a containing function, making the experiences of the patients meaningful to the workers.

The article "In Search of a Reliable Container" was written a year before I finished consulting at a drug dependency unit (DDU). The article considers the ways in which the addict searches for a container—sometimes in drugs alone and sometimes including the drug clinic. It then considers the stresses on the staff of the unit and the containment that they need.

Let me start with a description.

The clinic

The clinic at which I consult as a psychoanalyst is part of a large general hospital situated in central London next to a railway terminus. The building is on the outskirts of the hospital and is a temporary prefabricated structure. It has already outlived its intended life. One could say that this reflects the attitudes of the hospital administrators—a degraded speciality. The rest of the hospital, including psychiatry, has a brand-new permanent building opened by the Queen. However, I think that the issue is more complex than this. It is clear that it is a downgraded speciality in the eyes of the medical world, but perhaps this is what the addict needs, or, more specifically, what he or she can cope with. More about this later.

It is an outpatient clinic open on weekdays from 9 a.m to 6 p.m. The staff is made up of eight psychiatric nurses, two doctors, two social workers, one occupational therapist, and two secretaries. I go once a week for one hour and have done so for the past thirteen years. Everyone is on first-name terms; often I forget people's surnames. I am invited to the Christmas parties, but I don't go. There is pop music in the waiting room, ashtrays everywhere,[1] and lots of posters for self-help groups for AIDS, single mothers, and benefit entitlements. The patients refer themselves or are referred by an outside doctor or social worker. The majority of the referred new patients are on heroin, which they buy, and which, for the most part, they inject. The clinic is a prescribing clinic. The patients are given a prescription for oral methadone, which they collect from a pharmacy in their own locality. The methadone is intended to substitute for and replace the use of heroin. The philosophy is to offer them a reduction programme and weekly supportive psychotherapy in the hope that they will become drug-free model citizens. The reality is often very different. Most of the patients have a long history of addiction with many attempts at withdrawal, sometimes at this clinic, often at another. Often, too, they have been admitted as an inpatient to a detoxification unit elsewhere as a part of the overall programme, with support being offered by this clinic after discharge from the inpatient unit.

Methadone reduction programme

Before a patient is placed on a methadone reduction programme he or she must first have a urine test that detects the different drugs—opiates, barbiturates, benzodiazepines, etc.—and registers the level. After a history has been taken, the patient is assigned to a keyworker who negotiates the level of methadone to be prescribed and the time scale over which it will be withdrawn. Overall legal responsibility lies with the medical director. The clinic must notify the Home Office (the Government Department responsible for law and order)[2] of each new patient for whom they are prescribing an opiate substitute. All the prescriptions are signed by doctors and are sent by the clinic by post to the dispensing pharmacy. The patient collects his or her dose each day from the pharmacy.

For many, what I have described will be obvious, boring, or already known. For that I apologize. But I have described it in detail for various reasons. First, because some of you will not be familiar with the organization in England of which the clinic is in many ways typical, although it must be said that the prevalent philosophy in many other clinics is behavioural cognitive. There are, at most, two other psychoanalysts working in drug addiction.

Second, what is offered to the patients is psychoanalytically informed management (or part-informed). We are fooling ourselves if we think that we are working analytically within the transference or that any of the normal rules or precepts of analytic psycho-therapy are being followed. We are engaged in barter, coercion, support, and at times a small amount of thinking with the patient.

Third—and this is my first psychoanalytic point—we believe that, as professionals, we design organizations and programmes to suit the needs of our patients, clients, students, or whomever. I think this is an illusion. I think the patient/client designs the system according to his or her unconscious needs, and we, as professionals in our different roles, will, by a process of projective identification, try to meet those needs. This will be true of a hospital, a school, a prison, a residential home for the elderly, or a court of law—indeed, any institution. We will construct each institution in hundreds of subtle ways to meet those unconscious needs. The more cohesive the psychopathology of the client, the easier it will be to identify a healthy purpose within the institution—for example, a ward in a general hospital or an old people's home. The more fragmented the psychopathology of the client, the greater will be the tendency to splitting within the institution, and the harder it will be to iden-tify a single purpose. The most extreme example of this is a court of law, in which we find a prosecutor, a defence lawyer, a judge, a jury, a probation officer, a policeman, a prison officer, a social worker, a witness, a clerk of the court, and so on. Each of them believes that they are there because of their professional training, to fulfil the needs of society. This is in part true, but really they are there because they represent parts of the psychological structure of the accused, of which he or she is unaware. The accused needs all those people to be there, or they would not be there. But he or she could not tell you that he or she needs them, because he or she does not know it.

The role of the drug clinic

Anton Obholzer (Obholzer & Roberts, 1994) describes the National Health Service as a defence against the fear of death. I would like to expand this notion and suggest that (1) general hospitals are indeed a defence against death and dying (and loss and physical pain), (2) psychiatric hospitals are a defence against psychological disintegration, madness, and, to a certain extent, hopelessness, and (3) courts of law and forensic psychiatric services are a defence against corruption: corruption of the innate sense of justice.

The problem for the drug clinic is that it has elements of all three, and particularly the third, but it masquerades as the second or the first. It is hardly surprising, then, that the hospital authorities locate it at the periphery and resent spending money on it.

The confusion continues when we look at the names we give to the service: drug use, drug abuse, drug misuse, drug dependency. Each of them is correct, but each represents a different need of the patient. Perhaps we should also add that they represent different needs of the professionals. When we look at drug work, it has very little to do with medicine and less with psychiatry.

Question—why is it a clinic in a hospital?

The most healthy individuals find and relate to organizations in a defined, organized, and mutually beneficial way. Examples of organizations that benefit from such relationships might be a college in an old, established university or a religious order. Drug addicts are at the opposite end of the spectrum in their relationship to organizations. Their purpose is to destroy the structure, to create confusion and conflict, to corrupt, to bring out the worst in an organization—and yet have it survive.

If this is so, how can we relate it to the intrapsychic structure of the addict, his or her use or abuse of drugs, and institutions as a container for his or her anxieties? The next question is: what does the institution need for containment and survival itself, and, if it is a prescribing clinic, how does it cope with the compromises and contradictions inherent in this policy? I should at this point add that I do not disagree with this policy.

I think that a useful starting point is the "core complex" described by Mervin Glasser (1979). In this formulation he describes a situation where the individual is caught between a claustrophobic and an agoraphobic fear but with certain qualities. To get too close to the object is to be swallowed up and engulfed and thus to be annihilated. To be left is to be abandoned forever, again to be annihilated. The individual thus lives in a narrow corridor of safety and develops means whereby he or she regulates the distance from his or her objects. Glasser describes this state of affairs with particular reference to sexual perversions where the perversion is used as the regulator. The perversion has the following qualities: (1) It is sexually exciting. (2) It confuses erogenous zones and uses parts of the body for purposes other than those for which they were biologically designed. (3) It contravenes a moral code to which the perverts themselves subscribe. (4) The predominant affect is hatred and revenge, which are often masked by sexual excitement (although, as Glasser points out, the ultimate goal is to be reunited with a lost idealized—not ideal—good object). (5) The perversion is the individual's ultimate defence against negative affect—like an amulet worn to protect against whatever it is that is most feared, which is present consciously or preconsciously and to which they can turn whenever they need (yet even this defence is not totally trustworthy). (6) If the perversion fails as a defence, the individuals have only suicide or murder to protect themselves from total disintegration.

The perversion, in acting as a container, thus has many purposes and qualities and has as a requirement the fact that the body is partly split off from the self and used as a separate object—or part-object.

It will not be difficult to see how closely the addict and his or her drugs parallel the pervert and his or her perversion. (I think it is also legitimate to regard the pervert as a sexual addict.) It is important to recognize that drug addiction is a form of acting out.

Most clearly, with the addict, one sees the anaesthetic and physically addictive properties of the drug.

Reasons for attending the clinic

So why do addicts come to the drug clinic? The official message they transmit is that they want help to come off drugs—they want a methadone reduction programme. The real reason is, of course, more complex. I think that addicts usually come when their capacity to organize drugs as a defensive structure is seriously threatened. At a superficial level they want a steady supply of drugs, but for this they need to accept a dependency on the clinic and the staff. This is terrifying. They therefore adopt the defence of control by corruption. They score, sell the prescription, and tell the clinic that the prescription has been lost or stolen. The addict bites the hand that feeds him or her. It is a compromise dependency. At one level the addict is attempting to destroy hope in the staff and to replace it with cynicism. At another level he or she is desperately hoping that that hope will not be destroyed, that the object will survive the addict's attacks. But throughout, in a prescribing clinic, there is a compromise. We know our patients lie to us. We attempt to believe them, yet both addict and staff know that there will be lies for a long time into the therapeutic contact. Perhaps the first compromise is to prescribe in the first place—to condone their pathology in order to bribe them to come to the clinic in the hope that a relationship with a therapist can gradually be substituted for a relationship with a drug. Yet, if we do not prescribe, few will seek help.

The danger, however, is that in prescribing we run the risk of creating a system that is as pathological as the addiction itself and that, like the addict, the institution will resist knowledge of itself and thus resist change. It is here that I think my intervention as an analyst has made a contribution in counteracting a tendency towards corruption and the destruction of hope and its replacement with cynicism.

Crisis at the clinic

I first entered this particular system at a point of crisis. The consultant in charge was on the point of retiring. There was a pervading sense of cynicism and disillusionment, and there were suggestions that prescriptions were being sold by members of staff. His assistant was seriously injured in a road traffic accident (not suicidal). The building itself was crumbling and was frequently broken into by addicts.

My ticket of entry was that I was asked to sign the legitimate prescriptions. The senior nurse had to be made aware of the situation. She was, and a major review of the service ensued. When the assistant returned, he was promoted to being consultant in charge, and I started my weekly discussion group. The focus was, and always has been, the dynamic meaning of the interaction between the addict and the therapist, as part of the clinic, and to identify the depth of the psychopathology of the patient. The psychoanalyst Harold Bridger (personal communication) has pointed out that any new development within an organization will only survive if there is support from the top of the hierarchy. Throughout my time at the clinic I have had the unfailing and enthusiastic support of the consultant in charge. He has taken part in nearly all the sessions. Occasionally, we have had our own private discussions on the progress of the consultation.

Following an enquiry by the nursing hierarchy, a new system was set up. Nurses would only be allowed to stay in the unit for six months. It was as though the unit was on parole. We focused on the impact that this new contract would have on the therapeutic relationship with patients, as for the impact on the staff. There were two reactions: one of relief at only having to stay six months and one of regret, with many of the staff coming back in their off-duty to ask after their former patients. The staff started to battle with the authorities to stay longer. Eventually, they got back to having permanent staff posts for people who chose to work in the field.

The result was that they now had to face the disillusionment of patients who did not get better. They had to alter their perceptions of the purpose of treatment. They could see it now much more as a damage-limitation exercise, but that in itself could be worth while. As always, we examined, in the course of our weekly case presentation, the way the patient treated their keyworker/therapist, how they treated the rest of the staff in the unit (as well as outside agencies), and how members of staff felt about one another's reactions to the patients.

Progress

Three or four years have passed by now. The staff are staying about two years. They are beginning to enquire about the nature of the patients' inner worlds. Some of them mention casually that they have sought their own therapy.

An additional doctor is appointed on a permanent basis who has had her own analysis.

Meanwhile, the clinic moves to the larger and better, albeit pre-fabricated, accommodation, in which all are involved in planning. It feels as though some pride is coming into the staff's work.

The preoccupation in the sessions is with the very early stability of mothers and babies. The children of the addicts are rightly often seen as being at risk. There are many issues around adoption. I do not interpret the clinic's own anxiety about something valuable and fragile being born, yet all are aware of it.

The issue moves on to the patients' destructiveness and their attacks on the therapy and the clinic. Manipulativeness and deception become issues. How can one work with a patient when you don't know if he or she is lying? How do you cope with your own impotence? How do you say no without being punitive? The transference and countertransference can be named and explored.

Staff development

There is virtually no didactic teaching. The staff find out for themselves—they start a library. Predictably perhaps, it now emerges that three of the staff have enrolled on introductory courses in psychotherapy.

Two of them take me to one side and ask me if I will be a referee for them for further training.

But all does not go so easily. Two of the staff, perhaps as a challenge to me, perhaps in response to the concentration on negative transference, envy, and destructiveness in our case discussion, decide to break away. They start a family-therapy project, which changes into a cognitive restructuring programme. They offer the clients hope by concentrating on the positive aspects of their behaviour. Their purpose is to increase the clients' very damaged self-esteem. They see the exploration of negative transference and countertransference as destructive in itself.

By now AIDS is an issue for addicts, and the health authority decides to put a needle exchange next to the clinic. I point out that, by putting the two facilities next to one another and implicitly assuming that the addicts will use both services (i.e. will continue to inject despite being on a replacement programme), the health authority are undermining the therapeutic process. In addition, by accepting this juxtaposition, the staff are effectively condoning this state of affairs. Always the focus is on the patients. The staff appeal to the health authority, and the needle exchange is moved.

About three years later, they decide to convene a meeting (at the Tavistock but jointly organized) on the dynamics of drug abuse. Seventy people come from the drug clinics around London, with visitors from Rome. Two of the staff—a nurse and a social worker—present papers. It is decided to make it an annual event.

A new problem seems to be surfacing in the case presentations: that of the positive transference, which is perhaps less familiar to the staff. It is likely that they will be less confident in dealing with this than a more overtly negative transference. Later, and more dangerous still, there is a discussion of erotic transferences and even erotic countertransference towards some patients. The staff want me to help them understand and deal with such processes and how to differentiate feelings arising from the patient and feelings arising from the staff member. We discuss their pleasure, embarrassment, and tendency to make jokes when such material is presented.

Later I arrive to find the director of social work for the overall service in which the DDU is embedded being given a fierce interrogation by the staff of the drugs service, because she wants to replace a social worker who has left with a post shared between this service and another department. The staff of the DDU are furious; they want their own social workers. The social work director leaves with her tail between her legs.

Summary

How can we understand what has happened?

I think this is an unusual form of consultation. It is not a Balint group. It is not a normal consultation group. It is not a staff sensitivity group. It is not only a case discussion group. I think we have evolved a way of letting the patients tell us how they need the clinic to be and enabling the staff to know more of how they belong within that institution. Problems still abound, but I feel that over the past thirteen years the clinic has matured painfully into a more facilitating environment.

I think my part has been to encourage them to think, to tolerate frustration, disappointment, and not knowing. They are struggling to develop a structure that contains and accepts the reality of the patients' pathology but no longer mirrors it or reacts in such a counterproductive way.

I think that in many ways the clinic has learned from its patients in the way that Winnicott (1964) describes how a baby may teach a mother how to be a good mother. But, as Winnicott also says, "Mothers need mothering themselves." Perhaps I have been like that grandparent.

Notes

1. When this chapter was written, smoking was already banned in National Health Service institutions. The chapter does however pre-date the national ban on smoking in any enclosed places used by the public.

2. The legal requirements in the UK for medical practitioners to notify the Addicts Index at the Home Office of any addict they encountered was withdrawn in 1997. It was in force at the time this chapter was written. This comment has therefore not been removed from the body of the text here. (*Eds.*)

REFERENCES

Aichhorn, A. (1935). *Wayward Youth*. New York: Viking.

Alvarez, A. (1993). Making the thought thinkable: On introjection and projection. *Psychoanalytic Inquiry, 13*: 103–122.

Alvarez, A. (1996). Learning from Las Vegas. *The New York Review of Books, 43* (1).

Anzieu, D. (1989). *The Skin Ego*. New Haven, CT: Yale University Press.

APA (1980). *Diagnostic and Statistical Manual of Mental Disorders [DSM–III]* (3rd edition). Washington, DC: American Psychiatric Association. [*DSM-III-TR*: 3rd edition, text revision, 1987.]

APA (1994). *Diagnostic and Statistical Manual of Mental Disorders [DSM–IV]* (4th edition). Washington DC: American Psychiatric Association.

APA (2000). *Diagnostic and Statistical Manual of Mental Disorders [DSM–IV-TR]* (4th edition, text revision). Washington, DC: American Psychiatric Association..

Barnes, E. (Ed.) (1968). *Psychosocial Nursing: Studies from the Cassel Hospital*. London: Tavistock Publications.

Barnett, L. (1995). What is good day care? In: J. Trowell & M. Bower (Eds.), *The Emotional Needs of Young Children and Their Families*. London: Routledge.

211

Barrows, K. (1999). Ghosts in the swamp: Some aspects of splitting and their relationship to parental loss. *International Journal of Psychoanalysis, 80*: 549–561.

Beaver, K. M., Hoffman, T., Shields, R. T., Vaughn, M. G., DeLisi, M., & Wright, J. P. (2010). Gender differences in genetic and environmental influences on gambling: Results from a sample of twins from the National Study of Adolescent Health. *Addiction, 105* (3): 536–542.

Bellaire, W., & Caspari, D. (1992). Diagnosis and therapy of male gamblers in a university psychiatric hospital. *Journal of Gambling Studies, 8*: 143–150.

Bergler, E. (1935). On the psychology of the gambler. *American Imago, 22*: 409–441.

Bergler, E. (1943). The gambler: A misunderstood neurotic. *Journal of Criminology Psychopathology, 4*: 379–393.

Bergler, E. (1957). *The Psychology of Gambling.* New York: International Universities Press.

Bick, E. (1968). The experience of the skin in early object-relations. *International Journal of Psychoanalysis, 49*: 484–486. Also in: A. Briggs (Ed.), *Surviving Space: Papers on Infant Observation* (pp. 55–59). London: Karnac, 2002.

Bion, W. R. (1959). Attacks on linking. *International Journal of Psychoanalysis, 40*: 308–315. Also in: *Second Thoughts* (pp. 93–109). London: Heinemann Medical, 1967. [Reprinted London: Karnac, 1984.]

Bion, W. R. (1962). *Learning from Experience.* London: Heinemann Medical. [Reprinted London: Karnac, 1984.]

Bion, W. R. (1970). *Attention and Interpretation.* London: Tavistock Publications. [Reprinted London: Karnac, 1984.]

BJP (2009). *Mother, Madonna, Whore* 20 years on: Developing the work of Estela Welldon [Special Issue]. *British Journal of Psychotherapy, 25* (2).

Blackburn, R., Logan, C., Donnelly, J., & Renwick, S. (2003). Personality disorders, psychopathy and other mental disorders: Co-morbidity among patients at English and Scottish high-security hospital. *Journal of Forensic Psychiatry & Psychology, 14*: 111–137.

Blaszczynski, A., & McConaghy, N. (1989). Anxiety and/or depression in the pathogenesis of addictive gambling. *International Journal of the Addictions, 24*: 337–350.

Blaszczynski, A., McConaghy, N., & Frankova, A. (1991). Control versus abstinence in the treatment of pathological gambling: A two to nine year follow-up. *British Journal of Addiction, 86*: 299–306.

Bolen, D. W., & Boyd, W. H. (1968). Gambling and the gambler. *Archives of General Psychiatry, 18*: 617–630.

Bowyer, C. (2009). Around the table. *Psychoanalytic Psychotherapy, 23* (1): 41–60.

Britton, R. (1989). The missing link: Parental sexuality in the Oedipus complex. In: J. Steiner (Ed.), *The Oedipus Complex Today* (pp. 83–101). London: Karnac.

Britton, R. (1992). Keeping things in mind. In: R. Anderson (Ed.), *Clinical Lectures on Klein and Bion*. London: Routledge.

Brooks, M. (1999). Sex site surfers teach traffic watchers. *The Guardian* (online), 30 September, p. 3.

Brown, R. (1985). The effectiveness of Gamblers Anonymous. In: W. R. Eadington (Ed.), *The Gambling Studies: Proceedings of the 6th National Conference on Gambling and Risk-Taking*. Reno, NV: University of Nevada-Reno.

Brown, R. (1987). Gambling addictions, arousal and an affective/ decision-making explanation of behavioural reversions or relapses. *International Journal of the Addictions, 22*: 1053–1067.

Chasseguet-Smirgel, J. (1964). Feminine guilt and the Oedipus complex. In: *Female Sexuality: New Psychoanalytic Views*. London: Karnac, 1985.

Chasseguet-Smirgel, J. (1970). *Female Sexuality: New Psychoanalytic Views*. London: Karnac, 1985.

Chasseguet-Smirgel, J. (1985). *Creativity and Perversion*. New York: W. W. Norton.

Chodorow, N. (1978). *The Reproduction of Mothering: Psychoanalysis and the Sociology of Gender*. Berkeley, CA: University of California Press.

Cleckley, H. M. D. (1964). *The Mask of Sanity* (4th edition). St. Louis, MO: C. V. Mosby

Cooper, A., Delmonico, D., & Burg, R. (2000). Cybersex users and abusers: New findings and implications. *Sexual Addiction and Compulsivity: Journal of Treatment and Prevention, 1–2*: 5–30.

Copley, B. (1993). *The World of Adolescence*. London: Free Association Books.

Crane, A., Smith, G., & Treasure, J. (Eds.) (2007). *Skills-based Learning for Caring for a Loved One with an Eating Disorder: The New Maudsley Method*. London: Routledge.

Crome, I. B. (2007). An exploration of research into substance misuse and psychiatric disorder in the UK: What can we learn from history? *Criminal Behaviour and Mental Health, 17:* 204–214.

Custer, L. (1982). An overview of compulsive gambling. In: P. A. Carone, S. F. Yolles, S. N. Kieffer, & L. W. Krinsky (Eds.), *Addictive Disorders Update.* New York: Human Sciences Press.

Davidson, K. M. (1995). Diagnosis of depression in alcohol dependence: Changes in prevalence with drinking status. *British Journal of Psychiatry, 166:* 199–204.

Davies, R. (1996). The inter-disciplinary network and the internal world of the offender. In: C. Cordess & M. Cox (Eds.), *Forensic Psychotherapy: Crime Psychodynamics and the Offender Patient, Vol. 2* (pp. 133–144). London: Jessica Kingsley.

Delmonico, D. L., Griffin, E., & Carnes, P. J. (2002). Treating online compulsive sexual behaviour: When cybersex is the drug of choice. In: A. Cooper (Ed.), *Sex and the Internet.* New York: Brunner-Routledge.

Department of Health (1999). *Drinking—Adults' Behaviour and Knowledge, 1998: A Report on Research Using the ONS Omnibus Survey on Behalf of the Department of Health.* London: HM Stationery Office.

de Quincey, T. (1821). *Confessions of an English Opium Eater.* In: *Collected Writings of Thomas de Quincey, Vol. 3* (pp. 209–449). Edinburgh, 1889.

Dickerson, M. (1990). Gambling: The psychology of a non-drug compulsion. *Drug and Alcohol Review, 9:* 187–199.

Dolan, M., & Davies, G. (2006). Psychopathy and institutional outcome in patients with schizophrenia in forensic settings in the UK. *Schizophrenia Research, 81:* 277–281.

Dostoevsky, F. (1866). *The Gambler.* Oxford: Oxford University Press, 1991.

DrugScope (2012). *Heroin and Other Opiates.* Available at: www.drugscope.org.uk/resources/drugsearch/drugsearchpages/heroin

Edwards, G., & Gross, M. M. (1976). Alcohol dependence: Provisional description of a clinical syndrome. *British Medical Journal, 1* (6017): 1058–1061.

Eissler, K. R. (1950). Ego psychological implications of the psychoanalytic treatment of delinquents. *Psychoanalytic Study of the Child, 5:* 97–121.

Emmanuel, L. (2002). Deprivation × 3: The contribution of organisational dynamics to the "triple deprivation" of looked after children. *Journal of Child Psychotherapy, 28* (2): 163–179.

Emmanuel, L. (2008). *Deprivation × 3: The Contribution of Organisational Dynamics to the Triple Deprivation of Looked After Children Who Are already "Doubly Deprived"*. Paper presented at the OPUS conference, London, 21–22 November.

Etchegoyen, H. (1991). *The Fundamentals of Psychoanalytic Technique*. London: Karnac.

Farrell, E. (1995). *Lost for Words: The Psychoanalysis of Anorexia and Bulimia*. London: Process Press.

FDAC (2011). *Coram and the Tavistock & Portman NHS*. Available at: www.tavistockandportman.nhs.uk/FDAC

FDAC (2012). *The Family Drug & Alcohol Court (FDAC)—Evaluation Research Study*. Available at: www.brunel.ac.uk/research/centres/iccfyr/fdac

Fenichel, O. (1945). *The Psychoanalytic Theory of Neurosis*. New York: W. W. Norton.

Ferster, C. B., & Skinner, B. F. (1957). *Schedules of Reinforcement*. New York: Appleton-Century-Crofts.

Foster, A. (1984). *Women in Treatment: The Treatment of Dependence*. Paper delivered at the 8th World Conference of Therapeutic Communities, 2–9 September, Rome. [Published in Norwegian in *Stoff Misbruk* (1984, No. 5)].

Foster, A. (2002). The duty to care and the need to split. In: B. Bishop, A. Foster, J. Klein, & V. O'Connell (Eds.), *Challenges to Practice*. The Practice of Psychotherapy Series, Book One. London: Karnac.

Frank, M. L., Lester, D., & Wexler, A. (1991). Suicidal behaviour among members of Gamblers Anonymous. *Journal of Gambling Studies, 7*: 249–254.

Freud, A. (1965). *Normality and Pathology in Childhood*. New York: International Universities Press.

Freud, S. (1895d). *Studies on Hysteria*. [Chapter IV: The psychotherapy of hysteria.] *Standard Edition, 2*.

Freud, S. (1900a). *The Interpretation of Dreams. Standard Edition, 4–5*. London: Hogarth Press.

Freud, S. (1905d). *Three Essays on the Theory of Sexuality. Standard Edition, 7*.

Freud, S. (1920g). *Beyond the Pleasure Principle. Standard Edition, 18*.

Freud, S. (1927e). Fetishism. *Standard Edition, 21*.

Freud, S. (1928b). Dostoevsky and parricide. *Standard Edition, 21*.

Freud, S. (1930a). *Civilization and Its Discontents. Standard Edition, 21*.

Freud, S. (1933a). *New Introductory Lectures on Psychoanalysis*. [Lecture 32: Anxiety and Instinctual Life.] *Standard Edition*, 22.

Galdston, I. (1960). The gambler and his love. *American Journal of Psychiatry, 117*: 553–555.

Gamblers Anonymous (1989). *Gamblers Anonymous Leaflet*. Los Angeles, CA: Gamblers Anonymous Publishing.

Gambling Commission (2008). *British Gambling Prevalence Survey 2007: Executive Summary*. Birmingham.

Geha, R. (1970). Dostoevsky and "The Gambler": A contribution to the psychogenics of gambling. *Psychoanalytic Revue, 57*: 95–123, 289–302.

Gillespie, W. H. (1956). The general theory of sexual perversion. *International Journal of Psychoanalysis, 37*: 396–403.

Glasser, M. (1979). Some aspects of the role of aggression in the perversions. In: I. Rosen (Ed.), *Sexual Deviation* (2nd edition). Oxford: Oxford University Press.

Glover, E. (1932). On the aetiology of drug addiction. *International Journal of Psychoanalysis, 13*: 298–328. [Reprinted in: D. L. Yalisove (Ed.), *Essential Papers on Addiction*. New York: New York University Press, 1997.]

Goodman, R. (1996). *The Luck Business*. New York: Free Press.

Gordon, L., Tinsley, L., Godfrey, C., & Parrott, S. (2006). The economic and social costs of Class A drug use in England and Wales, 2003/04. In: N. Singleton, R. Murray, & L. Tinsley (Eds.), *Measuring Different Aspects of Problem Drug Use: Methodological Developments*. Home Office Online Report 16/06. Available at: www.homeoffice.gov.uk/publications/science-research-statistics/research-statistics/crime-research/hoor1606

Greenberg, D., & Marks, I. (1982). Behavioural psychotherapy of uncommon referrals. *British Journal of Psychiatry, 141*: 148–153.

Greenberg, D., & Rankin, D. (1982). Compulsive gamblers in treatment. *British Journal of Psychiatry, 146*: 364–366.

Greenson, R. (1947). On gambling. *American Imago, 4*: 61–77.

Griffiths, M. (2004). Sex addiction on the Internet. *Janus Head, 7* (1), 188–217.

Grotstein, J. S. (1980). A proposed revision of the psychoanalytic concept of primitive mental states—part I. Introduction to a newer psychoanalytic metapsychology. *Contemporary Psychoanalysis, 16*: 479–546.

Hale, R., & Dhar, R. (2008). Flying a kite: Observations on dual (and triple) diagnoses. *Criminal Behaviour and Mental Health, 18*: 145–152.

Haller, R., & Hinterhuber, H. (1994). Treatment of pathological gambling with carbamazepine. *Pharmacopsychiatry, 27*: 129.

Hamilton, P. (2006). *The Vodka Monologues. The Independent*, 22 October. Available at: www.independent.co.uk/life-style/health-and-families/health-news/the-vodka-monologues-women-now-drink-like-men-but-we-dont-have-the-livers-for-it-421150.html

Harris, H. I. (1964). Gambling addiction in an adolescent male. *Psychoanalytic Quarterly, 33*: 513–525.

Harris, J. L. (1989). A model for treating compulsive gambler through cognitive-behavioural approaches. In: E. M. Stern (Ed.), *Psychotherapy and the Self-Contained Patient*. New York: Haworth Press.

Hay, G., & Bauld, L. (2008). *Population Estimates of Problematic Drug Users in England Who Access DWP Benefits: A Feasibility Study*. DWP Working Paper No. 46. London: Department for Work and Pensions.

Hay, G., & Bauld, L. (2010). *Population Estimates of Alcohol Misusers Who Access DWP Benefits*. DWP Working Paper No.94. London: Department for Work and Pensions.

Heginbotham, C., Carr, J., Hale, R., Walsh, T., & Warren, L. (1994). *The Report of the Independent Panel of Inquiry examining the case of Michael Buchanan*. London: North West London Mental Health NHS Trust.

Hinshelwood, R. D. (1989). *A Dictionary of Kleinian Thought*. London: Free Association Books.

Hinshelwood, R. D. (1999). The difficult patient. *British Journal of Psychiatry, 174*: 187–190.

HM Government (2010). *Drug Strategy 2010. Reducing Demand, Restricting Supply, Building Recovery: Supporting People to Live a Drug Free Life*. London: HMSO. Available at: www.drugscope.org.uk/resources/drugsearch/drugsearchpages/heroin

Hodgins, D. C., Currie, S. R., & el Guabaly, N. (2001). Motivational enhancement and self-help treatments for problem gambling. *Journal of Consulting and Clinical Psychology, 69*: 50–57.

Hodgins, D. C., Currie, S. R., el Guabaly, N., & Peden, N. (2004). Brief motivational treatment for problem gambling: A 24-month follow-up. *Psychology of Addictive Behaviours, 18*: 293–296.

Hoffer, W. (1949). Deceiving the deceiver. In: K. R. Eissler (Ed.),

Searchlights on Delinquency (pp. 150–155). New York: International Universities Press.

Hollander, E., DeCaria, C., Mari, E., Wong, C. M., Mosovich, S., Grossman, R., et al. (1998). Short-term single-blind fluvoxamine treatment of pathological gambling. *American Journal of Psychiatry, 155*: 1781–1783.

Hollander, E., Frenkel, M., DeCaria, C., Trungold, S., & Stein, D. J. (1992). Treatment of pathological gambling with clomipramine. *American Journal of Psychiatry, 149*: 710–711.

Holmes, E. (1995). An educational intervention for young children who have had fragmented care. In: J. Trowell & M. Bower (Eds.), *The Emotional Needs of Young Children and Their Families*. London: Routledge.

Home Office (1992). *Crack and Cocaine in England and Wales*. RPU Paper 70. London.

Hopper, E. (1995). A psychoanalytical theory of drug addiction: Unconscious fantasies of homosexuality, compulsions and masturbation within the context of traumatogenic processes. *International Journal of Psychoanalysis, 76*: 1121.

Horne, A. (2001). Of bodies and babies: Sexuality and sexual theories in childhood and adolescence. In: C. Harding (Ed.), *Sexuality: Psychoanalytic Perspectives*. Hove: Brunner-Routledge.

Hughes, L., & Pengelly, P. (1997). *Staff Supervision in a Turbulent Environment: Managing Process and Task in Front-Line Services*. London: Jessica Kingsley.

Innes-Smith, J. (1987). Pre-oedipal identification and the cathexis of autistic objects in the aetiology of adult psychopathology. *International Journal of Psychoanalysis, 68*: 405–413.

Johnson, B. (1999). Three perspectives on addiction. *Journal of the American Psychoanalytic Association, 47*: 791–815.

Joseph, B. (1982). Addiction to near-death. *International Journal of Psychoanalysis, 63*: 449–456. [Reprinted in: E. Bott Spillius (Ed.), *Melanie Klein Today, Vol. 1* (pp. 306–318). London: Routledge, 1988.]

Kadish, Y. (2011). Autistoid psychic retreat in anorexia. *British Journal of Psychotherapy, 27* (1): 19–36.

Kalivas, P. W., & Volkow, N. D. (2005). The neural basis of addiction: A pathology of motivation and choice. *American Journal of Psychiatry, 162* (8): 1403–1413.

Kernberg, O. (1972). *Barriers to Being in Love*. Unpublished manuscript, The Menninger Foundation.

Kernberg, O. (2007). The almost untreatable narcissistic patient. *Journal of the American Psychoanalytic Association, 55*: 503–539.

Khantzian, E. J. (1985). The self-medication hypothesis of addictive disorders. *American Journal of Psychiatry, 142*: 1259–1264. [Reprinted in: D. L. Yalisove (Ed.), *Essential Papers on Addiction*. New York: New York University Press, 1997.]

Kim, S. W. (1998). Opioid antagonists in the treatment of impulse disorders. *Journal of Clinical Psychiatry, 59*: 159–164.

Kim, S. W., Grant, J. E., Adson, D. E., Shin, Y. C., & Zaninelli, R. (2002). A double-blind placebo-controlled study of the efficacy and safety of paroxetine in the treatment of pathological gambling. *Journal of Clinical Psychiatry, 63*: 501–507.

Klein, M. (1932). *The Psychoanalysis of Children*. London: Hogarth Press.

Klein, M. (1940). Mourning and its relation to manic depressive states. In: *The Writings of Melanie Klein, Vol. 1*, ed. R. Money-Kyrle. London: Hogarth Press.

Kroll, B., & Taylor, A. (2003). *Parental Substance Abuse and Child Welfare*. London: Jessica Kingsley.

Ladoucer, R., Sylvain, C., Boutin, C., Lachance, S., Doucet, C., & Leblond, J. (2003). Group therapy for pathological gamblers: A cognitive approach. *Behaviour Research and Therapy, 41*: 587–596.

Lamberton, A., & Oei, P. S. (1997). Problem gambling in adults: An overview. *Clinical Psychology and Psychotherapy, 4*: 84–104.

Laufer, M. (1966). Object loss and mourning during adolescence. *Psychoanalytic Study of the Child, 21*: 269–293.

Laufer, M. E. (1996). The role of passivity in the relationship to the body during adolescence. *Psychoanalytic Study of the Child, 51*: 348–364.

Lawrence, M. (2001). Loving them to death: The anorexic and her objects. *International Journal of Psychoanalysis, 82*: 43–55.

Lerner, H. E., Howell, E., & Bayes, E. (Eds.). (1981). *Women and Mental Health*. New York: Basic Books.

Lesieur, H. R., & Anderson, C. (1995). *Results of a Survey of Gamblers Anonymous Members in Illinois*. Park Ridge, IL: Illinois Council on Problem and Compulsive Gambling.

Lesieur, H. R., & Blume, S. B. (1991). Evaluation of patients treated for pathological gambling in a combined alcohol, substance abuse and pathological treatment unit using the addiction severity index. *British Journal of Addictions, 83*: 1017–1028.

Lester, D. (1980). The treatment of compulsive gambling. *International Journal of the Addictions, 15*: 201–206.

Limentani, A. (1989). Perversions: Treatable and untreatable. In: *Between Freud and Klein*. London: Free Association Books.

Lindner, R. M. (1950). The psychodynamics of gambling. *Annals of the American Academy of Political and Social Science, 269*: 93–107.

Lloyd-Owen, D. (2007). Perverse females: Their unique psychopathology. In: D. Morgan & S. Ruszczynski (Ed.), *Lectures on Violence, Perversion and Delinquency*. The Portman Papers. London: Karnac.

Lopes, L. L. (1983). Some thoughts on the psychological concept of risk. *Journal of Experimental Psychology: Human Perception and Performance, 9*: 137–144.

Lorenz, V. C., & Yaffee, R. A. (1988). Pathological gambling: Psychosomatic, emotional and marital difficulties as reported by the spouse. *Journal of Gambling Behaviour, 3*: 13–26.

McConaghy, N., Armstrong, M. S., Blaszczynski, A., & Allcock, C. (1983). Controlled comparison of aversive therapy and imaginal desensitisation in compulsive gambling. *British Journal of Psychiatry, 143*: 366–372.

McConaghy, N., Armstrong, M. S., Blaszczynski, A., & Allcock, C. (1988). Behaviour completion versus stimulus control in compulsive gambling: Implications for behavioural assessment. *Behavioural Modification, 12*: 371–384.

McConaghy, N., Blaszczynski, A., & Frankova, A. (1991). Comparison of imaginal desensitization with other behavioural treatments of pathological gambling: A two- to nine-year follow-up. *British Journal of Psychiatry, 159*: 390–393.

McGauley, G., & Rubitel, A. (2006). Attachment theory and personality disordered patients. In: C. Newrith, C. Meux, & P. Taylor (Eds.), *Personality Disorder and Serious Offending* (pp. 69–80). London: Hodder Arnold.

Meltzer, D. (1968). Terror, persecution, dread. *International Journal of Psychoanalysis, 49*: 396–400. [Reprinted in: E. Bott Spillius (Ed.), *Melanie Klein Today: Developments in Theory and Practice, Vol. 1* (pp. 230–238). London: Routledge, 1988.]

Meltzer, D. (1975). Adhesive identification. *Contemporary Psychoanalysis, 11*: 289–310.

Menzies Lyth, I. (1975). Thoughts about the maternal role in contemporary society. *Journal of Child Psychotherapy, 4*: 5–14.

Metherall, N. (1982). Doubly dependent: Some observations on the rehabilitation of women addicts. *Journal of Therapeutic Communities, 3* (1).

Minne, C. (2003). Psychoanalytic aspects to the risk containment of dangerous patients treated in high security hospital. In: R. Doctor (Ed.), *Dangerous Patients: A Psychodynamic Approach to Risk Assessment and Management*, ed. R. Doctor. London: Karnac.

Mitrani, J. L. (1992). On the survival function of autistic manoeuvres in adult patients. *International Journal of Psychoanalysis, 73*: 549–559.

Mitrani, J. L. (1993). "Unmentalized" experience in etiology and treatment of psychosomatic asthma. *Contemporary Psychoanalysis, 29*: 314–342.

Mitrani, J. L. (1995). Toward an understanding of unmentalized experience. *Psychoanalytic Quarterly, 64*: 68–112.

Mitrani, J. L. (2007). Bodily centred protections in adolescence: An extension of the work of Frances Tustin. *International Journal of Psychoanalysis, 88*: 1153–1169.

Mitrani, J. L. (2008). The role of unmentalized experience in the etiology and treatment of psychosomatic asthma. In: *A Framework for the Imaginary: Clinical Explorations in Primitive States of Being*. London: Karnac.

Mollon, P. (2002). *Shame and Jealousy: The Hidden Turmoils*. London: Karnac.

Money-Kyrle, R. (1971). The aims of psychoanalysis. In: D. Meltzer & E. O'Shaughnessy (Eds.), *The Collected Papers of Roger Money-Kyrle*. Strathtay: Clunie Press.

Moore, T. H. M., Zammitt, M., Lingford-Hughes, A., Barnes, T. R. E., & Jones, P. B. (2007). Cannabis use and risk of psychotic or affective mental health outcomes: A systematic review. *The Lancet, 370* (9584): 319–328.

Moran, E. (1970). Varieties of pathological gambling. *British Journal of Psychiatry, 116*: 593–597.

Moskowitz, J. A. (1980). Lithium and Lady Luck: Use of lithium carbonate in compulsive gambling. *New York State Journal of Medicine, 80*: 785–788.

Motz, A. (2008). *The Psychology of Female Violence: Crimes Against the Body*. Hove: Routledge.

Motz, A. (2009). *Managing Self Harm: Psychological Perspectives.* Hove: Routledge.

National Research Council (1999). *Pathological Gambling: A Critical Review.* Washington, DC: National Academy Press.

NICE (2004). *Eating Disorders: Core Interventions in the Treatment and Management of Anorexia Nervosa, Bulimia Nervosa and Related Eating Disorders.* National Clinical Practice Guideline Number CG9. Leicester & London: The British Psychological Society & The Royal College of Psychiatrists.

Niederland, W. G. (1967). A contribution to the psychology of gambling. *Psychoanalytic Forum, 2:* 175–185.

Nissen, B. (2008). On the determination of autistoid organizations in non-autistic adults. *International Journal of Psychoanalysis, 89:* 261–277.

Obholzer, A., & Roberts, V. (1994). *The Unconscious at Work: Individual and Organisational Stress in the Human Services.* London: Routledge.

Ocean, G., & Smith, G. J. (1993). Social reward, conflict and commitment: A theoretical model of gambling behaviour. *Journal of Gambling Studies, 9:* 321–339.

Ogden, T. H. (1989). On the concept of an autistic–contiguous position. *International Journal of Psychoanalysis, 70:* 127–140.

O'Shaughnessy, E. (1981). A clinical study of a defensive organisation. [Reprinted in: E. Bott Spillius (Ed.), *Melanie Klein Today, Vol. 1* (pp. 288–305). London: Routledge, 1988.]

O'Shaughnessy, E. (1999). Relating to the superego. *International Journal of Psychoanalysis, 80:* 861–870.

Pallesen, S., Mitsem, M., Kvale, G., Johnsen, B., & Molde, H. (2005). Outcome of psychological treatments of pathological gambling: A review and meta-analysis. *Addiction, 100:* 1412–1422.

Petry, N. M., & Armentano, C. (1999). Prevalence, assessment and treatment of pathological gambling: A review. *Psychiatric Services, 50:* 1021–1027.

Pines, D. (1980). Skin communication: Early skin disorders and their effect on transference and countertransference. *International Journal of Psychoanalysis, 61:* 315–323.

Plant, M., & Plant, M. (2006). *Binge Britain.* Oxford: Oxford University Press.

Prime Minister's Strategy Unit (2004). *Alcohol Harm Reduction Strategy for England.* London: Cabinet Office.

Rachlin, H. (1990). Why do people gamble and keep gambling despite heavy losses. *Psychological Science, 1*: 294–297.

Rado, S. (1933). The psychoanalysis of pharmacothymia (drug addiction). *Psychoanalytic Quarterly, 2*, 1–23. [Reprinted in: D. L. Yalisove (Ed.), *Essential Papers on Addiction.* New York: New York University Press, 1997.]

Ragan, P., & Martin, P. (2000). The psychobiology of sexual addiction. *Sexual Addiction and Compulsivity, 7*: 161–175.

Reilly, E. A. (2004). Skin deep: Psychic skin, second-skin formation and its links with eating disorders. *Free Associations, 11*: 134–174.

Rey, H. (1979). Schizoid phenomena in the borderline. In: J. Le Boit & A. Capponi (Eds.), *Advances in the Psychotherapy of the Borderline Patient* (pp. 449–484). New York: Jason Aronson. [Reprinted in: E. Bott Spillius (Ed.), *Melanie Klein Today, Vol. 1* (pp. 203–229). London: Routledge, 1988.]

Rhode, M. (2003). Aspects of the body image and sense of identity in a boy with autism: Implications for eating disorders. In: G. Williams, P. Williams, J. Desmarais, & K. Ravenscroft (Eds.), *Exploring Feeding Difficulties in Children, Vol. 1: The Generosity of Acceptance.* London: Karnac.

Riviere, J. (1937). A contribution to the analysis of the negative therapeutic reaction. *International Journal of Psychoanalysis, 17*: 304–320.

Robertson, J., & Robertson, J. (1969). *John, Aged Seventeen Months, for Nine Days in a Residential Nursery.* Available at: www.robertson-films.info

Rose, S. (2009). A Special K retreat: Dynamics which threatened the psychotherapy of an eating-disordered patient. *Psychoanalytic Psychotherapy, 23* (1): 78–91.

Rosenfeld, D. (1988). *Psycho-Analysis and Groups.* London: Karnac.

Rosenfeld, H. A. (1960). On drug addiction. *International Journal of Psychoanalysis, 41*: 467–475. [Reprinted in: *Psychotic States: A Psychoanalytical Approach.* London: Karnac, 1965.]

Rosenfeld, H. A. (1971). A clinical approach to the psychoanalytic theory of life and death instincts: An investigation into the aggressive aspects of narcissism. *International Journal of Psychoanalysis, 52*: 169–178. [Reprinted in: E. Bott Spillius (Ed.), *Melanie Klein Today, Vol. 1* (pp. 233–250). London: Routledge, 1988.]

Rosenthal, J. R. (1987a). The gambler as case history and literary twin:

Dostoevsky's false beauty and the poetics of perversity. *Psychoana-lytic Revue, 84*: 593–616.

Rosenthal, J. R. (1987b). The psychodynamics of pathological gambling: A review of the literature. In: T. Galski (Ed.), *The Handbook of Pathological Gambling*. Springfield, IL: Charles C Thomas.

Ross, G. S. (2002). *Stung: The Incredible Obsession of Brian Molony*. Toronto: McLelland & Stewart.

Roy, A., Adinoff, B., Roehrich, L., Lamparski, D., Custer, R., Lorenz, V., et al. (1988). Pathological gambling: A psychobiological study. *Archives of General Psychiatry, 45*: 369–373.

Sadock, B. J., & Sadock, V. A. (2003). *Synopsis of Psychiatry: Behavioural Sciences/Clinical Psychiatry* (9th edition). Philadelphia, PA: Lippincott Williams & Wilkins.

Schwarz, J., & Lindner, A. (1992). Inpatient treatment of male pathological gamblers in Germany. *Journal of Gambling Studies, 8*: 93–109.

Segal, H. (1957). Notes on symbol formation. *International Journal of Psychoanalysis, 38*: 391–397. [Reprinted in: E. Bott Spillius (Ed.), *Melanie Klein Today, Vol. 1* (pp. 156–174). London: Routledge, 1988.]

Segal, H. (1973). *Introduction to the Work of Melanie Klein*. London: Hogarth Press.

Segal, H. (1975). A psychoanalytic approach to the treatment of schizophrenia. In: M. Lader (Ed.), *Studies of Schizophrenia*. New York: Headley Brothers.

Simmel, E. (1920). Psychoanalysis of the gambler. *International Journal of Psychoanalysis, 1*: 352–353.

Simmonds, P. (1982). *Pick of Posy*. London: Jonathan Cape.

Sohn, L. (1985). Narcissistic organization, projective identification, and the formation of the identificate. *International Journal of Psychoanalysis, 66*: 201–213.

Steinberg, M. A. (1993). Couples treatment issues for recovering male compulsive gamblers and their partners. *Journal of Gambling Studies, 9*: 153–167.

Steiner, J. (1982). Perverse relationships between parts of the self: A clinical illustration. *International Journal of Psychoanalysis, 63*: 241–251.

Steiner, J. (1993). *Psychic Retreats: Pathological Organizations in Psychotic, Neurotic and Borderline Patients*. London: Routledge.

Stern, J. (1996). A small group experience. In: G. Edwards & C. Dare

(Eds.), *Psychotherapy, Psychological Treatments and the Addictions*. Cambridge: Cambridge University Press.

Stewart, R. M., & Brown, R. I. F. (1988). An outcome study of Gamblers Anonymous. *British Journal of Psychiatry, 152*: 284–288.

Stoller, R. (1975). *Perversion: The Erotic Form of Hatred*. London: Quartet. [Reprinted London: Karnac, 1986.]

Symington, N. (1980). The response aroused by the psychopath. *International Review of Psychoanalysis, 7*: 291.

Taber, J. I. (1985). Pathological gambling: The initial screening interview. *Journal of Gambling Behaviour, 1*: 23–34.

Taber, J. I., & Chaplin, M. P. (1988). Group psychotherapy with pathological gamblers. *Journal of Gambling Behaviour, 2*: 183–196.

Taber, J. I., McCormick, R. A., & Ramirez, L. F. (1987). The prevalence and impact of major life stressors among pathological gamblers. *International Journal of the Addictions, 22*: 71–79.

Taylor, P., Leese, M., Willams, D., Butwell, M., Daly, R., & Larkin, E. (1998). Mental disorder and violence. *British Journal of Psychiatry, 172*: 218–226.

Thompson, W. N., Gazel, R., & Rickman, D. (1996). The social costs of gambling in Wisconsin. *Wisconsin Policy Research Institute Report, 9* (6): 1–44.

Tustin, F. (1958). Anorexia nervosa in an adolescent girl. *British Journal of Medical Psychology, 31*: 184–200.

Tustin, F. (1972). *Autistic States in Children*. London: Routledge.

Tustin, F. (1981). Psychological birth and psychological catastrophe. In: *Autistic States in Children* (revised edition, pp. 96–110). London: Routledge, 1992. [Reprinted in: J. S. Grotstein (Ed.), *Do I Dare Disturb the Universe?* (pp. 181–196). Beverly Hills, CA: Caesura Press, 1981.]

Tustin, F. (1986). *Autistic Barriers in Neurotic Patients*. New Haven, CT: Yale University Press.

Von Hattingberg, H. (1914). Analerotik, Angstlust und Eigensinn. *Internationale Zeitschrift fur Psychoanalyse, 2*: 244–258.

Waddell, M. (1998). *Inside Lives*. Tavistock Series. London: Karnac.

Waller, G., Cordery, H., Corstorphine, E., Hinrichsen, H., Lawson, R., Mountford, V., et al. (2007). *Cognitive Behavioral Therapy for Eating Disorders: A Comprehensive Treatment Guide*. Cambridge: Cambridge University Press.

Walker, M. B. (1992). *The Psychology of Gambling*. Oxford: Pergamon.

Welldon, E. (1988). *Mother, Madonna, Whore: The Idealisation and Denigration of Motherhood*. London: Free Association Books.

Welldon, E. (1996). Perversion in men and women. *British Journal of Psychotherapy, 12* (4): 480–486.

WHO (1992). *International Classification of Mental and Behavioural Disorders, Tenth Edition (ICD–10)*. Geneva: World Health Organization.

Williams, G. (1997a). *Internal Landscapes and Foreign Bodies* (pp. 33–50). Tavistock Series. London: Duckworth.

Williams, G. (1997b). Reflections on some dynamics of eating disorders: "No entry" defences and foreign bodies. *International Journal of Psychoanalysis, 78*: 927–941.

Willner, A. (2002). Imperviousness in anorexia: The no-entry defence. *Psychoanalytic Psychotherapy, 16*: 125–141.

Winnicott, D. W. (1951). Transitional objects and transitional phenomena. In: *Through Paediatrics to Psycho-Analysis*. London: Karnac, 1991.

Winnicott, D. W. (1960). Ego distortion in terms of true and false self. In: *The Maturational Processes and the Facilitating Environment* (pp. 140–152). London: Hogarth Press, 1965.

Winnicott, D. W. (1964). *The Child, the Family and the Outside World*. Harmondsworth: Penguin.

Wood, H. (2007). Compulsive use of virtual sex and internet pornography: Addiction or perversion? In: D. Morgan & S. Ruszczynski (Eds.), *Lectures on Violence, Perversion and Delinquency* (pp. 157–178). London: Karnac.

Wood, H. (2011). The role of the internet in the escalation of sexually compulsive behaviour. *Psychoanalytic Psychotherapy, 25*: 127–142.

Wulfurt, E., Blanchard, E. B., & Martell, R. (2003). Conceptualizing and treating pathological gambling: A motivational enhanced cognitive behavioural approach. *Cognitive and Behavioural Practice, 10*: 61–72.

Yalisove, D. L. (Ed.) (1997). *Essential Papers on Addiction*. New York: New York University Press.

Yorke, C. (1970). A critical review of some psychoanalytic literature on drug addiction. *British Journal of Medical Psychology, 43*: 141–184.

Youell, B. (2005). Observation in social work practice. In: M. Bower (Ed.), *Thinking Under Fire: Psychoanalysis and Social Work Practice*. London: Routledge.

INDEX

AAI, *see* Adult Attachment Interview
acopia, 117
addict(s), female:
    particular needs of, 107
    psychopathology of, 70, 87
addicted mothers, 103, 105
addicted parents, 33, 36
addiction(s) (*passim*):
    in adolescence and young
        adulthood, psychoanalytic
        and psychotherapeutic
        treatment of, 69–86
    as affect regulation, 5
    alcohol, 2, 109, 124, 148, 151
    Anna Freud on, 71–72
    assessment of, prior to analysis,
        79–80
    vs. dependency, 2
    to gambling, 125–150
    to Internet social networks, 35
    nature of, 69
        in paraphilias, 151–173
        in sex addiction, 151–173
    neurobiological perspective, 4–5
    parental, impact on children, 33–49
    and perversion, relation between,
        8–11
    phenomenology of, 2–4
    psychiatry, 14
addictive behaviours, 2, 7, 10, 35, 49,
    185
adolescence:
    binge drinking in, 51–68
    development in, 55
    fear of dependence in, 56
    use of drugs in, 69, 78
Adson, D. E., 149

Adult Attachment Interview (AAI),
    117
affective theory, 136
affect regulation, addiction as, 5
Aichhorn, A., 76
AIDS, 201, 208
Al-Anon, 41, 148
Alateen, 41
alcohol, 14–22, 26–30
    cheap, availability of, 53
    dependence/addiction, 2, 17, 109,
        124, 148, 151
    increased tolerance of, 53
Alcohol Dependence Syndrome, 17
Alcoholics Anonymous, 148
alcoholism, 17, 45, 46, 72, 75, 78, 133,
    139
Allcock, C., 149
alpha function, introjection of, vs.
    omega function, 39
Alvarez, A., 128, 129, 196
American Psychiatric Association
    (APA), 53, 129, 130, 153, 154,
    167, 196
amphetamines, 75, 77
anal-sadistic universe of pervert, 139
analyst, as indestructible object, 80
Anderson, C., 133
anorexia nervosa, 175–197
    as addiction, 175, 185, 187, 195
    high morbidity of, 175
    as repetitive compelling behaviour,
        189
anorexic object, 175, 179, 181, 187, 193
    internal omnipotent, 191
antisocial personality disorder, 111
Anzieu, D., 192

227

228   INDEX

Printed in Great Britain
by Amazon